Sacred Keeper

a biography of
PATRICK
KAVANAGH

by Peter Kavanagh

Ireland 1979

THE GOLDSMITH PRESS
The Curragh Ireland

Published by The GOLDSMITH Press Ltd., The Curragh, Co. Kildare, Ireland.

Acknowledgments
We wish to acknowledge the assistance of The Arts Council (An Chomhairle Ealaíon).
The Index has been done by Mr. Fred Tuite.

Contents

Chapter one   page   9
Chapter two   page 21
Chapter three   page 40
Chapter four   page 54
Chapter five   page 70
Chapter six   page 84
Chapter seven   page 99
Chapter eight   page 117
Chapter nine   page 131
Chapter ten   page 145
Chapter eleven   page 161
Chapter twelve   page 174
Chapter thirteen   page 190
Chapter fourteen   page 203
Chapter fifteen   page 213
Chapter sixteen   page 227
Chapter seventeen   page 237
Chapter eighteen   page 247

Chapter nineteen   page 262
Chapter twenty   page 277
Chapter twenty one   page 292
Chapter twenty two   page 309
Chapter twenty three   page 323
Chapter twenty four   page 342
Chapter twenty five   page 353
Chapter twenty six   page 367
Chapter twenty seven   page 381
Epilogue   page 387
Appendix   page 391
Bibliography   page 397
Index   page 399

SACRED KEEPER

Aladdin*

Do not be greedy for these jewels,
Aladdin said to me,
For these that lie at the Cave's mouth
Are touched materially.

Any coward can pick these up,
Back to the world run
Bragging of how he robbed the nest
Of the Enchanted One.

But we will go farther and not fear
The monsters, Hatred, Hunger,
Meanness, greasy-faced Piety,
Defeat, whose stench grows stronger

As we grope through the Cave of Wonder.
Do not fill so soon
Your pockets out of that pile,
For time will wear out the tune

That flows in the brilliance of
The Truth you see.
At the foot of a Cross is the Utterness
Of humanity

Every atom of clay,
Every worn stone
Becomes your wish for beauty
The world cannot own

Or steal or buy for boasting . . . .
Friendless now, we
Are close to the Secret of Life's Cave
Aladdin said to me.

Patrick Kavanagh

* A recently discovered poem, published here for the first time.

Chapter One

My father strung for me
No genealogic rosary

When I write about Patrick Kavanagh I write as a partisan, as his alter ego, almost as his evangelist. Legends and lies invented about his life do not interest me. This is not a popular approach to biography — some would say it is not even a sensible one. The Spanish writer, Antonio Machado, would be one such when he warns of the dangers of dismissing the legends surrounding men of repute. *Every celebrity*, he writes, *must live with a legend from the time of his major successes — despite the fact that legend is the child of our inveterate misunderstanding of our neighbour. A life-time is not time enough to tear down one legend and erect another. And, lacking a legend, no one passes into history.*

I listen to the warning and pass on. Those who seek that kind of biography will find it easily in newspaper and television journalism where they may read of Patrick Kavanagh the eccentric, the drunkard, the *enfant terrible* of Dublin. *When someone sees you as picturesque*, wrote Patrick, *it is because that person refuses to see beneath your mannerisms, your peculiarities. Hate and evil are not deliberate acts as many*

9

suppose — they are negations, the absence of love. Love sees into the unique wonders of the loved one's heart.

As far as possible I shall avoid writing of him as a brother since my interest in him was mainly as a poet. So intense was this interest that I hardly knew him at all as a person. Even his physical appearance has scarcely registered on my memory. When we met we recognized each other, not by appearance, but in some other manner difficult to describe, perhaps in the same way animals recognize their own kind. Only the other day did I get a good look at him, as you might say, in the flesh. As I was contemplating the writing of this book he walked across my vision exactly as certain characters did to William Blake. And, like Blake, I quickly made a sketch.

Aged thirty-seven, close to six feet tall, with a lean athletic build and very virile. He is wearing an Irish tweed suit of softly woven grey herringbone, with wide-cuffed trousers. His hair is dark brown and his head equine, a weak chin but with great strength in his wide forehead. The eyes are blue tinged with green. He walks with an easy carefree swing but unhurried. He seems to hold a book or a rolled-up newspaper in one hand. He is not actually smiling but there is a pleasant absent-minded look on his face. When he sees me he stops short and quickly awakens from his reverie. He doesn't speak. No need to. Our personalities merge once again. The vision fades.

Towards the end of his life Patrick warned me in a letter that I was *the scared keeper of his sacred conscience.* To fulfil that command is one of the reasons for writing this book.

Patrick was an intense Catholic but reserved on the matter. He revealed his true position to no one, sometimes not even to me. He never blasphemed, never said *By God* or *By Christ* because for him poetry and God were the same thing and it would be unthinkable for him to insult the poetic fire, his most sacred possession and the reason for his being. He used broad language, the country language that appears in *Tarry Flynn* but never blasphemy. William Cooney, a neighbour of his on Pembroke Road, writes (14th November 1978):

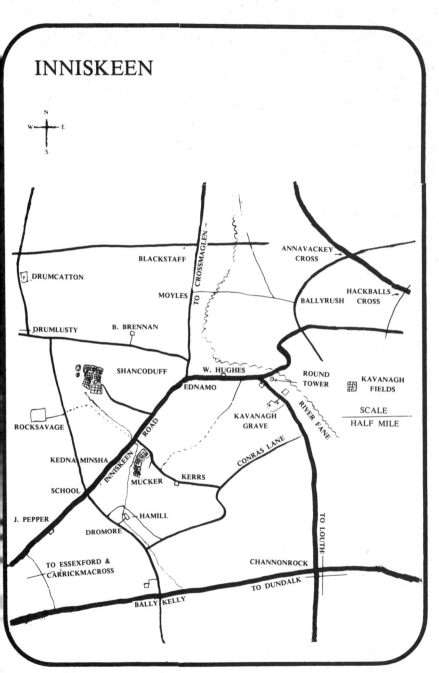

Map of Inniskeen: Peter Kavanagh.

11

*My outstanding recollection is of Patrick's kindness to all us
children. We would be playing, about six of us, and Patrick
would come down with his famous walk and spitting to the
left and right. He looked quite fearsome to us children but I
never heard him utter a bad word in our presence. He would
arrive at the steps of our house and produce from his pockets
a packet of sweets which he would share between us all. I
never saw him eat any sweets himself so I can only assume
be bought them to share with us.*

Another neighbour, Margaret Keyes, has much the same to say
(27th November 1978):

*I can still hear his poor harassed voice as we met him every
Sunday morning on our way to Mass in Haddington Road.
He never missed it. He certainly loved children. My children
were always with him. He would have them all gathered
around him quoting poems to them and giving them pennies.
My youngest girl, now thirty, was his favourite. She always
got six pennies from him. I remember the evening after the
result of the notorious libel case appeared in the paper and
we all said together: poor Patrick Kavanagh lost his case. At
once my little daughter said: 'No, he didn't. I just met him in
Baggot Street with his case in his hand and he gave me six
pennies'.*

*I would not like him to be misrepresented because he was
so fond of children and they were so fond of him.*

For most people Patrick was not an easy man to be around
because he would not observe the usual conventions of lying.
Had he been able to compromise a little he might have been
what the world calls a success. He could not do it; he had not
that wordly capacity. As a result he found himself an outcast in
Irish society, locked out from any means of making a living and
made the object of wisecracks and insults. He did not complain:
to whine was out of his character. *When a man chooses to be a
poet*, he wrote, *he must take the consequences.* He took them

and when success eventually seemed to be coming his way he died.

While it would be wrong to over-emphasise the religious element in Patrick's character it would be more wrong to ignore it. He was a Christian mystic with the spiritual element dominant. This then is the man whose life I recall.

Divine wisdom has its own logic – why for instance one family and not another should be honoured with the poetic torch — and why one person within that family and not three or four. Poetry is not a matter of education or of application. It cannot be learned. Education and application can at best produce only verse, that is to say, words dressed up like an actor in the garb of poetry but without the script.

Poetry is a gift but a gift that carries with it a heavy obligation, a compulsion at all costs to testify to the Divine Spirit in man. Patrick felt privileged

To carry the flame
On to the ultimate Olympic Game . . . .
(*Complete Poems*, p. 342)

but he also was sharply aware of the anguish. *Poetry*, he said, *is born of a curse/Which a New Moon Carnival cannot disperse* (The Albert Hall, London, June 1966).

There was nothing in our family history that would lead one to suspect the arrival of genius. Father was a shoemaker who in 1897 married a girl, Bridget Quinn, from a neighbouring parish. Almost each year thereafter a child was born until seven girls and two boys were produced. Patrick, born in 1904, was the fourth in line; I, born in 1916, was the last. There was a romantic note in Father's ancestry which possibly may have some significance. His father was a wandering scholar from the west of Ireland who happened along just as the local Kednaminsha school was to open, around the year 1854. He took lodgings in a nearby house and fell in love with a girl who worked there, Nancy Callan.

The full record of what happened was written down by Father but it was either destroyed or lost. The essence of the story is as follows. Nancy Callan was a widow with one child. The schoolmaster fell in love with her and in 1856 she produced twins through their union. One of the twins died at birth. The one that survived, my Father, was named James. Kavanagh, for that was the schoolmaster's name, was anxious to marry the lady but she being more than a hundred years ahead of the women's movement of the seventies told her lover that she would be happier without him and suggested he move off. She had enough of marriage. Her attitude so offended the local *mores* that her name was quietly execrated until recent times by those who knew the story. The schoolmaster reluctantly went off and settled in Tullamore where he married and became secretary of the County Council. But he did not forget his lover or his child: he contributed to Father's support and even arranged to meet with him occasionally in Dublin. Mail then was as risky as it is today and I heard it said that his method of insurance was to tear a five-pound in half and send each section to his son by a different post.

Nancy Callan lived with her mother and her brother Mickey in a thatched house on the site of the present house. It had been built in 1791 and had about ten or fifteen acres attached. This being the age of rackrents and absentee landlords their land was taken from them on the whim of the Land Agent and given to a neighbour. It has been said that this was because my family was late with its rent but a much more likely reason was that the Land Agent was offended by the dignity and independence of Nancy, much as Patrick was discriminated against in later life.

Fortunately the Callans were able to hold on to the old hovel and the Front Garden. Here Father grew up, from here he went to school in the local village, and from here he departed at the age of fourteen to be apprenticed to the shoemaker Campbell of Drumcatton two miles away. After four years of starvation on the thinnest of gruel and seldom getting even a piece of bread, Father set up as a tradesman in his own house. His mother, to whom he is said to have been deeply attached, died in

14

1896 and the following year Father married. Nancy's brother Mickey lived on into the twentieth century. He was a careful and intelligent fellow even though he could neither read nor write. In August 1896 he drew up a deed handing over whatever rights he had in the house to my father. Here is the document:

I Michael Callan of the Townland of Mucker in the Parish of Donaghmoyne, barony of Farney and the county of Monaghan do hereby agree to assign all the property I possess in the townland of Mucker as well as everything personal to James Kavanagh of aforesaid townland on condition that he clothe, house and provide me with food, the same as I was in the habit of getting, for the remainder of my life.

In virtue of and as proof of my good faith in said agreement I hereunto put my hand and mark this twenty-eighth day of August one thousand eight hundred and ninety six.

Signed Michael X Callan
his mark

Here is the world Patrick saw as he looked from his cradle in 1906:

When I was about two years old I was one evening lying in the onion box that had been converted into a cradle. I looked up and saw for the first time the sticky black-oak couples of the thatched roof. If I did not see the stars it was my child observation was at fault, for the blackbirds had pecked holes in the thatch — to the very bone in places. At three or four of a summer's morning the blackbird would begin his attack and by six, narrow sunbeam-ribbons like wedding festoonery would be stretched from roof to floor in peasant homes, or as happened more often, spitting rain would startle the sleeping faces of children in their beds, and indeed I often heard father tell of a wet night when he had to hold an umbrella over himself and my mother in their bed.

(The Green Fool).

15

When Father married in 1896 he was forty years old and Mother twenty-six. They were both the same height, five foot six. Father was a wiry fellow with intense eyes and a character to match. He did everything in a hurry and talked fast almost in staccato style. He was highly informed on a wide variety of subjects: history, law, medicine, geography, orthography. There was scarcely a work in the dictionary he did not understand — and he could spell them all. How he managed to collect such a mass of pedantry considering his meagre opportunities is a mystery. To some extent Patrick had the same capability — he educated himself out of two books, *Moby Dick* and *Gil Blas*. Of course the schoolbooks then were superior to anything we have had since; this no doubt was also a factor.

Father was considered by his neighbours a very intelligent man and they came to him for advice as well as to have their shoes repaired. He was reputed to be very well versed in the law. If there was a difficult case coming up for trial the litigant might be permitted to hold a rehearsal in advance of the real case. In the course of such a rehearsal the skin was perfected on many a good lie, though my father would not countenance such behaviour if he knew of it.

As I remember him he was not a man to attract affection even from members of his own household. He was too strict a disciplinarian. He gave Patrick many a thrashing *for his own good*. In *The Green Fool* Patrick states that he loved his father and that his father loved him. Towards the end of his own life Patrick took a more caustic view of their relationship, objecting to those beatings as psychologically damaging and unworthy of a father.

When I was a boy I recall that Patrick gave myself a beating and I am wondering if in later life he remembered it and if so was he concerned he had damaged my ego? However, this reconsidered view of my father by Patrick came when Patrick was a very tired and sick person. He was somewhat resentful at being born into so impoverished a family. Had we been

16

James Kavanagh 1856-1929   Bridget Kavanagh 1872-1945

(Photographs taken in 1897).

Family Group, 1913.

17

wealthy, how much suffering he could have avoided and how easily he could have written poetry. It was a false theory but one that in moments of depression was difficult to shake off.

Mother's character made a contrast to that of Father. She was quiet, unobtrusive yet efficient nonetheless. She hit nobody and in moments of difficulty conveniently left the chastisement to Father. She had a minimum of formal education but made the most of it. She always spoke of herself as illiterate — no doubt a method of self-defence in a family of readers. Though Father was not one to show affection, I get the impression that he liked Mother. Often I heard his remark about her quoted, that he never had a penny until he married her. Certainly I never heard an angry word pass between them. A cynic might explain this harmony between them in this fashion: that so many fights were taking place at all times between other members of the family, it would be necessary for them to schedule an appointment for a row.

Patrick was not isolated from such rows and was a worthy combatant who could take on two or more at the same time. Once in an argument with my very witty sister Sissie he made the rejoinder: *You are as ignorant as me arse! Well,* she replied, *you think enough of me to compare me to part of yourself. I wouldn't do that,* he replied, *only I have scabs on it.* He paused for a moment then added, *non-syphilitic.* That response is still recalled at family gatherings.

Of course this argument took place long after Father had died. He would not allow vulgarity in the house though he himself was not beyond using an occasional remark if it achieved a purpose. To an overly inquisitive child asking where he was going, his answer was short and deadly, *Out to shite! Will you come?*

Mother frowned on all fights especially on broad expressions involving the girls. Her comment would be, *Disgraceful conduct among girls who should be more refined. What would people think if they knew?* Cursing or taking the name of God in vain was never part of any conversation or row and this interdiction on cursing remained permanently as part of our style of expression up to this moment of writing. Mother's philosophy for living, especially for living in peace with her neighbours, was *the easy way is the best way*. This passive attitude with its lack of fire had a depressing effect on both Patrick and myself. It was a weakness in her character, hinting at remnants of slavery in the blood. She had been born into nineteenth century feudalism and the loss of our few acres of land was a constant drain on her courage.

How Father met his future wife I cannot say. It was probably through her brother Jimmy who had become apprenticed to my father. In the early years of their marriage the shoemaking business provided an adequate existence but as the children began to arrive in rapid succession (Patrick was born on 21st October 1904) this income had to be supplemented. The need for land on which to grow food and support a cow became crucial. The garden attached to the house was adequate only for growing vegetables and to supply running room for a dozen or two hens. Each year the neighbouring Kenny Estate rented out parcels of its land on the eleven months system. Father usually rented an acre or two and in this way our family survived until the year 1910 when we were able to buy a field adjoining our garden from Willie Woods. It consisted for the most part of bogland but for us it was *lebensraum*. It was in that section of the field nearest the house that Patrick later envisioned *The Great Hunger* and it was in the farthest corner of that field that he enjoyed the greatest days of his life — *there were stepping stones across a stream* . . . . (*Kavanagh's Weekly* 28th June 1952).

At the same time it was necessary to extend our living accommodation. The old thatched cottage was raised to two stories except for one section over which a loft was later raised. We did not own the garden at the back of the house then and since this was the only practical direction to widen the house — no compromise being possible — the new house was built on the

19

lower walls of the old cottage making the new house awkwardly narrow — only thirteen feet.

A section of the kitchen-livingroom four by six feet was marked off for the shoemaking business leaving only a small area for living and cooking. Just the same, our restricted living quarters never seemed to bother us. It was always a house full of interest and excitement with people constantly coming and going, information being exchanged and wild stories of faraway places, two miles distant, circulating.

After we had raised the house and acquired the field, we extended our farming business. Shortly we had three cows, four pigs being fattened and a large flock of hens. Mother took charge of this end of the economy — and a very good job she made of it too. There was a pot constantly on the fire, if not for the family, then for the pigs or hens.

Chapter Two

Returning I hear the lark

In 1909 Patrick went to Kednaminsha Primary School which was half a mile from home. He was taken there by his three oldest sisters. From a very wicked teacher named Miss Cassidy who believed in the virtues of the cane he learned the rudiments of what are called the three Rs. Some days he didn't go to school at all because of his fear of her. He would play truant and risk thereby the anger of his father. But despite its defects it was this primitive school that first introduced Patrick to the magic of poetry. He wrote:

> *If I had roots then they were in the schoolbooks. When I read 'Often I think of that beautiful town That is seated by the sea . . .' I am walking through a field called Lurgankeel away down in a shaded corner; it is an October evening and all around me is the protecting fog of family life. How shall I live when the fog is blown away and I am left alone naked? . . . But it is to the schoolbooks I must return for my virginal youth, for a winter morning in a desk near the fire, near the map of Scotland, with my head dipped in a new satchel*
>
> (*November Haggard* p.4)

21

The martinet Miss Cassidy never relinquished her authority even when dealing with teenage boys so that when Patrick was thirteen years of age she was quite confident of herself when she ordered him outside to the bucket to wash his hands. Patrick went — but when he didn't come back after five minutes another scholar was sent to bring him in. Patrick was not to be found. It was assumed that he had gone home and Miss Cassidy, her anger aroused, sent two scholars to our house to bring the truant back. But he wasn't there and Father came to the school in a fury threatening to murder Miss Cassidy if the boy were not found. Eventually he was discovered under the railway bridge unconcerned with schools and scholars. That was to be Patrick's last day at school. Father had enough of Miss Cassidy so he sat Patrick down on a seat beside him and began apprenticing him to the shoemaking trade.

Patrick had no great aptitude for shoemaking but by dint of practice, coaching by Father and an occasional word of irritation he managed after five years to turn into a tolerable tradesman. If you can manage to avoid much hand-sewing, shoemaking can be a pleasant and dreamy occupation. Father talked constantly to himself while working, taking swipes at imaginary objects with a hammer or a knife. Patrick had the same habit. And when not talking to himself Father or Patrick would be talking to some customer who was spending a leisurely hour while his boot was being repaired. Such conversations covered aspect of this life and of the life to come. The Great War was still raging and when one tired of that subject more local wars received attention:

> *Who owns that half a rood of rock, a no-man's land*
> *Defended by our pitchfork armed claims . . .*
>
> (*Complete Poems*, p. 238)

Then there was the boot, a very personal item and in working on it a strong element of creativity was involved, as well as the personal element — two important qualities in art.

22

A. K. Smith, London.

Two views of the Kavanagh house, Inniskeen.

I remember this period of Patrick's life, 1918-1925, somewhat imperfectly. I was a boy, sleepy and mostly unaware. To me then he was just another member of the large household getting his share of insults. I remember him playing checkers with me — a game to which I was then addicted — and of course I remember him playing tag with me in the Front Garden. Years later he celebrated in verse those early associations with me:

> *Remember well your noble brother*
> *Whose constant heart embraced no other*
> *But you, and when love's arteries harden*
> *Evoke the image of the Front Garden*
> *Yellow with sunlit weeds, and there*
> *You are the hound and he the hare*
> *And round and round you run and laugh*
> *This moment is immortal stuff.*
> *Name his name, beloved name Peter*
> *And only regret that words must fail*
> *To tell that marvellous brotherly tale.*

(*Complete Poems*, p.276)

I slept through the so-called War of Independence and even through the Civil War. Fortunately for Patrick he was too young to become involved with either. Not that he would have, had he been older: Father would not have allowed it. We were never involved in politics. In recalling this early period of Patrick's life it must be taken into account that we in our area were still in the Middle Ages. The automobile was a novelty and even the bicycle was rare enough. When going places people walked or if it were a distance, went by horse-drawn trap or side-car. We were still in the age of ghosts, fairies and legends. Entertainment had to be home-made.

In winter-time darkness fell around four o'clock. The lamp would be lighted and the house gradually begin to fill up with people who needed boots repaired and even with casual visitors coming for entertainment. The conversation and the storytelling continued all evening until ten o'clock when everyone went home and the Rosary was recited before going to bed. Patrick would not always be present – he might be down in the Village with one of his friends to watch the evening train come in, or he might be playing cards in a neighbour's house or at a Gaelic language class or bag-pipe class in the school. He was always home for the Rosary. Then up to bed, checking my shirt before going to sleep to make sure the top button was open and there was no danger of me choking.

Occasionally he would delay coming to bed and stay sitting at the fire reading a book or newspaper. He might perhaps make himself cocoa. Mother would be listening upstairs and could tell from the slightest tinkle exactly what he was doing. *Will you come up to bed out o'that and stop using the good sweet milk we need for our breakfast – and may the devil pull it up out of your guts*, she would call in a mock angry fashion. She might have to make many such imprecations before he finally came to bed. Mother of course was model for Mrs. Flynn in the later work, *Tarry Flynn*.

In the summertime the routine was more or less the same except that the entertainment might be more varied; Patrick would be in some neighbouring field kicking a football with his friends or at the crossroads playing pitch-and-toss.

Does any of this matter? Not a great deal I suppose but it is recorded here for the benefit of those readers who may be able to see in these activities greater influences than I can. What does seem to matter is that every evening for as long as I can remember Patrick wrote verse. He never failed to spend at least an hour writing, in wintertime upstairs in a corner of the bedroom, where we kept the sewing machine or in summertime out on the loft where he sat on a bag of oats. Nothing could prevail on him to break this routine. It was as important to him as eating. Oftentimes it annoyed Mother that a friend of his should be downstairs in the kitchen while he was upstairs writing. There was an old wooden trunk upstairs packed to overflowing with verses written by Patrick with a straight pen and a bottle of ink. He wrote with a very clear hand. No amount of abuse from Mother could dissuade him from writing. I don't know what Father's reactions were to Patrick's verse-making and Patrick never spoke of this matter to me which, now that I think on it, is very odd. Father went into dotage at an early age — when he was about seventy. Senility with him took the form of trying to recall some date or event that he had temporarily forgotten. He wanted to hold on to the mass of information he had accumulated during his life. And since Father was a musician with knowledge of every Irish jig, reel and hornpipe there was an added complication. Patrick was a great help to him in solving these problems and his patience and charity made a lasting impression on my mind. He expressed extraordinary devotion and I do not remember that he ever became irritated with Father, as well he might, for this phobia of Father's could become active even in the middle of the night.

Patrick, who never missed an opportunity of turning an experience of his into cash, wrote about his early days writing verse. There was the nearby railway gatehouse called The Chunk outside of which teenagers gathered; and there was the dancing deck in a nearby bog which was stolen one night:

That famous society called the Chunk
I never hear of it today
For it has into oblivion sunk
And fled like morning mists away . . . .

* * *

Can I believe the boards were stolen
For which I paid seven darling notes
Collected through the country
By myself and patriot friends . . . .

* * *

In Gusher's the dance of the season
Was held in the gentleman's hall

1910: Sissie, Annie, Mary and Patrick at Kednamisha N.S. (Patrick aged six).

And to every boy there 'twas real pleasing
To see every lass with her shawl . . . .

* * *

That riotous little village
That never was surpassed
For shooting, loot and pillage
Is peaceful now at last.
All the roads around are clear
For those who aren't blind
Too well we see the fighting here
Has left its mark behind . . . .

* * *

Oh see the boots being cobbled while the cobbler sings a song
About the pleasures of the time when he was young and strong
When he could make a pair of boots in less than half a day
But now his hands are getting stiff and his hair is turning grey.
But his heart is light as ever it was in youthful days gone by
He takes the world easily and makes grief look like joy.

Although it was well known in the neighbourhood that Patrick was practising verse no one would mention it unless in a quarrel. *Your brother's a Bard*, they would jeer. It was Patrick himself who eventually made the exposure:

Around about twelve or so I took to the poeming, as it is called. Quite a lot of terror filled the hearts of my parents when they heard the news. Was he going to be another Bard? We had a local Bard in our district, the Bard of Callenberg he called himself, and he worked hard at his craft. The ordinary people appreciated their poor poet too and the local Arts Council of Inniskeen organized a football tournament to buy him an ass and cart and set him up in the

28

crockery business. I should have mentioned that the Bard was a cripple. My only memory of him is seeing him in his ass and cart among his crockery talking to the local women and the news was that the language he was using was a total dread. He got himself a wife in spite of his failings and the week after his wedding he had a ballad in the local paper telling of the misfortune of his rival who watched the wedding procession go by:

'A look of sorrow lingered on Owen's wrinkled brow
Like rain fell down his tears
But his offer she had spurned
For he was advanced in years.'

During World War I or thereabouts our Bard who managed to get a bit of travel sued a neighbour and addressed the court in rhyme:

'My heart with indignation swells
As I state my case to Mr. Wells
Alas to tell how I was done
By Pat the Miser and his son.
I was in Scotland far away
When they drew home my cock of hay
And when I returned home I seen
My stack of corn growing green.
They promised to thatch my mother's cot
But no, they left it there to rot,
The rain came percolating through
And smashed a couple, sad to view . . .'

And sadder still to relate, the Bard lost his case in court.

(*Lapped Furrows*, p.5)

During his juvenile years Patrick recorded in rhyme several of the more interesting local events. Some of these rhymes were recited locally until recent times. Here is a sample:

> *Farrelly climbed in the window*
> *But Dooley fell back with a shout*
> *And the singing and ructions were dreadful*
> *Around the half-barrel of stout.*

And another:

> *The band turned out at early morn*
> *Upon St. Patrick's Day*
> *Down the ould Bog Road they march*
> *In wonderful array . . . .*

Patrick did not spend all his early years sitting on the shoemaker's bench pulling a waxed-end. There was our small holding to be taken care of, cows to be milked, bedding to be cut, pigs to be fed. Further, we had no farming equipment, not even an ass and cart and twice a year when we had pork to take to Carrickmacross market we had to borrow this facility from Kerrs up the road:

> *We borrowed the loan of Kerrs' big ass*
> *To go to Dundalk with butter,*
> *Brought him home the evening before the market*
> *An exile that night in Mucker*
>
> *We heeled up the cart before the door,*
> *We took the harness inside*
> *The straw-stuffed straddle, the broken breeching*
> *With bits of bull-wire tied;*
>
> *The winkers that had no choke-band,*
> *The collar and the reins . . . .*
> *In Ealing Broadway London Town*
> *I name their several names*

30

Until a world comes to life
Morning, a silent bog,
And the God of imagination waking
In a Mucker fog.

(Complete Poems, p.254)

When we needed our crops planted, we had to depend on a neighbour who had horses, ploughs and the other farming equipment. We paid the neighbour by bartering help with him. This meant Patrick, though other members of the family were also engaged. Patrick was a very lazy worker and it took a most skilled slave-driver — of which there were a few around — to get value out of him. In a piece of journalism written in 1939 Patrick quotes one of these farmers: *I'd be into pocket if I paid you to stay at home. You ought to have been a preacher.*

In an interview some years later Patrick asked Owney Hanratty, a light-hearted neighbour of eighty-five:

'Did you ever know me to do any work?'
'You carried bags for me at the mill and I found you all right. Of course you never killed yourself.'
'I was fairly intelligent?'
'Sure you were intelligent. Only you were intelligent you'd have to work the same as the rest of us.'

Here are two pieces by Patrick evoking those early years.

Some months ago I spent the best part of four weeks in my native place in County Monaghan and I found it difficult to recapture the emotions that once moved me in this place. And one of the causes, at least to some extent, was my inability to find gaps where gaps once were.

Trying to dig up my past I sought the ruined dwelling of Johnnie, a relative of mine and a neighbour. His little house on a height was the usual piece of Irish architecture of its kind and day, a little room on each side of a kitchen, clay floors with potholes in them where hens drank, a jamb of a

31

wall between the door and the fireplace in which there was a small window, and in the chimneypiece itself small square holes for holding pipes and so forth.

The picture was perfectly in my mind, but I wanted the pleasure of refreshing it. I could hardly believe that any place could be so smothered in bushes and weeds; it reminded me of some famous ancient city that was discovered in the Indo-China jungle some years ago. To dig out Herculaneum would be little more difficult. I couldn't even see into the orchard. It used to contain some very sweet apples and red gooseberries.

So I was left to muse on the way things were. And this I did as I stood there, shut out in exterior greenness.

Johnnie's father was a school-master of the old school, a crank and a character. He was a land surveyor for con-acre and once upon a time he let a portion of his own meagre holding to my father and measured it himself.

My father, a good man at stepping ground, told old Tom he doubted the measure.

'Did you measure the headland?' asked Tom.

The headland was a big swamp and in con-acre for cropping you were supposed to get one headland free for turning on. So when my father said that he couldn't measure a bog, the other made a statement which I heard repeated as droll wit, 'Turn on your own ground,' says he. 'Yes,' says he, 'turn on your own ground.'

I don't think I remember a happier family than those cousins of mine. As a child I remember them well, the whole family and father and mother roaring with laughter, and joking as they sat around drinking tea out of jam-pots and bowls.

Johnnie was a good-looking, handy fellow of six feet with curly black hair and no desire whatever to kill himself working. Yet I heard a slave driver of a farmer declare that 'Johnnie would fill as much dung into a cart as any three men I ever had about the place.' He was also noted as a

Kednaminsha School today and (top) when last in use.

33

great man with a crowbar. It was his handiness he was noted for. Such was fame in those days.

Johnnie died in New York a few years ago, too young for a man of such a youthful heart and too soon for me to meet him again to live over those simple, amusing and (looking back) moving times.

I cast one last look at the green forest that once was house and garden and tried to visualise the path that led to it. Difficult till I had got away from that whitethorn, bramble and boortree.

Delving into my past I had better luck, or at least no worse, at Barney's old place. The architecture here had been similar to Johnnie's, except that one room of the house had been slated and this remained standing. The thatched part was quite gone except for the fireplace where, in the chimney wall or the hob or whatever you call these parts, there were the two square holes where Barney kept his clay pipes and tobacco. Even now after all the rains one can discern the stains of burned tobacco.

As I reflect on these simple lives I also am aware of the enormous and peculiar courage and persistence that inspired these lives. It was the Life Force carrying on in spite of everything. They were stuck by love to their little patches of land.

Patches they were; the recognised economic holding in those parts was five Irish acres. They lived on it too, mostly off praties and oats, and it was probably the stirabout staple that saved the day. They saved the landlords, too, without knowing it, for if they had walked off those patches of starvation where would the landlords be?

This area is rapidly going into larger holdings which are still not large enough, and with the untrimmed whitehorns overwhelming the countryside . . . .

A part of our estate was known as The Meada, a bit of land easy on the feet where I used to practise at high jumping, my great ambition then. Today that Meada has about twenty crops of its own wiry grass rotted and half rotted on top of each other. A man would need his health to make his way through that Meada. You might as well be walking over the middle of a newly-built stack of hay. Still, I didn't do so bad.

And I got a job for a while. I was posted with a gun on the side of a hill to keep the crows away from turnips and later from barley. Waiting with a gun is conducive to patience, like angling. When I arrived with the gun you'd think every crow in the country had emigrated.

I shot the first one I got a bead on, and by Lord Harry it was hard to stand me after that. The temptation to boast is very great and I thought of Nicholas, a noted gunner and a man of imagination. He never dropped less than three or four foxes with one shot.

It was wonderful to be back in one's native fields, but a little unsatisfactory when one is not part of the general activity. People are worried and talking about certain things, and you are out of it.

Oh, it is wonderful to be involved in life and to be worried by it.

Harvest Time

It is harvest time now, eight o'clock on a late August morning. Rather foggy, the corn is damp and drooping but it will soon be dry and lively. The sun is coming through the mist and if this day is anything like the days past it will be a hot one.

I have been harvesting during the last few days for a neighbour at five shillings a day. There are three others along with me and together we wait among the stooks till the reaping mill is ready to start. We are smoking cigarettes and talking about football and other things. The horses are yoked to the reaping mill, the driver who is also the owner of the corn, is stooped over the gears greasing them. Now and then he lifts his head to speak to the horses which are striving to snatch at a nearby stook.

'Will yez hould up there,' he says, 'a man would think yez were starved.' Between the little hills we can hear the sudden music of other reapers as they start.

The man at the reaping mill puts a knot on the reins and ties them around his neck, he drives and makes the sheaves at the same time; he can do this because his horses are quiet and well trained. He gets to his seat, the sheaving rake poised.

'Go on in the name of God the same as if it was morning,' he addresses the horses. Down along the ledge the mill roars and I experience a sort of heroic moment.

'Every man to his ould place,' is the order. We take up the positions along the ledge that we held yesterday. I am at the beginning of the cut; my neighbour is the slowest harvest-man in the country I think, that is the man who is next to me in the cornfield. When he lifts the sheaf onto his knee he holds it there for a space of a minute while he drinks in the beauty of the immediate landscape. The next man is nick-named The Sniper because he has a long nose like a snipe, and the fellow at the opposite end is an old-time harvestman who can appear busy doing nothing. 'He'd do a lot of work in a long time,' as the saying goes.

My neighbour is working towards me, a little quicker than usual because he is anxious to talk on the eternal subject. We meet before the reaper comes again and sit together on a sheaf.

From the far end of the field a shout comes; 'Move down yous, five sheaves apiece,' the boss orders us.

We shift down a few yards. The reaper is coming again. 'What's that she said to Joe?'

The answer is lost in the roar of the reaper.

We have now settled down to work, developing a good rhythm. Ledge after ledge falls and is tied into sheaves. We

36

26 - 9 - 1917

Dear Teacher, The cause of my absence from school yesterday was because we were drawing home the corn and I was sorry I could not attend my lessons.

I remain

your fond pupil

P. Kavanagh

Miss Cassidy

Handwritten letter from Patrick, 1917.

have off caps, coats and vests, and the old-timer has his braces hanging down behind him. We have all tied straw ropes around our knees.

'Sittin' down, sittin' down. What the devil do yiz mane sittin' down at such an hour of the day? Are there no heads to be gathered? Thrust up the brow of that ledge.'

That is the boss. As he drives back idle he gives us a vicious stare and passes on growling to himself for our benefit. 'A bleddy pack of gets coming to lie up on a fella.'

The other two harvestmen are still stooped over their sheaves.

'Time the ten o'clock tay was here,' my neighbour remarks.

'Talk of the devil, there's Mary comin' across the stile,' I say.

We sit around on sheaves while Mary hands the mugs round. The boss takes his tea sitting on the mill seat; one of our men is standing up.

'Sit down ye oul' hathen; the man that ates standin' up is on the road to hell.'

'Who's yon fella?' Mary says, looking towards the stile.

'A harvestman from the city of Crossmaglen.'

He is welcomed, he is a stranger, a traveller, a romantic to us.

'Hard man, Peter.'

'Yer lookin' for a start?' our boss says.

'I was' he says.

'Well, I'm sorry I don't think I can give ye a start. What wages are ye lookin'?'

'Five bob.'

'There's no five bob going, but on account of who ye are four-and-six and throw off your coat.'

'Very well,' the Cross man says, throwing off his coat.

'There's a sup o'tay in the can,' Mary says, 'maybe you'd like a drop.'

He drinks a mug of tea. In a few minutes we are back at

work. There are five of us now, so we can almost keep the mill moving constantly. It is a heavy crop of oats and has lodged in many hollows.

We shout lies to one another as to the relative hardships of our particular sections.

'I'm in an awful hole here,' the old-timer says; 'more thistles than oats and every bleddy one of them as big as your leg.'

'If ye were up here, Tommy, ye'd have something to talk about,' the Sniper says; 'the oats is lying flat on the ground and the scutch is growing up through it; it would drag the sides out of a fella.'

'I wish some of you chaps had my place,' I say; 'I'm up here on a spellick where the crows would have to go down on their knees to get at the grain.'

We sometimes burst into a fit of idiotic laughter or give a cheer. It is a harvest morning.

(November Haggard, p.6f.)

Chapter Three

*Fondling the rushy beards
of Shancoduff*

Two of the farmers we swapped labour with were Paddy *Jemmety* Meegan and Peter Hamill of Dromore. Both lived near to each other. Patrick helped both of them during the busy season:

*On an apple-ripe September morn
Through the mist-chilled fields I went
With a pitchfork on my shoulder
Less for use than for devilment* . . . .

(Complete Poems, p.141)

In 1920 a loft was added to that section of the house not raised in 1909. Access to it was by means of an outside stairway. It was a convenient place for Patrick to slip up there unnoticed and write his verse undisturbed.

In 1918 a piper's band was started in Inniskeen under the instruction of Dick Keelan. Patrick joined and became a tolerable player. There was also a Gaelic language class in the village and yet another in Drumlusty school, both of which

Patrick attended. He became a fluent Gaelic speaker for a time, even though his interest was not in the language but in the girls he would meet at the classes. Even more curious than the language class was the step-dancing class which he also attended, ending up tapping the floor with the best of them, *as light on his foot as a Tyrone ragman.*

Patrick's delight in nature extended to his taking an occasional drink from running streams. The result was that he contracted typhoid fever in 1923 and on August 23 he was sent in a hearse wagon to Carrickmacross Fever Hospital. The wailing in our house and even among the neighbours was fierce. No one expected him to recover and the house was fumigated lest other members of the family come down with it. Memories of the plague that followed the Famine still haunted the imagination of the district. How he survived that wretched institution is a mystery. He was home after a stay of about two months with a permanent thrombosis in his leg and his hair falling out. While he was in hospital Father visited him every Monday — the traditional shoemaker's holiday. He walked the six miles each way. He didn't have a bicycle and couldn't bother waiting for a train. My sister Lucy, then in High School in Carrick visited him every day.

With Patrick safely on the side of the living once more, my parents began to plan for the future of the family. I, the second man in the family, had to be provided for. The traditional course of action in this part of the country was to hire out excess members of the family to prosperous farmers who needed extra help. Thus twice a year in Carrickmacross there was held the Hiring Fair, Ireland's version of the slave market. Men and women gathered in two separate groups on the Main Street opposite New Street and stood around like slaves waiting to be bought. A buyer would come along and a bargain would be struck for a half year. The winter half would be for five months and the summer half for seven. The hired person would go home to his new master and for a pittance work at least fourteen hours a day, and at night sleep out on the loft or in some outhouse. That in brief is what hiring meant and that was the position of Jemmy Pepper in *By Night Unstarred*. It was Mother's proudest boast that no member of her family ever went for hire.

The problem of my existence was solved in a way that astonished the neighbours. In May 1925 my parents for the sum of two hundred and sixty-seven pounds bought a farm then for sale in Shancoduff called Reynold's Farm. What matter that the seven rushy fields faced north. Here was a farm of sixteen acres three roods and nineteen perches for the second man! The countryside was mystified: how in God's name could the Kavanaghs have got that amount of money? They surely must have received a legacy from America from some criminal relative who had murdered someone. The bad drop was always in them.

Not long afterwards we amazed our neighbours further by buying a secondhand cart and an old mare that, as it turned out, would kick the stars out of the sky. The amusement caused by the kicking mare did something to mollify the envy of the neighbours. An account of the kicking mare is to be found in *The Green Fool*.

Shancoduff was more than a farm for Patrick: it was a wonderland. Almost mountain-high the fields provided us with a scenic view that stretched fifteen miles to the Mourne mountains. On a clear day you could see not only Glassdrummond chapel but even houses on the side of Slieve Gullion. Lying there on a headland you could observe the activity of the whole parish. Of course some work had to be done but Patrick managed to treat it most of the time as a branch of relaxation.

In a column in *The Irish Press*, 26th June, 1943, he describes in a light fashion how his true autobiography ought to begin:

Once upon a time there was a boy of eighteen who lived in a little house in the country. His father was a hot-tempered

*man and his mother a wise woman. The boy was as lazy a
boy as ever slept on a headland in the sunlight of a June
afternoon. The boy was awakened from his headland sleep
by his father. 'The cows are broke into the oats and you lazy
robber, you are lying here like a churn a-drying. What do
you intend to make of yourself?'*

*The young man was in love — or thought he was — with a
beautiful young girl whose name was Julia. As he drove the
cows out of the oats he was thinking of her and wondering if
it wouldn't be a good idea to make a poem about her and
send it anonymously to her.*

Patrick engaged in every type of athletics popular in the parish.
In 1925-26 he captained a Junior Tug O'War team that out-
pulled the Senior team. He practised the high jump, ran the mile
in under five minutes, threw weights and played football with
the Inniskeen Rovers. Yet all this time he was writing verse and
I had become his sole audience and literary critic. I held that
position almost until his death forty years later.

As Patrick read his verse I would listen not for the rhythm,
nor for the obvious sense in the lines but for some superior
sense beyond the actual words, some harmonics,
communicating a sacred message or incantation delighting me
with the knowledge that there was a God. If a verse has none of
this no matter how well it may be composed it is dead. That has
been my standard and when I praised something of his Patrick
knew what I meant. He himself many times tried to explain this
quality in verse which transforms verse into poetry. He spoke of
it sometimes as *the flash* and sometimes in a more roundabout
way:

*One often hears of men who declare that they love the ground
some lady walks on. It is no exaggeration: we do love in that
way . . . . Love is an enslavement against which we hold out
as long as we can. But surrender is happiness . . . . I do not
know anything I love so much as a potato field in October. A*

friend I once knew used to say that I wrote too much about
potatoes and cabbages and not — I suppose — about roses. But I
might pause to ask a question. What is the quality of beauty in
art or in nature? It is what happens to you when you look at
something. And looking at a cabbage can be a more thrilling
experience than looking at a rose. Beauty is an energy.

(*The Standard*, 5th October 1945)

Technique is important is poetry only so that it may reveal the
supernatural. I could sense this unique quality in Patrick's early
verse, struggling to be revealed though it seldom came through.
He had not the technique to release it; some influence other
than his own personality intervened. The Divine Spirit does not
sparkle unless the pure personality of the writer is laid bare in
surrender to it.

Although I was only a boy then, I encouraged Patrick to
continue, even urged him to submit verse to the Poet's Corner
in the *Weekly Independent*. Then one day in the summer of
1928 the thrilling news came that the paper had accepted three
of his pieces, *Summer*, *The Pessimist* and *Freedom*. Patrick
was up in Lennons' working at a threshing when I raced up to
him with the news. It was the most thrilling moment of his life.
There were to be two others comparable but this was the first.

On September 1st 1928 *Freedom* appeared; here is a stave:

Oft did I look into her eyes —
That were of greyish splendour —
To catch their secret lover-wise
And crush their proud defender.

There was shock felt throughout the parish as well as in our
own family — here was the uneducated son of the local
shoemaker having pretensions to being a poet. A gulpin who
hadn't even reached the sixth grade in school! But there was no
denial by Patrick and there at the foot of the verse for all to see
was *P. Kavanagh, Mucker, Inniskeen*. He didn't have to put in

1927: Peter (in background) and Patrick in the front garden. [Annie Kavanagh].

Mucker but did it just the same! Two weeks later he struck again and for the next six months. The man was becoming a menace and it was generally agreed that Patrick had a slate loose. It had to be so, the way he was acting. Now, were it his sister Lucy — who had recently become a schoolteacher — then such behaviour would be understandable.

As the months passed and Patrick continued to publish, fear began to grip the hearts of the parish that they might have another bard on their hands. There was quiet consternation in many people's eyes. From the scourge of a bard, may the Lord God deliver us! No doubt prayers were said by those neighbours with a guilty conscience who saw retribution on the way. To those who so prayed it seemed their prayers were answered for Patrick apparently went silent. What in fact happened was that accidentally Patrick had discovered the world of literature.

1927 was a momentous year for Patrick. His uncle, Jemmy Quinn, suffering from arthritis, presented Patrick with his old bicycle. From today's point of view with everyone in the parish having a car this statement seems excessive, even amusing. But not so. Such was the condition of poverty then that owning a bicycle was a luxury. *Ould Quinn*, as the bicycle was affectionately named, gave Patrick freedom: he could now travel to public events several miles from home, taking me with him — as it turned out — on the crossbar. He could visit Dundalk or Carrick any time he was free. The trains were there but they cost money and tied one to a schedule.

It was on one such trip to Dundalk that Patrick came across a copy of AE's *The Irish Statesman*. Here in its pages Patrick for the first time became aware of contemporary writing. It was writing in the style of the so-called Celtic Twilight tradition that he later came to detest. Writers in this tradition invented the myth of Mother Ireland and wrote about it in prose and verse as if it were a fit subject for serious literature. Writing based on such a lie is unreal and worthless. The only valid subject for literature is the expression of the writer's personality, the heart laid bare. Patrick at this time was unaware of this immense defect in writings of the Celtic Twilight. For him it was literature on a high level: certainly it was an improvement on anything he had so far come across.

Every week Patrick rode on his bicycle to Dundalk, close to ten miles away, to pick up his copy of *The Irish Statesman*. He began submitting verse. Shortly he received another thrilling letter: AE wrote returning the verses he had sent but encouraging him to send more. Finally in 1929 three were accepted, *The Intangible*, *Ploughman* and *Dreamer*. Here is *The Intangible* as it appeared on 19th October 1929:

Rapt to starriness — not quite
I go through fields and fens of night,
The nameless, the void
Where ghostly poplars whisper to
A silent countryside.

Not black or blue
Grey or red or tan
The skies I travel under
Indian
Vision and Thunder.

Splendours of Greek,
Egypt's cloud-woven glory,
Speak no more, speak
Speak no more
A thread-worn story.

Death and birth! Father died 27th August 1929 and Patrick was born a poet two months later.

The other two poems were published on 15th February. Two months later the magazine folded for ever. It had lasted just long enough to open the doors of the literary world for Patrick. He was lucky and the following summer (1930) in a half-aware tribute to his good fortune and in an endeavour to stretch it a bit, he walked all the way to Dublin to visit AE. It took him three days. AE received him with warmth and enthusiasm and when was about to make the return trip, gave Patrick a load of books to take home with him. These Patrick wrapped in his raincoat and carried on his back at least to the railway station for he came back by train.

These were real books, not just school anthologies: Emerson, Dostoyevski, Whitman, James Stephens, *Gil Blas*, *Moby Dick*, Plato, Victor Hugo and many others. He also presented him with copies of *Poetry Chicago*. After sampling the books, Patrick set his mind to two — *Gil Blas* and *Moby Dick*. These he read and re-read for the rest of his life. I read all the others.

In addition to presenting Patrick with the library of books, AE introduced Patrick to Frank O'Connor, to Seamus O'Sullivan editor of *The Dublin Magazine* and to one or two others. Further, he began to announce to all who would listen that he had found a poet! Dublin listened but did nothing. When AE died in 1935 Patrick scraped up enough money for the train fare and went to Dublin to attend his funeral. He was pictured in *The Evening Herald* 20th July 1935 at the graveside ceremonies. Yeats too is in the picture but they were not introduced. Yeats was in Patrick's proximity only one other time, in the Abbey foyer in 1936. Neighbours who saw Patrick's picture in the paper growled because he had attended the funeral of a stranger while ignoring that of a prominent neighbour.

In a BBC interview in 1946 with W. R. Rodgers, Patrick paid this tribute to AE:

He was the first man who published and paid for a poem of mine, and I was astonished when I got a guinea from him, from The Irish Statesman. I didn't meet actually when he was editing The Irish Statesman, I met him after it closed. I met him as a country gobshite, rather pretending, and I didn't meet him honestly, sincerely, though I recognized him as a great and holy man.

It was the first time I ever came to Dublin. I went up to see him as a country boy, which probably I was, without knowing it. He received me marvellously, with great kindness, considering that he wasn't altogether very well at the time. He was very good to me, quite friendly. He made tea for me. I admired the fact that he was a good man, and I know that there is a tendency now to make little of him on account of his work, but I think he himself was a great work. I never met Yeats but I would say AE was a much holier man. I'd say greater in every way, except that Yeats was a very fine writer, but I liked AE. I think that any man who contributes virtue, goodness and that kind of nobility which really is something, produces a union of hearts far more than any Wolfe Tonery.

Patrick had broken through the boundaries that confined him to his parish and from 1930 onwards his perspective was Dublin, London, even America. He wanted to escape the bondage of Inniskeen, the little farm, the slavery, the muck. He wanted to meet intellectuals, learned people, those with an interest in literature, music, painting. Inniskeen was a jail. He had relatives in Chicago and wrote them to ask if they would sponsor him should he decide to emigrate. Fortunately they ignored him. Whenever he had the train fare he would be off to Dublin deserting his work to the great annoyance of Mother. What would he get out of that carry-on she would enquire. Only the Poorhouse in the end. And in a way she was not far wrong. But neither Patrick nor I saw it that way until perhaps thirty years later. Had he sat where he was and kept writing, the world would have come to his door — but here again this is speculating after the fact.

By 1934 only Mother, Patrick and my sister Josie remained in the family holding. Most of my sisters had moved off into branches of the nursing profession except Celia who had joined a convent in England. I myself was on the way to becoming a schoolteacher. When Father died in 1929 it was decided at a family conference that I should be educated. A collection was made, a bicycle bought and off I went to the High School in Carrick, six miles away. For four years I cycled in and out each day except Sunday and in 1934 I was called to St. Patrick's Training College in Dublin. Patrick was delighted with my success. I was breaking out and he could surely follow.

Patrick was now the nominal head of the household and had to decide on the planting of crops, the buying of supplies, the selling of cattle and all the other duties that fall on a small farmer. He made a fairly good job of it considering he was dissatisfied with his position. His policy at a fair was to sell quickly even if that meant selling cheaply. At least he didn't have to drive the beasts home. Nor did he believe in overworking the potato drills which has since turned out to be scientifically correct. Mother loved him even though he caused her lots of small problems such as stealing money for the accursed cigarettes that were eventually to do him so much harm. He was also the household correspondent with other members of the family. Some of his letters to my sister Cecilia survive and here are a few extracts which will give some idea of his activity at this time 1933-1935. (The reader must understand that these letters were written to a convent and that Patrick knew they would be scrutinized by the authorities before they were passed along. He therefore did a bit of boasting and put on a thick veneer of poetic swank mixed with a splash of piety.)

I think Sissie mentioned in her letter your desire to have some of my poems. Well, you couldn't do better than read real poetry; 'tis more religious than prayer.

* * *

I am sending you some of my published poems. I hope you find something lovely and holy in them. Unless you find 'a thing which is beautiful' in them they are useless to you — the Holy Breath. Poetry is a piece of earth in which the Holy Ghost is manifest.

Agreement

I Michael Callan of the townland of Mucker in the Parish of Donaghmoyne, barony of Farney and county of Monaghan do hereby agree to assign all the Property I possess in the townland of Mucker as well as everything personal to James Kavanagh of aforesaid townland on condition that he clothe, house and provide me with food, the same as I was in the habit of getting, for the remainder of my life.

In virtue of and as proof of my good faith in said agreement I hereunto put my hand and mark This twenty-eighth day of August One thousand eight hundred and ninety six.

                   his

Signed   Michael X Callan

               mark

Witness present: Patrick Meegan

1896: Agreement between Michael Callan and James Kavanagh, father of Patrick.

This letter isn't clean but then Francis Thompson scarcely ever washed his hands or his face. Dirt, the prerogative of poets.

Last Monday I was in Dundalk fowl market with two turkeys in a hamper of Meegans, the one Paddy was cradled in, and it was an experience. I sold one in five minutes at sixpence a pound and it took me three hours to get fivepence for the other. If I'd have waited half an hour longer I'd have got sevenpence or eightpence as they rose in price.

Peter says I should be chained to my desk like a Greek slave, or a mediaeval monk. He's a tyrant.

Yes, I have written a number of poems this late while but I am sorry to say they are frightfully mannered, bad . . . . Perhaps now that I have turned to objective reality I may be able to write something honest and beautiful, as chestnut trees or horses out on grass.

I believe you pray a lot and now let me utter a little heresy. I think quite a lot of the orthodox praying has no more spiritual value than a Dipper's bath.

Here I am at half-past eight December 18th 1934 sitting in my den. The rain is beginning to sing on the slates. There are a few poems of mine in the Dublin Magazine. I'll send you a copy when I get it. . . . There is an Irish class at Drumlusty School three nights a week and Josie, May Crawley and this kid attend. (Patrick fell in love with a girl he met there). Mother is looking forward to Peter's homecoming with great joy. Do you know, Mother is very wise; she could buy and sell the lot of us. She is doing well this long time. Indeed her health is remarkably good. I haven't mentioned her or hardly anyone because I'm a terrible egotist.

I had a letter from Helen Waddell, the novelist. It had to do with the publication of my poems. She is a reader for Constables and if any good comes out of it I'll tell you.

Peter had some good fun in college and, lest I forget, he was appointed to the Civil Service but declined. . . . I had a few rounds of boxing with him. The radio hasn't made a sound since Peter deserted it. I myself never look at the baste, as Betty Taaffe used to say. I played the melodeon for Mick Shevlin. He said I'd hardly ever be better but one consolation I had was that I could hardly ever be worse.

My poems in the Dublin Magazine are thin, cold and intellectual and folk who expect delicate emotions are often disappointed.

Chapter Four

Alive when April's ecstasy
Dances in every whitethorn tree

Shortly after Patrick entered what may be called the world of real literature he began sending out selections of his verse to publishers. He was encouraged in his hopes by Thomas Moult who included *Ploughman* in his anthology, *Best Poems of 1930.* Eventually, and after many rejections, on 9th April 1936 he received the following letter of acceptance from Macmillans:

> *Dear Sir,*
>
> *We have now carefully considered the Ms. of your 'Ploughman and Other Poems' and we write to say that we should be pleased to undertake its publication if the following proposal would be acceptable to you. You possibly know our Contemporary Poets Series, a specimen volume of which is enclosed. This series was primarily intended to introduce to the public, authors whose work had not yet appeared in any collected form, as we felt that a writer who had not yet produced any large body of verse, but who wished and deserved to receive the attention which the publication of a small collection should ensure him, might find it a suitable means of achieving that result.*

June 1931: Portrait of Patrick. (Photographer unknown).

If you would be willing to allow us to produce your poems in this form to be sold at one shilling we should be pleased to pay you a royalty of 10% on all copies sold and a payment of five pounds on account of such royalties on publication. It is unfortunately true that, like ourselves, we would be unlikely to obtain any considerable financial return, but this arrangement would no doubt allow us to add to this first group any further small collection of poems you might subsequently write which could then be placed on sale in the usual cloth-bound volume at a higher price.

If this proposal is, as we hope, acceptable to you we shall be glad to send the usual forms of agreement embodying these terms for your signature.

Patrick signed the agreement and collected the five pounds. The book was issued in the autumn, paper-covered with thirty-five pages. It was well received by the press but no mention was made of it around Inniskeen, nor were any copies bought. There was not the high excitement for Patrick or for myself that we had experienced earlier when his first verse was published.

The reader for Macmillans was Helen Waddell and when one reads her verse it is not difficult to see why she should be attracted to Patrick's early verse. Patrick refers to the magic of the East:

A strange unquiet wonder.
Indian
Vision and thunder,
Splendours of Greek,
Egypt's cloud-woven glory . . .

Furthermore, it was written by candlelight and Helen Waddell loved the candlelight image. In her Introduction to her translation of *Chinese Lyrics* (1913) she writes:

It is by candlelight one enters Babylon; and all roads lead to Babylon provided it is by candlelight one journeys . . . . One

sees most by candlelight, because one sees little. There is a
magic ring, and in it all things shine with a yellow shining,
and round it wavers the eager dark . . . . All men meet at
Babylon who go on pilgrimages for all roads end in Babylon,
the Road of the San Grael, the Road of the Secret Rose . . . .

With a book of poems published in London, Patrick now felt
that he was on the move. On 20th February 1936 he read his
poems over Radio Athlone. I asked permission from the Dean
of the College to listen to him in the library over the
loudspeaker. He had a most impressive voice, the best reader of
verse I ever heard.

In June 1936 I graduated as a National Teacher. I could
hardly believe it, so great had been the effort. I hadn't yet a job
but I was at least technically out of poverty. A vacancy turned
up in our parish but the parish priest, Bernard Maguire, turned
me down, saying a prophet is never accepted in his own
country. I suspect his reason was resentment at Patrick's
pretensions at becoming an intellectual. That role already had
been filled by himself. Just the same I managed to latch on to a
temporary teaching job in Dundalk at forty-seven and three
pence a week. I performed so well there that I was officially
rated Highly Efficient and with that special qualification I had
no difficulty getting a teaching position with the Christian
Brothers in Westland Row, Dublin. I began there in October
1937.

My job in Dundalk, so near home, had this exceptional
advantage: it allowed me to take care of the farm and release
Patrick from all family obligations. With the publication of his
book of poems, Patrick saw the possibility of conquering
London or at least of finding a place in its literary world —
which would amount to the same thing. So in the late spring of
1937 Patrick set off for London, I providing him with the fare
and as much pocket money as I could afford. After he had paid
for his ticket to London he would have about two pounds ten
shillings, according to my estimate. But he could make money

there. It did not occur to either of us that we were engaging in wild delusions, so full of hope and confidence were we. No one invited him to London so there were no free lodgings awaiting him. He made for Rowton House, the well-known shelter for the down-and-out. He was aware of only two literary people in London: Thomas Moult, the anthologist and the other, Helen Waddell who had recommended his poems to Macmillan.

He first called on Moult who opened the window to him but not the door. He was sitting in a pleasant room writing. Patrick gave his name saying he had a poem in one of his anthologies. Moult feigned ignorance and closed the window. Patrick was shocked at the time but later told me he understood the position. Moult was making a living as a journalist and Patrick had interrupted him as he was trying to write to a deadline: that was all there was to it. Still it was a disappointment.

Helen Waddell, when he called, received him with enthusiasm and at once arranged with Constables that Patrick should write his autobiography for them. But a contract to write a book in this instance didn't bring any advance on royalties and Patrick had to send out begging letters to several people including of course to myself. I sent him what I could and Seamus O'Sullivan of *The Dublin Magazine* sent him a pound. Patrick's letter to O'Sullivan is extant and was on exhibition in Dublin a few years ago.

London astonishes the newcomer, he wrote in another letter (*Lapped Furrows*, p.39) *but I hit back by not being astonished*. Just the same, things were looking up and he moved to a room at 20 Williamson Street. There he began to work on the book that was to become *The Green Fool*. Soon he ran out of money and had to return to Ireland where he finished it. The original title *The Grey Dawn Was Breaking* was considered too awkward, and we had to search for a better one. There was a phrase common in our area, *an iron fool* — used to describe someone who was pretending to be a fool only to protect himself. The idea was good but the word *iron* in the phrase would be lost on most people. So the title was changed to *The Green Fool*.

After reading the manuscript Constables decided it wasn't for their house so they graciously passed it on via A. M. Heath, the agent, to Michael Joseph then a young publisher starting up. He advanced Patrick forty pounds *half on delivery of a new final chapter in accordance with the suggestions made by the Publisher, and half on the day of publication in advance on account of royalties.*

The book, published in the spring of 1938, was killed at once by Oliver Gogarty who sued for libel. Patrick had innocently mentioned that he had called on Gogarty and had mistaken his maid for his mistress. So instead of the extra twenty pounds Patrick got a bill for two hundred pounds court costs!

Apart from its being a bad blow to Patrick's momentum, the killing of the book was not a great loss. It was permeated by the lie of Mother Ireland, so much a part of the Celtic Twilight. In it Patrick was dreaming just before awakening. As I write I have before me the small pocket diary in which Patrick wrote the notes for this book. It is noteworthy that on the first page is a verse by Helen Waddell, a translation from the Chinese:

I cannot come to you, I am afraid
I cannot come to you there, I have said
Through all the night I lie awake and know
That you are lying waking even so.
Though day by day you take the lonely road
And come at nightfall to a dark abode.

Yet if so be, you are indeed my friend
There is the end
There is one road, a road I've never gone
And down that road you shall not pass alone,
And there's one night you'll find me by your side
The night that they shall tell me you have died.

Only the first verse was in the notebook but I quote the lot. As far as I know there was no romance between Patrick and Helen Waddell (1889-1965). Nor did he ever meet her again. She was a brilliant translator of mediaeval lyrics and obviously a person of sound judgement.

The Green Fool is not an autobiography: perhaps it is a good book of fiction. I cannot say; I have not read it in forty years. I do recall several bare-faced lies in it, for instance that he went out for hire. As the story of his early years the book is unreliable.

I mentioned earlier how in October 1937 I moved to a teaching job in Dublin. Now I had made my own escape from the country I planned to help Patrick do the same. My employment was in the sweat-shop category but even so at a push I could support Patrick as well as myself. But moving Patrick away from the fields he loved was not easy. Towards the end of his life, with the benefit of hindsight, he regretted having made the move:

> *There I was, in a city that was not a city. Scores of cunning rogue writers, drinking and talking about poetry. With no background, no job or prospects of one, I came to Dublin and since then I have never stopped regretting it. Living in a fusty bed-sitting room on the Drumcondra Road. Living in another fustier bed-sitter at the top of O'Connell St. near the bridge — six stories up.*

The rights and wrongs are hypothetical.

He wanted the best of both worlds. He loved the fields but detested the society. He was constantly complaining how hard work killed the creative spirit; of the ignorance of his neighbours; of the country girls who liked nothing better than to insult his ego. A choice had to be made and I made it for him. Nor do I now regret that decision — it was the correct decision in the circumstances.

He began tentatively with excursions into Dublin making what are called *contacts*. He now had a modest reputation with a book of poems and a book of prose to his name. There was as

1933: Harvesting, with Josie and Peter (right). [Annie Kavanagh].

yet nothing to his discredit: he seemed harmless enough to Dublin literary society. Through T. J. Kiernan, head of Radio Eireann, he was invited to do several broadcasts in the *I like that Book* series. Patrick chose the title *I Hate that Book*, this book being *Pilgrim's Progress* by Bunyan. No one objected; he wasn't being taken seriously.

In 1938 Patrick did another talk, this one for BBC Northern Ireland in a series on Irish counties. He talked on County Down. I toured the county with him looking for information and even ascended Slieve Gullion (in County Armagh), that mystical mountain peak that had haunted our view for so long from the splink of Shancoduff Hill. The talk was a success but like all these early talks there was no recording made. I do however have the notes he took on the county.

Before trying Dublin, Patrick decided to give London a second try. He had reason to be more hopeful this time. In August 1938 he had received a blue envelope from Peter Fleming, editor of *The Spectator* informing him that he was accepting a poem he had submitted to the periodical. This was the third great thrill of Patrick's life. It meant he had broken the barrier into the British literary world. No longer was he an Irish poet — he was *the* poet. Peter Fleming was a brother of Ian Fleming, later to become famous at the author of James Bond. Curiously enough the poem accepted and published on 16th September was another poem called *Ploughman*:

In these small fields
I have known the delight
Of being reborn each morning
And of dying each night.

And I can tell
That birth and death
Are nothing so fierce
As the Preacher saith.

But when a life's but a day
The womb and the tomb
Press lips in fondness
Like bride and groom.

And when a man's a ploughman
As I am now
And Age is a furrow
And Time a plough.

And Infinity a field
That cannot stretch
Over the drain
Or through the ditch.

(Complete Poems, 63)

Patrick was in Inniskeen when he received that thrilling letter. He was wondering what his next move should be when he received a letter from two ladies who lived at Gerrards Cross, outside of London, inviting him to come and stay with them. They had read *The Green Fool*, they said, were impressed by it and felt Patrick could achieve big things if he came permanently to London. They would guarantee him board and lodgings. What their motives were Patrick did not enquire: he jumped at the offer and in the late spring of 1939 he settled in with these two ladies. They ran a café and it turned out they were middle-aged and unattractive. They bought him his first typewriter and Patrick began his assault, not on the women, but on London. Here are a few of the letters he sent me at the time:

Gerrards Cross, Bucks., July 1939
Dear Peter,
   I was disappointed not being in when you phoned either time. I therefore hasten to write.
   There is no news except that today Harold Macmillan wrote saying that he was going up to Scotland for a few days

and bringing The Green Fool with him. When he has read it he will write again.

He signed himself 'Believe me, yours sincerely' and it looks good. Well, I am almost sure that I'll get books to review for The Observer. I'm going over there on Tuesday as arranged. I was told that she would do whatever she could. There were no books this week as it is a scarce period in the publishing trade.

I finished another chapter of my novel.

I am displeased with the person who answered your phone call because she knew everything I'm telling you and didn't want Miss Blois to hear. To tell you the truth, I violently dislike these people and my dream of a job includes getting away. Anyway, they serve a purpose, and that itself. I think you need not worry as things are sure to break. I have complete confidence in my future. And I know I was right in coming to England. I'd prefer that you weren't taking so deep an interest in me as that is a burden. I shall not fail. Of that be certain. I am glad you had a good journey. Write and let me know anything strange. Did The Irish Press publish my stuff, etc?

Don't mind the reference to your interest in my life; it's purely philosophical. Anyway, ties of friendship are things that impede. Luck.

PATRICK

* * *

Gerrard's Cross, Last Sunday in July 1939

I wrote last evening after you phoned but it is doubtful the letter will get to you as soon as this one. I am going over to see the editor of The Observer on Tuesday. I have had my coat cleaned and that will be money. I wonder if you would be able to raise ten bob for me by return— to arrive by second post on Tuesday morning. In my other letter which I wrote yesterday and may not arrive so soon I told that H.

Lunch in the fields: Peter (left) and Patrick, 1934.

Macmillan wrote a friendly letter. I'll hear from him and you'll hear then.

* * *

London, 1st August
Got your card and letter today — thanks. I wrote the letter you got today after you phoned me and when I was a bit worried. Ignore it. Well, I didn't see Miss Garvin today either but just the same I'll get the books to review — or I'll be surprised. Am expecting word from Harold Macmillan any time now. Might apply for radio. Great fun over Halls surely. Glad you got safe home.

(The reference here to the two halls is to a row in Inniskeen between a hall run by the locals and another by the parish priest. It was this row that formed the original plot of *Tarry Flynn*.)

* * *

33 Great St. James Street, London, August 1939
Dear Peter,

Those women gave me a great education. I'd be fit for a job now if I got one.

I wouldn't write only I know you'd be expecting a note. So far nothing. Observer, nothing doing. I'm out of Gerrard's Cross and things aren't going too well with the girls and owner. I'm waiting till next week as I have one more chance. Every time I told you about a chance I had none and this time I hadn't a mind to say. Anyway, it is a dull chance but it might mean my going back to Dublin. It is Macmillan, of course. He wrote saying that he had no opening. I saw him today and he gave me three pounds to tide me over. Will let you know. Hope this letter-writing doesn't jinx me. Superstition of course.

All the best,
PATRICK

66

London, 15th August, 1939
*I know you'll be expecting a letter. I'm afraid to talk lest . . .
. Saw Macmillan* today. He offered me three pounds a
week for six months if I got Joseph to release me from the
option. Will see Joseph tomorrow. If he doesn't do so I'll
send him a wad of stuff. I could come back to Ireland and
write if I had three pounds weekly. I applied for a job in
Dublin. Hope everything comes right but expect nothing now
till it happens.*

* * *

16th August 1939
*Joseph refused to free me from the option so now I must try
to get together a Mss. for him. I haven't the typewriter now.
I'll see Macmillan again tomorrow and maybe he'll do
something in any case. Big disappointment. Don't be
surprised if I land in Dublin Saturday morning. You never
know.*

Patrick was no diplomat; worse, he began making passes at the
pretty waitress who worked in the café. Hard words were
uttered and Patrick took off for Dublin leaving behind two very
angry women as well as his recently-acquired typewriter.

But though Patrick may appear to have been incompetent
when dealing with the world of commerce, as soon as he sat
down to write, the man of genius, the assured intellect took
over.

Here he is writing just three months later after returning to
Dublin:

Christmas Eve Remembered (1939)
I see them going to the chapel
To confess their sins, Christmas Eve
In a parish in Monaghan.

(* Later Prime Minister).

67

Poor parish! And yet memory does weave
For me about these folk
A romantic cloak.

No snow, but in their minds
The fields and roads are white
They may be talking of the turkey markets
Or foreign politics, but tonight
Their plain, hard country words,
Are Christ's singing birds.

Bicycles scoot by, old women
Cling to the grass margin
Their thoughts are earthy but their minds move
In dreams of the Blessed Virgin
For One in Bethlehem
Has kept their dreams safe for them.

'Did you hear from Tom this Christmas?'
'These are the dark days'
'Maguire's shop did a great trade,
Turnover double — so Maguire says'.
'I can't delay now Jem
Lest I be late for Bethlehem'.

Like this my memory saw
Like this my childhood heard
These pilgrims of the north.
And memory, you have me spared
A light to follow them
Who go to Bethlehem.

(*Complete Poems*, p. 71)

1938: Portrait of Patrick by Duffner Bros., Dundalk.

Chapter Five

I follow the blind dog
Over the twisted trail

World War Two had just begun as Patrick arrived from London to live with me in Dublin. At the same time, from England and from the continent came crowds of refugees, draft dodgers, spies posing as artists, artists posing as spies, American intelligence people posing as folklorists, German agents, Japanese, Australians, Bulgarians, French and those of every race. Dublin was a lively spot if you could afford to live there in comfort. I couldn't and as it turned out neither could Patrick.

I was in digs out beyond Drumcondra at the time. Patrick stayed a few days with me while searching for an adequate flat. He got one he thought was good enough on Drumcondra Road. We moved in but moved out within a month. Too expensive. Then off to 35 Haddington Road where I rented a bedsitter at twelve shillings a week. It was a room about twelve feet square, had two beds, a table, a chair, a gas cooker, gas fire and gas lights. We squeezed into it and stayed a year. Extraordinary, our resilience then, and how we managed to live in such quarters. We were like those orientals you sometimes

70

hear about who live twenty-four to a room. Patrick of course was always on the point of hitting it rich and moving out. He would take care of me then, he assured me; I'd have the best that money could buy. That's the way he was, a great man for promising especially if he were about to borrow a shilling.

I don't recall that I was overly worried by the domestic situation: I was as full of hope as he was, perhaps more so. I had a cause in which I believed — Patrick's genius; nothing else seemed to matter. That the Germans sank ten ships as well as the Ark Royal didn't bother us too much. What concerned us was literature, finding Patrick a job that he could support himself on, and trying to ration our money so we could pay the rent and eat at the same time.

Patrick had matured since writing *The Green Fool*. He was shortly to reach the top of his intellectual power and could out-write anyone within sight. Why shouldn't he be a success? He was bursting with energy and bursting with good looks. He belonged to the corduroy set, his pants singing as he strode along. He wore a fashionable sports jacket, his hair was neatly combed, his shoes polished. He washed not only his hands three or four times a day but also his wrists, of first importance according to Rilke for the man who wants to succeed. The only thing he wasn't bursting with, was money. But never mind, he'd get that, buckets of it.

Dublin literary society gave him a great welcome, not knowing what they were getting. They saw him as the ploughman with mud on his boots, the authentic Irishman, the one who had written a Celtic Twilight novel and had produced a slim volume of, for the most part, slimmer poems. For years he had been writing verse for Seamus O'Sullivan's *The Dublin Magazine* — Seamus O'Sullivan known in Dublin as the synthetic Hibernian. Patrick seemed to be exactly what the doctor ordered. They had had enough of synthetic Irishmen — here was the real thing, elemental.

Almost at once he was given the AE Memorial Award of one hundred pounds even though he hadn't properly applied for it.

He took the hundred and didn't even stand the committee a glass of porter each. This was a shocker but it could be explained by the fact that Patrick was a teetotaler. All sorts of literary types, male and female, began to show up outside our house on Haddinton Road to invite him to parties and other social events. Principal among these welcomers was loud and raucous Delia Murphy, the ballad singer. Her husband was T. J. Kiernan head of Irish radio. Patrick froze her out: he was a romantic with interest in young girls. Had his sensibilities permitted him to be interested in her very likely he would end up, as others had done, with a lucrative programme on the Irish radio.

It didn't take long for the word to get around that Patrick wasn't a man to play the game. People started to do a double-take. In spite of his conservative appearance his genius burst through. He couldn't hide it even if he tried. People took notice of the casual word dropped by chance which denoted a dangerous arrogance.

Our routine in those days — one that didn't change for several years — was as follows: we got up about seven-thirty. I made breakfast while Patrick went out for the newspaper and our morning milk bottle. Reading the paper took about three minutes unless it happened that Patrick had an essay in it which was seldom. We discussed the war news and, after a few speculations on the day ahead, I went off to school to arrive there at nine. Patrick stayed in the room writing until about noon when he joined me for lunch in an underground restaurant near Westland Row. *Those were queer times*, wrote Patrick later, *I remember I used to get lunch in a cheap café near Westland Row. It was a time of the phoney war when Hitler and Stalin had a pact. What would Uncle Joe do, we wondered as we sat around our comfortable cheap table. I used to pay by the week and the pay was one-and-threepence a time for the lunch which usually consisted of the best of fresh spuds and butter with some meat also. It saved my life, living as I was on the edge of starvation.*

It was I, of course, who paid for the lunch. During the

afternoon Patrick toured around Dublin visiting offices looking for work. We met again at six at our bedsitter for tea. Afterwards I went to the library to study for a university degree while Patrick went off seeking entertainment or diversion at some political or social gathering. We met again at nine in a café for coffee and walked home together along the docks, commenting on the foreign ships and cargoes, sometimes discussing literature. We were both in bed by ten-thirty.

On arriving from London, Patrick's first stop was the Palace Bar in Fleet Street. There the editor of the *Irish Times* held court each afternoon. Smyllie was his name, huge, rotund, puffed cheeks and rimless glasses. He was a Protestant and — I understand — came from the west of Ireland. I have never seen even a brief biography of the man. He is dead now of course. A year or two ago I tried to encourage someone to write a short biography but so far it has not appeared. The old story of when you are no longer in power.

Smyllie was approachable and pleasant. He feigned an interest in literature which is more than the editors of the other dailies did. He liked to think that the Leaders he wrote each evening were written in prose and not in journalese. He had been interned during the first war in Germany, had picked up the language and now spattered his writings with German phrases. Each Saturday he had a page in his paper devoted to books, and usually a poem or two decorated the top half. He drew a large miscellaneous crowd to his salon each afternoon, all looking for some space or notice in his paper. He was pro-British.

He already had published several things by Patrick and the hope now was that he would make the large gesture and appoint him to a job on the paper. Not a chance. He saw Patrick as someone with talent, eccentric and without power. Why should he befriend him? He was someone to be used, no more. Openings were available on the newspapers but not for Patrick. Paul Carroll who had written a number of sentimental plays and who seemed on the way to world fame showed up in the Palace Bar towards the end of 1939 bringing his younger brother, Niall, in tow. He started ordering whiskey by the bottle and sandwiches by the hamper, overwhelming Smyllie with his hospitality. Before the night was out Smyllie had landed a job on *The Irish Press* for Niall — a chap with no writing experience. But as Patrick warned me years later, in Dublin you are worse off if you have written books than if you are illiterate. Patrick and I were deeply shocked — savaged in fact — by the incident. We never could explain it.

In compensation for the insult, Smyllie invited Patrick to write 'specials' for the paper. Hence *The Gaelic Final* (September 25th 1939), *Europe is at War* (October 25th), *The Corn Goddess* (November 8th), *A Winter's Tale* (December 7th) and *Christmas in the Country* (December 30th). Patrick didn't pay for many lunches with what he got from *The Irish Times* in payment — just a miserable guinea a time.

Ten years later when he was writing an autobiographical novel Patrick described The Palace Bar and its patrons. He himself is the Michael in the story. In the published version, *By Night Unstarred* (Goldsmith edition, p. 162 ff.), I changed the 'Michael' to 'Patrick':

> *He called into the pub where the poets who did not write met on Monday and Thursday evenings. There they were all of them sitting praising each other and talking literature all the time. 'That line had what Belloc calls the unwanted spondee' he heard one small particularly stupid versifier say. Although he had written much verse in his time Michael did not rightly know what a spondee was. The last time he had seen the word was in a text book for the Intermediate Examination.*
>
> *Those men who sought emotional satisfaction by being in the company of writers and artists were there in strength this evening. As soon as a new 'writer' (none of these men was known to have written anything except undergraduate stuff in a college magazine and they were living on the strength of*

Funeral of George W. ('AE') Russell.
The scene in Mount Jerome as Mr. Frank O'Connor made an oration at the graveside. Patrick, second from right, back. *(Evening Herald).*

1935 (?): in Dublin with Frank O'Connor.

it) came in the door every one of these men who liked the company of writers gave him a wink and arranged a place at their tables for him.

A fellow with a corrugated face and wearing a large black hat over an expression of profound poetic pessimism entered and was immediately seized by three fat fellows who were dying to taste the company of a son of Apollo.

The editor of The Irish Smile sat alone, as if in a huff. He was the mountain that forced all the literary Mahomets to come to him, he did not go to them. Now he was waiting there testing his drawing powers. Finally the poet with the corrugated face went over to the editor and leaning on his shoulder made a few solemn humbug remarks.

How seriously these men took themselves!

'Are you coming in or going out?' a little fellow with a long straight pipe in his mouth said to Michael who was still in the doorway, looking on. 'Don't be so bloody difficult,' he said through his teeth. 'Will you have a drink? Joe, Joe . . . . Of all the men I have met yet you're the most impossible . . .'

'No, I'll have nothing, I'll have nothing; I only came in to see a fellow that's not here. I'll be going away in a minute.'

'Have a drink' he said with a hard ironic bite.

'I will not'.

'Impossible man'.

The conversation at the tables was usually drivel. There were no standards of criticism. That destructive element of inarticulate Dublin society which became articulate in Gogarty and James Joyce was here represented. A poisonous element, bitter, clever, good at making hurtful witticisms about their neighbours. But they had nothing creative to their name. Some of them achieved a reputation for scintillating wit but the final effect was injury to the soul. They had had their innings but that inning was over. Serious-minded men of talent and some of genius came in from the country with fertile imaginations.

Michael should have felt sympathy instead of dislike for

76

these witty jackeens who could imitate but could not create. He was brutally cruel to their efforts. Why did he not understand these men would be creative if they could?

They could get jobs, that was the trouble, that was their compromise. They could beat him for all the good jobs. They may have said to themselves: we may not have the joy of writing as well as he does but we will see to it that that is the only pleasure he will have. Michael came to the pub because that was the only way he had of hearing about jobs. . . .

The editor was a great friend of Michael's insofar as praising him in his newspaper went or of allowing him to say his say in his columns for a small fee. But to take him into the inner ring of his confidence where the gossips plan the commercial future of the state he had not done. Remarkable too how uninterested really all these pub writers were in literature or in art. The chief topic was jobs that were going or gone and how to circumvent someone's chances in favour of one of 'the boys'. Michael vaguely guessed this at the time. But a reasonably intelligent man, a man with an average sense of the realities of society as it operates would have a full conscious knowledge of it all and would not even consider it sufficiently interesting to comment upon. To Michael some of the elemental principles of capitalist society were sensational discoveries for him — when at length he did discover them.

'I didn't see you there last night' said a lantern-jawed fellow with a crooked pipe in his fingers looking across his glass at Michael, thinking he had cought the thread of the discussion.

'Where was that?' Michael asked.

'De Vanay's gramophone recital'. He turned to the editor and spoke in a different, far more intimate voice. 'That was a good thing, that recording of Menuhin'.

The editor took a hurried sip of his drink, looked wise, lit his pipe, then answered by asking another question — directed at Michael.

77

'What happened George Flabb that he isn't going back to that radio job?'

'Tired of it, he told me'.

The editor drank that in with his whiskey. The other man made a casual remark about golf.

'Where is he living now?' asked the editor.

Michael explained as innocently as the child in these job affairs which he was.

'Have a drink?' said the editor. 'Joe, Joe,' he called the barman.

'What is it?'

'I'll have nothing,' said Michael.

'Fair enough' said the editor.

The man with the lantern jaws whispered something to the editor and the editor inclined his ear. 'Surely' he said. To Michael: 'Do you know anything about this job that's going in the Plastics company?'

'What job?' said Michael and looked a little too surprised.

The other man interrupted again and the conversation between the editor and him continued in a whisper — that was insofar as the main threads were concerned.

Wasn't it queer, thought Michael, that these big men should be interested in such a small job as that vacant in Plastics? He was rather shocked, but not unduly so, for he had gone all out and pulled all the strings.

The lantern-jawed individual was a high official in the Civil Service. He was on terms of deep intimacy with all the leaders of trade — and art, so far as was possible. He was one of that numerous body of the public who are for ever on the lookout for some harmless act of which the ordinary layman and humbug can be a noisy part. Music, the theatre, painting, the people who in general carried on these arts were of the middle and lower-upper classes, of recent years of the business classes almost exclusively. Writers were different; they were harder to get on with — except the ones who drank in pubs and who didn't

78

1936: Peter (left) and Patrick, Inniskeen.

write. Men like this civil servant found much emotional satisfaction in being in the swim of music, art, the stage, etc.

'A wonderful family,' the civil servant remarked aloud after a short whispered discussion.

'The de Vanays?' said Michael. 'I wonder if they are. I shouldn't be surprised if they come from vulgar company. I know the pianist to see and to hear — unfortunately —and I'd say she hasn't a great deal of breeding".

The civil servant was very angry. The editor smiled. The former said: 'They are the de Vanay's of Dirnaugh, a well-known family'.

'I see,' said Michael drily.

A young man wearing outlandish clothes at the far side of the pub cocked his ear. The editor gave him a friendly nod. The young man picked up his glass and came across the floor carrying it which seemed to the ironic eye of Michael somehow a little undignified. Rather like bringing what is called a set-in with him.

The rest of the conversation was mainly about literature and art. But beneath all the talk the currents of the de Vanay river gave a direction to the most casual remarks. You could sense it. Michael sensed it, but that was because he was in the market himself with something to sell. These others would have been experts on the trends of such markets even when they had no interest in the business proceeding — which, indeed was very seldom.

The discussion turned for awhile on the skill of various musicians in the city. Was Jane de Vanay the greatest pianist in Europe?

She had the poetic touch, it was agreed.

The editor talked about prose. He referred to his Leaders as prose though they were merely a higher type of cliché than was usual in journalism. He asked Michael what he thought of certain poets and Michael said they were execrable.

The editor smoked his pipe and took all in without showing any signs of unusual interest.

Closing time. They all went into the street and about their different businesses.

Michael began to analyze the debate. Now he was reading more into it than was implied and that was as bad as his usual way of reading less. The wise man takes the crookedness of life and of society as a matter of course and always acts on the principle that the other fellow is trying to doublecross him.

He suspected that editor of being unfriendly which was not quite the case. The editor was as near friendly as it is possible for a man to be to another who is neither in a position to return the friendship in tangible form, or a relation or a member of the same Lodge or Old School club.

An Australian caricaturist, Alan Reeve, did a drawing of the Palace Bar in 1940 as well as individual drawings of most of the customers. Patrick wasn't considered sufficiently important to have an individual drawing made of himself but he appears in the composite picture, standing overlooking a table, no drink in his hand, ready to flee the company.

What never occurred to Patrick or to myself was the fact that Patrick had not the vaguest chance of breaking into Dublin's world of jobbery unless he compromised himself totally. Strangers from abroad came to town and within a few months were what people call successful. They had the right formula and cynically applied it. This formula, deriving from Machiavelli in the fifteenth century changes little over the years. A friend of Stendhal explained what this was. When I enter a town, he told him, I always find out first who the twelve most beautiful women are, who the twelve richest men are and which man could have me hanged if he so wished.

Patrick could have followed some such formula as others had done but he refused success at any price. He sought success only because he wished to preach integrity. But even if he had done the unthinkable and compromised, success would not have been achieved easily. During those years Dublin was

The Palace Bar by Alan Reeve.

controlled by a few political families who for years had been racketeering in the 1916 revolution. Without a nod from one of these families you couldn't get even the most menial job.

Apart from the politicians, there were other groups in this tight situation, huddled together for protection and self-promotion — the Freemasons, the Knights of Columbanus, the academics. Some of these groups overlapped each other. Patrick belonged to none and had contempt for them. His genius would carry him through, he thought. Not for long could a man of true genius be excluded — that would be immoral.

Patrick assailed every barricade but always head-on and without any over-all strategy. He phoned, he wrote letters, he went for interviews. When rebuffed by the husband he tried to influence the wife. He wrote to Mrs. McEntee, wife of the Minister of Industry and Commerce. Here was the response:

Further to the acknowledgment of the contents of your letter of 24th Ultimo addressed to Mrs. McEntee . . . . I should perhaps explain that in general all posts in the Government Service, particularly those requiring clerical qualifications, are filled competitively through the Civil Service Commission. On occasions when very special circumstances warrant it the Departments are authorised to recruit temporary staff through the Labour Exchange. These occasions are few and far between but before any candidate can be considered for a vacancy so arising it is an essential rule that he must be registered as unemployed at the Labour Exchange.

He also thought he might get a job lecturing on poetry at some school and in the course of investigating this possibility met a priest who taught at Blackrock College. Patrick was invited by him to give a talk to the students. He didn't get much in the way of cash for the assignment but he did better — he met John Charles McQuaid who very shortly was to be made Archbishop of Dublin. At that time he was head of the College.

Chapter Six

A simple man arrived in town

It is now forty years since Patrick and I lived together in that small bedsitter at 35 Haddington Road. The miseries and the frustrations as well as those that occasioned them are fading from my memory. There is very little left except the memory of some wild laughter. A few friends, too, that supplied Patrick with the occasional pound when he was in desperate straits. Roisin Walsh, head of the city libraries, was one; H. L. Doak, editor of The Talbot Press, another. Doak had Patrick make up a collection of verse for schools and though it never was published it supplied Patrick with a few pounds to help him survive. The collection is not extant.

Doak was himself a writer of verse, much of it superior to what passes today for Irish poetry. Four lines remain in my memory:

As into Dublin I rode down
With wonder I was filled
The way they said in Blanchardstown
Poor Johnny Durney's killed.

After the editor of *The Irish Times* had demonstrated that he had no intention of helping Patrick in any large way Patrick turned his attention to that mountain of prosperity *The Irish Independent*. At this time it represented the ultra-pious wing of the Catholic Church and was highly smug and capitalistic. The editor was a fellow called Geary and I have no knowledge that he ever wrote a line much less an editorial. Nevertheless he was in the job and he was the man to approach.

Patrick began rounding up his clergymen acquaintances from minor as well as from major orders; he planned strategy and finally he was able to meet the great editor of *The Independent*. The outcome of the meeting was that Patrick would be sent books for review at ten shillings a time. It was taken into account that he could sell the review copies to bookstores. In addition, he would be invited to do *specials* at three pounds each. This was long before the National Union of Journalists organized the trade. For *The Independent* Patrick wrote several articles: *Strange Company at Punchestown, Mystery of our Irish Bogs*, and notably an essay on a visit he made to Croagh Patrick. Here is an extract from the opening of this piece:

> . . . . *everybody is gay with a gayness that is the ecstasy of the pure of heart. Gay piety is not a contradiction. And one of the differences between this and Lough Derg is that while Lough Derg is quiet and austere Croagh Patrick is flamboyant and colourful as some warm-faithed corner of mediaeval Christendom. Westport tonight is like something one might read about but never experience: Christmas Day in a poet's childhood or a page of the Canterbury Tales.*
>
> *It is much better than any of these imaginings for it is real, it is happening here in Ireland in the year 1940. There is a war raging and we pray for peace.*

By chance on the day this article appeared (29th July 1940) Patrick was in court suing the B. & I. Steamship Co. because one of its horse-drawn drays had knocked him off his bicycle, doing him grevious bodily damage and causing him great mental anguish. The judge had read the piece in the paper, congratulated Patrick publicly on it and promptly awarded him thirty-five pounds damages when in fact he deserved nothing.

At the back of his mind Patrick had the notion that he might be able to write a bestseller on Irish pilgrimages. For years he held on to the idea but he never wrote the book.

In June 1940 he had visited Lough Derg, the most famous Irish place of pilgrimage. His first impressions of the place were not favourable; he wrote them down but did not publish them. Here is what he wrote:

The moment you think of Lough Derg your mind goes blank, your mind atrophies . . . . It has the terrible qualities of a tourist attraction . . . . The crowds which gather in such a place as Lough Derg act like one enormous creature, almost; and it is doubtful if one can develop a defence against it. The heart of this creature is one boiling mass of suspicious insultability . . . . Familiarity and peasant fear of the unconventional began when we were preparing to embark in the big boats for the Island. I had taken a stand on a height and was gazing over the lake trying to make myself believe the pious lie, trying to think what I ought to think, to feel what I ought to feel. I was thinking 'poetically' about Lough Derg and in my idiotic mood was building the scene up . . . I earned what came to me.

A thick-set peasant with a gnarled face, one of the boatmen, one of whose jobs apparently was to screen pilgrims and to ensure that nobody was allowed on the Island whose motives had anything to do with spirituality, came up to me as I stood locked in a bogus trance.

'Are you a pilgrim?' he asked.

'Certainly,' I answered.

'And were you ever there before?'

'No'.

He didn't like my tone of voice. He called another fellow.

P Kavanagh

4th Floor
9 h. O'Connell St.
Dublin

LOUGH DERG

om Cavan and from Leitrim and from Mayo,

om all the thin-faced parishes where hills

e perished noses running peaty water,

ey.come to Lough Derg to fast and pray and beg

th all the bitterness of nonentities,and the envy

the inarticulate when dealing with an artist.

eir hands push closed the doors that God holds open:

ve-sunlit,is an enchanter in June's hours

d flowers and light. These to shopkeepers and small lawyers

e heresies up beauty's sleeve.

e naive and simple go on pilgrimage too .

vers crying to take God's truth for granted...

         Listen to the chanted

ening devotions in the limestone church

r this is Lough Derg,Saint Patrick's Purgatory,

came to this island acre of greenstone once

be shut of the smug too-faithful. The story

different now.

Facsimile of page 1, *Lough Derg*, only mss. surviving.

'This fellow says he's a pilgrim'.

The second boatman scrutinized me policeman-like and in third-party manner while I stood in helpless humiliation. Lough Derg is typical of what may be called the Irish mind. No contemplation, no adventure, the narrow primitive piety of the small huxter with a large family.

Two years later Patrick once more visited Lough Derg and this time he wrote a long poem about his experience. I published it after his death.

All this activity, hunting for a job so he could settle down and marry; writing articles for newspapers; reviewing books . . . was apart from his real life, that is to say, the writing of verse.

He was working on a long poem at this time, *Father Mat* or as he was later to title it *Why Sorrow?* It told the story of an intellectual priest caught in the darkness of a rural parish. The place he had in mind was Inniskeen and the priest was Bernard Maguire who later on appeared in several of his books. Immediately on leaving Maynooth Father Maguire was sent to Salamanca to teach theology and hence the nickname *Salamanca Barney*. He fell in love with Spain and when he was withdrawn ten or more years later to become curate, then parish priest of Inniskeen, instead of committing suicide he turned to drink. No one in the parish knew of his weakness, not even Patrick, until after the priest died. He was a great preacher whenever he deigned to address the locals. Here then was the main character in Patrick's long poem. It opened as follows:

It was the month of May. Father Mat walked among
His cows that evening dreaming of a song
That Christ had closed the window on.
Now the priest's pride
Was a Roman poet hearing of the Crucified.
Apollo's unbaptised pagan who can show
To simple eyes what Christians never know —

Was it the unspeakable beauty of Hell?
The priest looked once — twice — and fell.

(*Complete Poems*, p. 167)

No matter how Patrick tried, he was unable to finish this long poem. For years he worked on it. Clearly there must have been something false in it which neither of us could determine. The false note, I have since decided, is this: that Patrick had no experience as a priest, was writing from the outside. There are however a few good lyrics in it notably *Garden of the Golden Apples* which was published separately in *The Listener* 19th December 1941. Another section called *Father Mat* was published, in *Irish Writing in 1946**.

In October 1940 a new literary magazine was started entitled *The Bell*. The editor was Sean O'Faoláin. A Board of Directors comprised Roisín Walsh, Peadar O'Donnell, Maurice Walsh, Frank O'Connor and Eamon Martin. The magazine according to O'Donnell was to be a magazine of life rather than of opinion. It was also founded to fill any gap in Irish letters that might have been caused by the war. For ten years on and off Patrick had been contributing to *The Dublin Magazine*. He had stopped writing for it because he smelled death there. Its beautiful format reminded him of a mortuary slab. The inside was decaying matter. *The Bell* promised to be lively. He had two poems in the first issue, both good ones, *Stony Grey Soil:*

O stony grey soil of Monaghan
The laugh from my love you thieved;
You took the gay child of my passion
And gave me your clod-conceived . . . .

You flung a ditch on my vision
Of beauty, love and truth.
O stony grey soil of Monaghan
You burgled my bank of youth! . . . .

(*Complete Poems*, p. 73)

* *The complete poem is of course available in Complete Poems* and *Kednaminsha.*

> *You wore a heather jumper then*
> *A hat of cloud and on your feet*
> *Shoes made by craft-gods out of peat.*
> *No poet ever drew a pen*
> *To bind with words wild goats and men*
> *In such a glen. O, Time's deceit*
> *Flirts here in Dublin's Grafton Street . . . .*
>
> (*Complete Poems*, p. 74)

Another excellent poem, *Christmas Childhood*, appeared in the December issue. It contains the popular lines:

> *My father played the melodeon*
> *Outside at our gate*
> *There were stars in the morning east*
> *And they danced to his music.*
>
> *Across the wild bogs his melodeon called*
> *To Lennons and Callans.*
> *As I pulled on my trousers in a hurry*
> *I knew some strange thing had happened . . . .*
>
> *Cassiopeia was over*
> *Cassidy's Hanging Hill,*
> *I looked and three whin bushes rode across*
> *The horizon — the Three Wise Kings . . . .*
>
> (*Complete Poems*, p. 144)

Patrick's method of publication was as follows: he wrote each day and when finished would throw what he wrote aside. When an opportunity came for publishing something he would sort through the pile of writings and select one that he considered appropriate for the occasion. This was his general method but

1941: in Dublin with friends.

now and then he departed from it to celebrate some immediate event.

Writing for *The Irish Independent* would have posed no problem for Patrick if they would employ him regularly and if they paid him. Patrick could write pietistic trash with the best of them. But they didn't want him. In fact it seemed they didn't want to be thought literary. Books, except religious books, were bad business. *The Irish Times* at least had literary pretensions so Patrick drifted back there.

In July 1940 he was given a book by *The Irish Times* for review call *The Hill is Mine* by Maurice Walsh, a director of *The Bell*. He was famous as a contributor to *The Saturday Evening Post*. Patrick's review cuased a riot of letter-writing and controversy. Here is an extract:

> *Literary weeds are sometimes popular. Suspicion haunts the book which sells ten thousand copies. In our world ten thousand perceptive readers is an optimism too large for ears of ordinary credulity. There is the popularity of stupid boring books like Gone with the Wind which hit the fashion, but there is also the eternal popularity of Don Quixote, Gil Blas and Hans Andersen's fairy tales. There is a common denominator of the spirit where the vulgarian and the artist meet . . . .*
>
> *There is here a little too much of the open-air, the boy scout type. The boy scout may be said to represent civilization at its lowest. The jamboree is the academy of illiteracy.*

The controversy that ensued continued for six weeks. Patrick did not participate. Leading off were those in defence of the Boy Scouts represented by Harold C. Brown. Then followed a great many witty people writing under pseudonyms, Oscar Love, N. S. Harvey, Jno. Ruddy, Lir O'Connor, Whit Cassidy, Flann O'Brien (later Myles na gCopaleen), the editor under a pseudonym with his address *Chateau Egout*, and one fellow signing himself Cu So4, the chemical used in spraying the potatoes — a reference to Patrick's poem *Spraying the Potatoes* which appeared on the book-page during the controversy, surrounded with a border that made it look like a five pound note. Here are sample extracts from the letters:

This controversy has arisen through The Irish Times having readers with a love for the decent things, for aims such as those included in the Scout Laws, for honour discipline and purity . . .

Harold C. Brown

The boy, not the boy scout represents civilization at its lowest and long may he remain so. Only the grown man develops and rejoices in the art of destruction.

Oscar Love

Mr. Kavanagh's stuff smells strongly of the Goebbels midden and I wonder you allowed it to stray into your paper which is not supported by guttersnipes or the type of individual who enjoys strolls through the sewers conducted by Mr. Patrick Kavanagh and his ilk.

N. S. Harvey

In Germany last year I had only to raise my hand to have my tricycle mended every day.

Flann O'Brien

My eye lighted on Spraying the Potatoes and I naturally enough inferred that our notes were being treated periodically with a suitable germicide, a practice that has been a commonplace of enlightened monetary science in Australia. When I realised that the heading had reference to some verses by Mr. Patrick Kavanagh dealing with the part played by chemistry in modern farming my chagrin may be imagined . . . . First, I think it is time somebody said a

*seasonable word on the question of sewage. Mr. Harvey who
lives in the honky-tonk-ridden West End of Cloughjordan
accuses Mr. Kavanagh of preoccupation with middens,
backyard cesspools and of seeking to conduct the public
through the city sewers. Mr. Harvey thinks that when Mr.
Kavanagh lays down his Homeric fountain-pen for the day
he strolls down into the street, opens a manhole and disappears
for the evening.*

Flann O'Brien

*My librarian and I have searched every shelf and combed
every catalogue in quest of some of this Mr. Kavanagh's
words. I have skimmed through The Utility of the Horse by
Paul Kavanagh, What to do with your Pulsocaura by Pietro
Kavana, Yoga & Rheutmatism by Pav Ka Vanagh and a
series of others whose names approximate to that of the man
whom I set out to vindicate. At the end of six hours research
I was forced to give up. Sir, in the entire compass of a library
which I should add is the largest collection of books in any
private establishment north of a line drawn from
Williamstown to Cabinteely, and passing through Glasthule
there is not one single work from the pen of Mr. Kavanagh.*

Lir O'Connor

*The hour has struck when I must relinquish the burden of my
lifework, A History of the Wheelbarrow, in all its aspects and
so setting aside my half-completed manuscript of volume
seven I return again to the jostle of the market place and
brave perhaps for the last occasion the raillery of Oscar
Love, my victual (and doubtless virtuous) neighbour.*

Whit Cassidy

Finally after six weeks the editor asked Patrick as a favour to
write a letter closing the controversy. This he did in the issue of
7th. August 1940 and since he almost never replied to criticism
I give this letter in full to show his style of rejoinder:

Sir,

Now that the ball is over it might be no harm if I address a few words to the stragglers on the gallery steps.

In my review of Maurice Walsh's The Hill is Mine I referred to the empty virtuosity of artists who were expert in the art of saying nothing. Ploughmen without land. One of my critics said it was a wistful remark, and maybe it was; but if ever a critic was proved right all around by his critics it happened this time. It is to be feared that the dilletantish disciples of Joyce and Eliot are no more a credit to their masters than are the followers of Baden-Powell and of Margaret Mitchell. I am referring chiefly to the undergraduate-magazine writers who reached the height of epic literature in a balloon with verbal gas. It was all very adolescent though at times faintly amusing.

As I write these words a feeling of deep pity comes over me, the pity that is awakened by the contortions of a clown's funny face, or when listening-in to a certain radio less than a million miles from Athlone. There is tragedy here and I, for one, am shy to bring their literary scouts and touts to a raw awareness of their tragedy. Too soon they will know the misery of literary men without themes, poets without burdens, ploughmen without land. Such grief has Higher Education brought to simple-minded, decent fellows who might have developed in happiness as Corporation workmen in actual sewers.

I hardly expected boys like these to realise that the predicament of the wasp in the poem was due to a misplaced full stop. Some people may say that I have taken the thing too seriously, but life is a serious business. These silly letters are significant because, as I have suggested — or have I? — the face of truth is often most truly reflected in the mirror of folly.

On the serious letters I do not intend to comment here. Yours sincerely,

Patrick Kavanagh

c. 1949: Portrait by The Green Studio, Dublin.

This was the first of many controversies over Patrick's writings aided and abetted by *The Irish Times*. Readers had great fun at his expense. Patrick was being built up as a character, a stage-Irishman who says wild things. Patrick and I enjoyed it immensely. There lay the danger — for, deliberately or not, there was malice in the campaign under the guise of publicity. Patrick of course saw it for what it was — an exploitation of his poverty — that is one reason he didn't join in. The object was to invent a character for him, encourage him to conform to it and from there push him further and further into folly. With this in mind Patrick wrote in *The Standard* (18th. September 1942) on a related topic:

> *There is no sin more to be condemned than putting the fool farther. It does keep him happy but it is far better to grieve in truth than to rejoice in the untrue. I myself cannot help when I meet a man — or even moreso a woman — trying to awaken him to a realization of things as they are. People think i'm a gay fellow, said a man of the foolish kind to me one day after I had given him a sense of discomforting reality . . . . Sometimes my heart is breaking, he said, and still the people laugh.*
>
> *Yes, I said, but the fault is largely your own. Why can't you act serious and say the dull stupid things like everybody else . . . . The world will not accept a laughing philosopher.*

Patrick returned to this theme many times later, for this attitude was an upsetting element in his life. Here is *Inscription for the Tomb of the Unknown Warrior*:

> *Passers-by on the bridge of your Charity*
> *Forget that my least sin was my vulgarity*
> *For underneath the motley I affected*
> *A nasty piece of goods might be detected.*
> *Sometimes I assumed the role of clown*
> *With the intention of knocking talent down.*

Or with a fund of anecdotal wit
Parroted from all sources, I was It.
Genius if it happened to appear
I saddle-marked with some belittling smear.
The technique I employed to blast the serious
Was laugh in the face, go quite delirious.
If someone were to say 'God's good' I'd answer
'His tongue is in his cheek, the bloody chancer'.
When another ventured to speculate
Too earnestly about man's ultimate fate
To his cunning peasant background I did draw
Attention with an organized 'Haw-Haw',
That rascal who deserted pick and shovel
'Ephemeral trash' was what he called my novel.

(*Complete Poems*, p. 273)

Outsiders could easily get the impression, from all the publicity, that Patrick was making a fortune when in fact he received no more than the original guinea for the article that started the row.

Chapter Seven

Among the unholy ones who tear
Beauty's white robe

At Christmastime both of us went back to Inniskeen. To pay for his train fare he began the habit of writing a Christmas poem for *The Irish Independent*. He wrote the following in 1940:

Oh is it nineteen forty
Or a thousand years ago?
We are not going home by train
We're riding through the the snow,

Riding our horses warily
Among the ancient trees
Strange beasts are howling fearfully
Somewhere deep in Meath.

We saw beside the Boyne
A kern keeping guard,
But we waved our green silk banners
As we galloped across the ford.

We saw upon a hill
A Christian church in flames;
Some said it was a candlelight
But it might have been the Danes.

'Oh listen to the chanting
Of the monks in Monasterboice'
An old man said, and pulled
His horse's bridle tight.

There's John De Courcy ahead of us —
What! It cannot be
Perhaps 'tis Collier the Robber
Heading for Dunleer.

Though our lamps are cold blue ghosts
We ride in triumph north
Cheering, laughing . . . . What voice said to me
'Change at Dundalk!'

Some thought that we were in a train
But my cloak was stiff with snow!
We were riding home to Christmas
A thousand years ago.

(*Complete Poems*, p.75)

At the beginning of 1941 we moved to a slightly bigger
bedsitter at 122 Morehampton Road. Here the cooker was
outside the living quarters. Our room was on the street level and
was separated by folding doors from an adjoining room where
the landlord lived. Every word we said could be overheard. We
paid fourteen shillings a week rent.

1941 produced fewer assignments for Patrick but the rows
his writing created stayed at the same high raucous level. *The
Irish Times* asked him to write a special account of the opening

Mrs. Kavanagh with two neighbours (top) in 1942; and c. 1944 'Going to Mass on a summer Sunday'.

of The Irish Academy Exhibition in April. Here is the section of the article that caused most offence:

Women add slickness to an art but in proportion as women succeed in that art the level of criticism sinks . . . . No real struggle seems to have been responsible for the birth of anything in this show. There is no passionate grief to express the quintessential mind which is the angel caught in clay . . .

We experience no God-crazy emotion.

'But do you get that in poetry today?' a painter asked me. I can only answer, no. But then in poetry of the present day in Ireland the standard is as low as it can be . . . .

It was about this time that the dreadful news was broken that owing to rationing no tea would be served. Bang went the most interesting part of the show. Queueing-up with a cup and waiting for the spout of the tay-pot. No tay! What a blow!

The controversy began with both Brigid Ganly and Norah McGuinness, members of the Academy, declaring that a writer has no business criticising painting. The carnival was now on and everyone with an ounce of wit joined in. Here is Angela McCaffrey (a pseudonym):

A literary man, a journalist, a philistine, a ?, has criticised Irish painters and what is more has been rude to my sex. That shall not pass. The whole R.H.A. will rise up as one man, I mean as two-thirds man and one-third lady, and smite Mr. Kavanagh for his insolence. Things have come to a pretty pass indeed when a literary man can say what he thinks about pictures.

Flann O'Brien joined, too, with a witty letter:

What a world it would be if you could not complain about the quality of a pint unless you were a brewer, or complain about a play unless you were born and bred in the Abbey. We could do with a little less of this sort of childish precosity! (sic).

Incidentally painters are the last people in the world to talk. They discuss and criticise everything without any shyness and even write queer books about life. A well known continental painter has found time in recent years to meddle in a lot of matters that have nothing to do with Kunst.

As usual Patrick did not join in the controversy nor did it inhibit him from writing once more about art — this time seven months later when he reviewed Jack B. Yeats' exhibition.

His fantastic humour is one of the two million points by which he is to be distinguished from the nest of insects who live in synthetic garrets and who paint the queerest and most depressing nothings. I feel it is blasphemy to mention such lousy creatures in the same breath with a genius like Jack Yeats but they do hang around so . . . .

An aesthetic sense is the only thing required to enjoy or criticise a work of art. You may have visited all the galleries of Europe and lodged in the Louvre but it is useless unless you have sensibility. After that all you need is plenty of money and a reasonably good digestion. In art there are no comparisons. Either a man is or he isn't.

One afternoon when I came home from school Patrick showed me three or four pages of a long poem he had begun. What did I think? he asked. I read it in glances of wonder. Great, I told him; don't write another thing until you finish it. He took me at my word and finished it within ten days. This was later to be called *The Great Hunger*. At this moment Cyril Connolly was in Ireland collecting material for an Irish edition of his magazine *Horizon*. Patrick gave him the poem and it was published in part in January 1942 under the title of *The Old Peasant*. Immediately there were ructions.

Detectives called on Patrick to discuss the poem and there was the implied threat that he would be arrested for writing indecent words. Here is the passage that caused the authorities offence:

O he loved his mother
Above all others.
O he loved his ploughs
And he loved his cows
And his happiest dream
Was to clean his arse
With perennial grass
On the bank of some summer stream,
To smoke his pipe
In a sheltered gripe
In the middle of July —
His face in a mist
And two stones in his fist
And an impotent worm on his thigh.

(*Complete Poems*, p.83)

I wasn't present when the detectives arrived and was infuriated to learn that Patrick treated them graciously, discussing Chaucer and the nuances of language. He should have run them out of the place or given each of them a kick in the arse in a practical explanation of that word. He didn't do it. That was the way with him, giving the gentle response. A few days later the magazine *Horizon* was seized by the police. The presumption was that it was because of Patrick's poem but later information suggested that in reality what offended was an article in it on contraception by Frank O'Connor. Later in the year *The Great Hunger* was published separately by the Cuala Press. It was not seized or censored and circulated freely.

Before the liberated reader gets locked into his paroxysm against the moral values of the Irish authorities he must be warned that when Macmillans published this poem in *A Soul For Sale* in 1947 the above passage was censored.

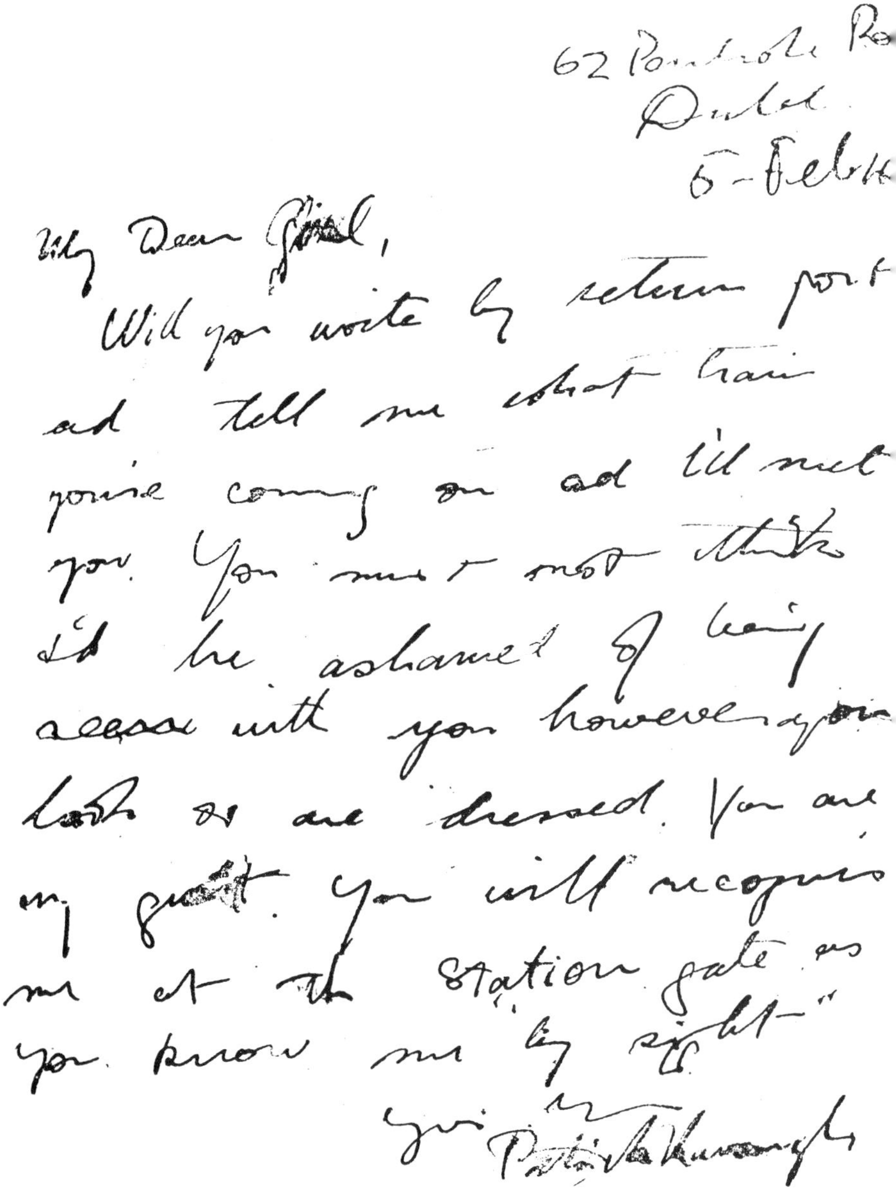

62 Pembroke Rd
Dublin
5 Feby

My Dear Girl,

Will you write by return post and tell me what train you're coming on and I'll meet you. You must not think I'd be ashamed of being seen with you however you look or are dressed. You are my guest. You will recognise me at the station gate as you know me by sight—"

Yrs Patrick Kavanagh

1948: Letter to Renée Kilfeather (later Dougherty).

The news that Patrick had ruined himself by writing an indecent poem caused great satisfaction in literary quarters. There was much head-shaking in mock sadness. To the great embarrassment of these people the Censorship Board did not ban the poem nor did the Catholic *Standard*, for which Patrick had begun to write specials, ostracise him. Only Frank O'Connor was genuine and loud in his praise. Patrick, he said is not merely the greatest Irish poet, he is the only Irish poet.

Patrick himself looked on *The Great Hunger* with a cold critical eye and in a B.B.C. broadcast eighteen years later he commented:

> *In this poem you get this concern for the woes of the poor — the social land: it is far too strong for honesty. And can a thing be truly compassionate if it is touched with hypocrisy? The poem remains a tragedy because it is not completely re-born. Tragedy is under-developed comedy. We can see it and are not afraid . . . . I will grant that there are some remarkable things in it, but free it hardly is for there is no laughter in it.*

He is here groping for some philosophic answer as to why he cannot be enthusiastic about the poem. He doesn't quite get the point which is that he himself is not Patrick Maguire and that he is not really concerned about him that much. Patrick with his highly developed imagination actually took delight in such a scene, at least in retrospect as will appear in the following passage written in 1958.

> *It was a great pleasure harvesting potatoes especially if the Octobers were fine, as in my memory they seem to be. There I was with my sister, one each side of a basket, gathering away. The cart was heeled up in a convenient spot and we filled it until it was about half full and then pulled down the shafts and filled it in the front. Our cart held sixteen baskets . . . . What pleased me about gathering the potatoes was the*

rhythm we worked to. Then home with the load . . . . Now I am sitting in an oil-lamp kitchen eating a feed of flour bread and tea and eggs with an appetite I wish I had these days. Outside, the moon is bright in the sky and over the countryside there lies some mysterious beauty which affects me though at the moment I cannot analyse it . . . .

Contemporary with the publication of *The Great Hunger* was the affair of *The Capuchin Annual*. This publication was fat, slick and with pretensions to art and to literature. It was edited by Father Senan who was mighty proud of it. He himself was one of the great sources of power in Dublin. The word got out that Patrick had received the *Annual* from *The Irish Times* for review and Father Senan rushed out to our place to present Patrick with a five-pound note hoping thereby to influence Patrick's judgement. Patrick accepted the gift because, as he explained to me, it is unlucky to refuse money.

Patrick's review was awaited anxiously. The tension increased as *The Irish Times* in a boxed notice explained that the review was held up because of pressure of space. Finally it appeared on 10th January 1942. There was shock and consternation. Instead of the fulsome praise expected here is a sample of what he said:

Here is my review which pressure of space kept out last week. It is substantially the same as the original so I will leave it at that and see what is to be thought of this revival of interest in art and letters which has been taking place in Irish Catholic circles during recent years . . . .

I suggest here that all new things like artistic revivals or arrivals are like new shops in a district: they attract all the bad pays, all the disreputable. Yet even allowing for that there is still a margin of doubt as to whether art is not the devil's brew. I don't believe it is.

The fiction that a man could never be a good Catholic and a true artist or poet at the same time was given additional

107

credibility by certain groups and newspapers in this country who made anti-literature a plank in their platforms Whenever an Irish writer wrote a book that was not in slavish yes-man agreement with their illiterate ideas of Catholicism he was sure to be damned by some scribbler who had failed to make the grade among the pagans . . . .

True patronage consists as much — if not more — in keeping the wrong kind down as in assisting the right kind up. You can form a better opinion of an institution by the people who are excluded than by the ones included . . . .

How I blame my father for not doing one day's fighting for Ireland instead of fifty years hard work. If he had, he would have a good national record and I by his proxy be I ever so contemptible. I might mis-quote John Bunyan: The milk and honey of easy, well-paid jobs are beyond the wilderness of the ruined G.P.O. and the burned-out Custom's House.

No extensive controversy followed this review. *The Irish Times* might permit a slating review but it would not expose the powerful Father Senan to the caustic wit of its readers.

No surprise that financially 1942 turned out to be one of the worst periods of his life. Poverty. Just a few reviews in *The Irish Times* and an occasional special article in *The Standard*. Patrick comments:

One thing I ought to have learned, or known, is that any man who attempts to write verse, the most time-wasting of occupations, must first acquire a private income. In Dublin I found what at the time seemed like enthusiasm for the poetic spirit but which later I learned was dark enmity. I could have gone to England and dug ditches and why I did not will always remain one of the mysteries of my life. I could have burst out with the truth and to the devil with the begrudgers but for some mysterious reason I remained a man with a stake in the country.

In June Patrick re-visited Lough Derg, not to do the pilgrimage as such but to write about it. Life was providing him with sufficient canonical punishment so I packed sandwiches for him and a bottle of whiskey which he concealed on his person to help him keep alert on the island of fasting and prayer. This time Lough Derg didn't seem so menacing after his two years experience of life in literary Dublin. He wrote in *The Standard* when he returned:

> *The thing that struck me most forcibly was the freshness and the recency of Christianity. Lough Derg is no museum piece. The old stalk of Christianity ends in flowers that have colour and scent — and thorns too. The absence of thorns I might remark is one of the signs of senile decay in a bush. It might have been A.D. 100 or thereabouts and all the excitement of the New Truth was stirring the imaginations of men and women. Perhaps there were people present who had seen Christ. From the way they prayed a man would think so. That was my first and strongest impression . . . .*

Writing an article for *The Standard* was only a side issue: his main reason for visiting Lough Derg was so that he might write a poem about it. This he did, and in an Introduction to a special edition of this poem published in 1978 by the Goldsmith Press * I explained the position as follows:

> *Patrick Kavanagh was a Catholic with emphasis on the mystical element. He did not dismiss the penitential approach as wrong. He wanted to understand it. That is why he went to Lough Derg, first in 1940 and again in 1942. Everyone in our district, indeed everyone in our family, went there often for spiritual renewal. Lough Derg was part of our environment. Not only did he want to understand it, he wanted to capture it permanently in verse. He did not go as a*

---

* Lough Derg, Edited, with Introduction by Peter Kavanagh, (The Goldsmith Press).

pilgrim: he went as a poet. Falling in with his mood I not only supplied the train fare, I also supplied him with sandwiches and a naggin of whiskey. He was going to offer the most supreme prayer of all — a poem about the pilgrimage.

When he returned to our flat, then at 9 Lower O'Connell Street, Dublin, he began writing and within a week had produced the poem as it now stands. He asked me for my opinion. I told him I thought it superior to The Great Hunger. He took this opinion in silence. I particularly did not wish to see this poem lost so, with his acquiescence, I took possession of it. I kept it safely for twenty-five years.

Patrick as a rule was never much concerned how anyone might misinterpret what he wrote but this was a special case. There was a danger that he might appear to be intruding sinfully on the prayers of sincere people. The risk is still with us today but I choose to ignore it. I am certain Patrick would agree with my decision to publish it at this time. It is a dazzling and sensitive picture of the social and religious life of the people of our area during the 1930s and 1940s. For these pilgrims Christ had only lately died and

The apostles's Creed

Was a fireside poem, the talk of the town.

They remembered a man who had seen Christ in his thorny crown.

By this time my sense of history had signalled to me that perhaps one day I might be recording these savage years and that it would be a help if I kept a diary. It didn't last long — only two months until I found my landlady reading it and realised how dangerous a weapon it could be. A few extracts may perhaps re-create the mood of those days:

17th May 1942

I have been thinking all week of keeping a Diary and just

this evening at about half-past six Patrick suggested I should keep a Diary. I wonder was it telepathy?

* * *

19th May

Patrick is away tonight at the Craobh Ruadh meeting in the Country Shop. He thought it was on last night but was mistaken. I partly made up the speech for him, a vicious philippic on political-religious Ireland. Attacked De Valera and all the crooks.

* * *

20th May

Patrick is in a fury. He made the speech I suggested. Said that the 1932 election, when De Valera came to power, was the greatest blow to Anglo-Irish literature ever received. The Irish Times printed the speech and Patrick was worried lest he had made a fool of himself. I ridiculed his concern.

* * *

21st May

Methuens replied to Patrick re his novel Stoney Grey Soil (an early version of Tarry Flynn). Patrick had asked them for suggestions for improving it but they in response merely repeated his own criticisms. Patrick will hardly alter the novel. Frank O'Connor says it should stand as it is. He liked Patrick's speech at the Craobh Tuadh a lot.

* * *

28th May

When I came home from the library Patrick met me at the gate. He had a stick with him. He told me that earlier

111

he had a girl visiting him. In the middle of the visit the landlady and her husband broke into the bed-sitter shouting and stuttering (for the husband had a stutter) and accusing Patrick of sleeping with a girl for two nights. The husband made a swipe at Patrick, prudently missing him. The girl had run home. When we came in the house Patrick announced in loud voice that the wife was jealous of him, and much else. I rather enjoyed the show as it brought back memories when I myself used to be fighting with landladies. I decided for now to say nothing. As luck would have it I had and ad. in the Evening Mail that very evening for a new flat.

* * *

31st May

Went to a soccer game at Dalymount Park. Patrick had told me he was going home to write as we parted at Westland Row. I strolled up town and delayed a bit. Just as I was crossing the street who did I see but me bould Patrick hurrying off to the match. When we returned I didn't let on that I knew where he had been.

* * *

1st June

We got up at 8.15 a.m. The gas was off but I managed quickly to make breakfast for Patrick who is going to Lough Derg — as a poet, not as a pilgrim. I make great haste as the train leaves around nine. He packed his provisions — German sausages and bread and dashed for the train.

* * *

3rd June

Moved to a new bed-sitter in Percy Place.

Just now with the advent of Spring

We agree that all poets must sing,

For the poems I have made

Put all verse in the shade,

For the " spring " in **O'DEAREST'S** *the thing.*

TRADE INQUIRIES TO—

O'DEA & CO., LTD. WOLFE TONE HOUSE, DUBLIN

1949: Ad. in *The Irish Times.*

5 June

Patrick arrived back from Lough Derg. He thought the new quarters were excellent. He was home part of the way on the train with the Protestant Archbishop of Dublin. He recognised Patrick and they talked.

* * *

8th June

Patrick wrote an article on Lough Derg for The Standard and handed it in today.

* * *

9th June

Had a note from Methuens. They will advance Patrick nothing to help him improve his novel.

Patrick also had a note from the Irish Travel Association saying his application for the job of Tourist Reporter was late. It was a good job paying six pounds a week, going round the country writing articles about places of interest. Graft and religious influence with the politicians picking their own man. Patrick was less vexed than worried, worried to think that he would not be given a job for which he was undeniably the best qualified in the country. I felt sorry for him. He said he would go over to England even if it meant working on a farm. He visited D. L. Kelleher of the Tourist Association in the afternoon. Kelleher suggested that Patrick write a few articles for his paper, perhaps write a play. Patrick replied that he could sell his stuff where he wanted. Kelleher actually had the giving of the job.

* * *

10th June

In the National Library Joe Bouch, librarian, asked me

what Patrick was doing these days. Writing for The Standard I replied. That must be the joke of the year, said Bouch in great merriment.

* * *

15th June

Patrick tells me he is considering going to England and getting his card at the Labour Exchange — he is so frustrated with Ireland and his inability to make a living. Curry has been talking to the Archbishop of Tuam who had asked Curry to see if he could arrange a job for Patrick. Curry is the editor of The Standard.

* * *

18th June

Patrick was speaking to Curry yesterday. Tuam asked him to find Patrick a job and Curry is going to do his utmost.

* * *

22nd June

Patrick came in late. He had been over with a letter to McQuaid, Archbishop of Dublin.

* * *

26th June

Patrick is waiting for a letter from the Archbishops of Dublin and Tuam. Both are busy at Maynooth. Meanwhile if nothing happens Patrick says he will go to Belfast and screw bolts for a living.

* * *

27th June

Patrick went off to do a Retreat with the Jesuits at Milltown Park.

30th June

Once more on the move. This landlady also objected to Patrick's habit of bringing in his girl friend. We were amused by our manner of flitting, Patrick with bundles of books, I with my cycling cape stuffed with clothes, etc. Patrick was joking about our stragetic withdrawal saying we should have been sending out propaganda for a week previous to the move explaining how worthless our present place was — just as the different military commanders are doing at the present time to explain their defeats.

We moved to a sixth floor walk-up at 9 Lower O'Connell Street. Very tiny place and only a single bed but we managed to sleep.

* * *

2nd July

Patrick had an article in The Standard on his Retreat. He got a great display on the billboards. Discussed the international situation with Patrick until 1.00 a.m. and then went to sleep on the floor. Very sultry and hot.

END OF DIARY

Chapter Eight

Those savage years

During the summer of 1942 I toured Ireland on my bicycle but kept in touch with Patrick by letter. Here are two letters that survive:

> *9 Lower O'Connell Street 29 July 1942*
> *Dear Peter — Pity you didn't send me your ration book. I'd register for sugar and so be collecting for both of us while you are on holidays. If I have any good news you'll hear; anyway, good news can wait. I am not poor at all. However I may be able to tell you more when you return.*
>
> *All the best,*
> *PATRICK*

> *9 Lower O'Connell Street, Tuesday*
> *Dear Peter — Thanks for the pound. Regarding McQuaid you may rest assured I have him under observation.*
> *In a few days D.V. I may have news of a job in Ireland and I'll let you know if it comes. I just don't want to talk until —*
>
> *All love,*
> *PATRICK*

Nothing came then or later of Patrick's association with John Charles, Archbishop of Dublin, except the odd five-pound note *to tide him over*. The Archbishop of Tuam was much better and even might be called a fan. He made it clear to *The Standard* that he would like them to put Patrick on the staff. There was no vacancy then and Patrick had to be satisfied with writing *specials*.

Cynics may laugh when I choose to say here that Patrick's pilgrimage to Lough Derg and his poem tribute were rewarded. In September 1942 quite unexpectedly he was given a job as a twice-a-week columnist for *The Irish Press*. He named the column *City Commentary* and chose the name Piers Plowman as his pseudonym. He was to be paid two pounds a column — not riches but something steady to live on. The feature lasted until 8th February 1944 with a total of one hundred and twelve columns.

It was an interesting enough column but he was not at his best in it because it forced him to fall between two stools. Were he to lean towards the gossipy side he would feel embarrassed and were he to write out of his own integrity the newspaper wouldn't print it. Even as it was it stank of literature, as Villiers de l'Isle Adam would say, and there were days his column would not be printed. This killed the quality of inevitability of appearance which gives journalism the suggestion of power. Anyway, it threw Patrick off his stride. Unless he were in great distress for copy he would avoid praising somebody he thought poorly of. He reached his lowest depth when he wrote a verse in memory of Joe Holloway who apart from writing an endless diary was a severe bore. Patrick didn't like to be reminded of this fall from dignity and while alive refused to all the verse to be reprinted.

On the other hand he was ready to be enthusiastic about someone with genius as for example Brian O'Nolan (Flann O'Brien/Myles na gCopaleen). He asked Patrick to give a puff to the premier of his first play, *Faustus Kelly*. Patrick immediately agreed, making the humorous remark, *I'm not that honest!* Here is what he wrote in his column for January 25th 1943:

> *Myles na gCopaleen has a play on at the Abbey tonight. Myles is the pen-name of a young Civil Servant about 30. Under the pen-name of Flann O'Brien he wrote a book called At Swim Two Birds and under his present name is the author of a book in Gaelic. A product of the National University he is a clever, destructive wit. As he has provided me both in his writings and as a personal acquaintance with some of the richest laughs of my life I naturally look forward to a big laugh tonight at the Abbey.*

The passages in Gaelic that appeared in his column were part of my contribution. Patrick could speak Gaelic fluently in the late twenties but by the forties he had forgotten it completely. Where Gaelic or Latin phrases appear elsewhere in his writings my authorship may be assumed.

One of Patrick's best columns was on how he felt when he returned to visit his native fields. Here is an extract (25th December 1942):

> *Whenever I return to my birthplace I always take a walk through the tillage fields of that rolling hilly country and say to myself as I see some familiar spot: 'In that sheltered corner I often drank my evening tea, sitting on the dry stones on the back of that very ditch'. And I recall every circumstance: the rock in the middle of the field, the clear stream on my right, on a lower level than this field, tumbling brightly over the black shiny stepping stones . . . . And so it was with me on Christmas Day, every field, rock and lane, every bush and stream, was part of my geneology.*
>
> *At one time I wanted to forget but now I try to remember. My past in these fields is like the memory of some dear one dead. In the beginning we want to banish the memory that holds our grief but, as the years go by, we strive to build up*

pictures of them in our imaginations. Every incident: the more painful, the more beautiful. Every pang of sorrow is a joy. But they slip from us, they slip from us.

Christmas Day is family re-union day. Doors are closed. Nobody is abroad but myself. The crows caw as they flutter in the sunlight down to the pits of potatoes on the side of the hill. I walk slowly on trying to take in every place I have known intimately. Whins are in blossom. The fluffy tops of the cushogs by the bogside are silvery with melted white frost like the tinsel they sell in Henry Street for Christmas decorations. Looking across the country from a height I think I have never seen the landscape so black with ploughing at this time of year . . . .

And here I come to a well-known field where the wheat is six inches tall . . . . I wish I had time to tell the miraculous story of the farming feats of the man and his sons who own this wheat. Sometime I will write that story; it will be a long book and as great a subject as the siege of Troy . . . .

And so here I am leaving my native fields again. I look around me at the gates and stables and the old plough against the bank. I wish I could feel the heartbreak of lovers parting as I once did. Once these fields had greedy arms of passion that held me in their grip. They hold others now. The power of the fields to make a man love them never dies. Suddenly I remember something that makes me sad and, curiously enough, I am happy then.

Patrick peppered his column with original verse. Here are a few examples:

*And have you felt that way too
That someone was in love with you
And was afraid to speak? The air
Vibrated with your mutual prayer . . . .*

* * *

120

Through Gone with the Wind I yawned my way
So I might know what magic lay
In this slow story that to its author
Three million sterling must have brought her.
And here's the secret I found in it —
Barnum was wrong — there's two a minute.

* * *

Jack Doyle

Some think he might have won the crown
That now to Brown Joe's head seems glued
But he got tangled in the gown
Of Venus waiting as she would
For the handsome boy who comes to town

* * *

Julstifiable Homicide

'I killed a verse speaker', said the Playboy
'Through my radio he attacked with that cry
So banshee-like I followed him through Dublin
And split him down the middle with my loy'.

* * *

Tarry Flynn

On an apple-ripe September morning
Through the mist chill fields I went
With a pitchfork on my shoulder
Less for use than for devilment . . . .

* * *

Restaurant Reverie

O half potato on my plate
Is it too soon to celebrate
The centenary of '48
Or even '47.
You're boasted in the centre too
And wet, in soapy soil you grew
But I am thankful still to you
For hints of history given.

There's something lonely far away
In what you symbolise today
For me — the half that went astray
Of life, the uncompleted.
But up brown drills new pink buds start
With truer truth than truth of art,
Ignoring last crop's broken heart
And a generation defeated.
O here is life
Without a wife
A half potato. Eat it.

(Complete Poems, pp.130-146)

Three months after he started *The Irish Press* column, *The Standard* gave him space to review books each week. He named this column *The Literary Scene*. It began 26th February 1943 and continued until 11th June when it was dropped in favour of a new column by Anna Kelly, *Ireland's most pungent writer.*

Now for the first time Patrick was surviving on his own earnings. I went back into digs leaving him the small flat to himself. We both still kept in the closest intimacy. No longer did we lunch together at the underground restaurant near Westland Row: now we dined in style in the Trinity College cafeteria at which university I was working towards a Ph.D.

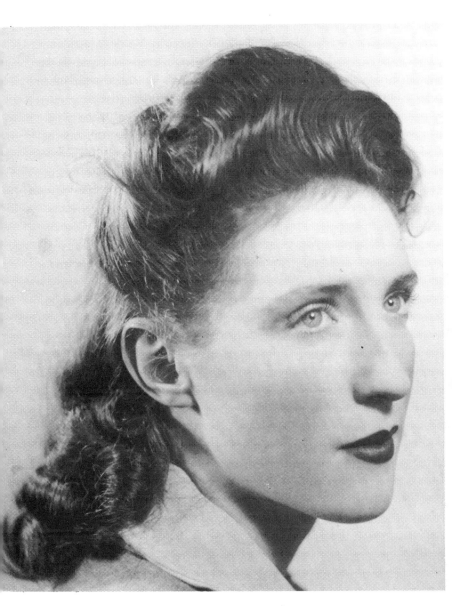

Renée Kilfeather (née Dougherty).

The flat at Lower O'Connell Street, though very convenient, was much too small for a man as large as Patrick. Besides, it was infested with ants so tiny that no screen we could devise would keep them from the food. Patrick consulted with Julian Huxley, then giving a special lecture at Trinity. Huxley advised pouring kerosene down the cracks in which these South American ants lived. This method might get rid of the ants but it might also burn the house down so Patrick moved out in the spring of 1943. He took up residence in a high-class lodging house on Raglan Road. Robert Greacen was a fellow lodger and he recalls:

He stayed for a few months in the same guest house in Raglan Road, near Ballsbridge that I lived in. This was a somewhat genteel establishment and there he seemed to enjoy outraging the other residents. He would clump into the dining room, march heavily as far as possible from the others, and without a word of greeting open a newspaper noisily. Friendly to me outside, he usually ignored me when we met in the house. I tried to stick up for him but the teachers and sales reps simply refused to believe that such a man could be a significant poet, the most significant in fact then writing in Ireland.

Stories about Kavanagh abounded during the 40's and these legends have grown still more colourful with the passage of time. Yet Kavanagh in my presence emphasised his belief in God and Mother Church. Nor would he listen to a dirty story much less tell one. I think he was somewhat afraid, as well as respectful, of women. As for the poets then writing, the only one I heard him praise was W. H. Auden. He also spoke kindly of Harold Macmillan whom he had met through his connection with the publishing company of that name, a real gentleman.

Kavanagh liked to think of himself as a real gentleman, free from the shams and hypocrisies of the lace-curtain Irish. That is why he was so openly contemptuous of the people who stayed in the Ballsbridge guest house. Savage indignation lacerated him. Disappointment and lack of money frustrated him.

From time to time as our acquaintance grew he would call me a Protestant bastard in a most affectionate tone of voice. This of course was a kind of signal to the effect that he liked me for he used really savage phrases to describe certain good Catholic bards who incurred his wrath. Once or twice he even went so far as to admit that some poems of mine had merit, that being his favourite for expression of approval. Occasionally he ate in T.C.D. buffet along with his brother Peter who taught in a Christian Brother School. It was obvious that a strong rapport existed between them; their opinions on important matters were identical but Peter, the younger, had an impish sense of fun.

We never met once by arrangement but central Dublin is small and we would meet accidentally in one of the coffee houses or a bar or just in the street. Kavanagh always prowled around the streets like a hungry wolf before the evening papers appeared. He devoured news of all kinds, political, racing or gossip — with avidity.

While Patrick was moving around Dublin in the course of collecting interesting material for his column he met a girl he liked. She was a niece of Michael Collins. He asked her to marry him and in fact he gave her an engagement ring. He began searching for a suitable flat and eventually in September 1943 settled on one at 62 Pembroke Road. For some reason now not fully remembered the engagement was dissolved. One obvious reason was that his *Irish Press* column had not been expanded into a daily and in fact was foundering. Shortly he would once again be out of funds. Another reason, never stated by him but now advanced by me, is that he had met a girl he liked better, Hilda, for whom he wrote many verses:

On Raglan Road on an autumn day
I met her first and knew
That her dark hair could weave a snare
That I might one day rue . . . .

And rue it he did. Some three years later Hilda married a politician and Patrick wrote me expressing his relief. Just the same he got something out of it — three or four excellent poems. Curiously enough the Raglan Road poem did not carry Hilda's name. It was titled after a girlfriend of mine and published in *The Irish Press*, 3rd October 1946 as *Dark-Haired Miriam Ran Away*.

The lease for 62 Pembroke Road was signed on 20th September 1943. The rent was six pounds ten a month. That was a lot of money then and Patrick asked me to come and live with him to help pay the rent. It was an immense flat, almost what might be called a duplex for it was on two levels. However to reach the second level you had to go outside into the hall. Down below and to the back was a breakfast room, bathroom, kitchen and cabinets while up a flight of six steps were two large drawing rooms divided by a folding door, and a small bedroom. In each room was a large marble fireplace. The windows were six feet high but were leaky and even when the shutters were locked tight a breeze blew through the rooms. Because of the war there was a shortage of fuel but even if we had tons of coal it would be hard to heat such a place.

Our furniture was the minimum for survival: two tables, some chairs and sleeping accommodation. Patrick had a rug on the floor and even bought a large couch. He also ordered and had delivered to the hallway a bedroom suite of the cheapest quality. Fortunately he couldn't pay for it and it had to be picked-up by the store and returned. Patrick was like that ordering something and forgetting that he had not the money to pay for it. Years later he met my sister Lucy in Dublin with two of her children. In his enthusiasm he brought them into Elvery's and fitted them out with new coats. When it came to paying he found he hadn't the money and the children had to abandon the gifts.

We bought a load of turf and had it stored in the breakfast room. We seldon lit the fire except in the morning when Patrick was writing. We spent as much time as possible in places that were heated — coffee shops, libraries and such. When both of us arrived home around ten we sometimes lit the the fire and spent an hour or more chatting.

The job of cooking was shared by both but since our cuisine consisted mostly of chops and sausages this presented no problem. In the morning the gas went off at eight and if you were late getting up you had to do your cooking in the fireplace using newspapers and now and then old broken editions of eighteenth century sets of books. A help in this regard was about two tons of manuscripts off-loaded by Patrick Little, Minister for Posts. He had a very pious brother called Philip Francis who wrote immense quantities of verse for which he failed to find a publisher. Patrick being hard up agreed to edit his manuscript so a collection could be published. Patrick took the job as piece work. Whenever he needed a pound he would scatter a bundle on the floor, put a stroke or two here and there, and go off to collect. The remainder of the bundle we would use as fuel. Yet in spite of all our burning there were still bundles around when I cleaned the place out in 1955.

Patrick spent very little time on journalism; he was a fast writer on light topics and had seldom to re-write. His main energy was spent on verse and on the novel that was later to be called *Tarry Flynn*. He had begun work on it in 1940, his object being to set down the authentic speech of the people, something that had not been done since Carleton. As he explained later, he had closed the door on that class of novel and no one for a generation would attempt to write about the Irish countryside.

The original version was built around a row in the parish of Inniskeen between the Parish Priest and certain locals. The locals built a parish hall which was very much needed. When the Parish Priest, Bernard Maguire, realised the money he would be missing he protested against the granting of a license to the hall and then built a parochial hall himself and collected on it. The Mullagh Hall, as it was called, still stands but is used as a warehouse. The parochial flourishes.

Patrick had great difficulty with *Tarry Flynn*. My suggestion to him was that he should write it in verse and in that way was sure to succeed. He tried it but except for a few verses gave up on the idea. Later he filleted out the theme entirely and published the work as it now stands.

With his *Irish Press* column defunct, (8th February 1944), Patrick turned once more to *The Irish Times* for a forum and for pocket money. Hence a number of special articles on Carleton, Lord Dunsany, Philip Francis Little. Here is one entitled *The New Art Patronage* (I pass over the controversy which followed).

The New Art Patronage

At this exhibition I heard some healthy criticism from ordinary visitors. But among those who take on in newspapers or otherwhere to be appraisers of painting there is only the tentative piety of well-wishers who know that the god of Art is a great god and who are therefore afraid to say anything lest they say the wrong thing. Schoolgirls admiring an actor. And we find that pseudo reverence which we also note at symphony concerts, the hushed and empty awe; the faces upturned with a strained look; the glassy stare into vacancy of those who are pretending to be in love.

To pretend to feelings that we have not got is, as has often been remarked, destructive of the ability to feel on any subject. Side by side with this false reverentiality for safe arts are like painting and music we have everywhere a strong dislike for the writer which takes the form of starving him.

The revival of Gaelic is no more, strange as it may seem, than anti-intellectualism in disguise.

The way to test a proposition of this kind is to measure the patronage for art against something we know — the support given to the writer — which is, as I have said, hatred and starvation. Their ideal of an artist (I do not mean painters now) is a fashionable actor, an executant of music, whatever is intellectually female, not liable to cause a revolution or a great heresy. I should hate to appear to attack other artists in the process of showing humbugs up — but the truth can never do harm.

I was at the exhibition of Continental Paintings and found on the walls a collection of work very safe, very pretty, and with just exactly the right amount of harmless shock to please the conventional middle-class mind. In all this exhibition there is hardly a suggestion that there are men and women in the world who work and love and struggle for a place in this world — and the next. The romantic frills of sexual love without its purpose.

The exhibition is middle class and destined to delight the middle-class mind. There is nothing wrong with the middle classes — they are the humus of society; but when they try to come across with the idea that they are deeply involved in the artistic life, when we see their suburban selves looking at us through as much phoney poetic convention as is good for trade we are liable to get a bit vexed. Vexed not so much with the painters as with the alleged critics, the reverential young girls who have taken up art because — well, didn't the other sister join a school of acting, the other one has gone in for the law, and yet another has been cultivating with horsey heels the members' enclosure of a racecourse.

Here is a nude by Renoir. A fat, very seductive female is going to the bath, presenting to us a back view in which I have failed to find any transcendent — that is, artistic — purpose. When the masters painted a nude woman they were merely trying to express in an earthly symbol something of

129

the wonderful, the intangible creativity of God. If this picture is in any way superior to a photograph I'd like to be told how. Here is a very pleasant landscape by Monet. There is something in Monet, a touch of childhood nostalgia. His paintings would make ideal decorations for a bungalow in Killiney.

Oh, these painters must have lived very complacent lives. Complacency, well-fed respectability. Braque, Bonnard — no merit as artists, whatever they may have as painters.

If the purpose of art is immediate sensual pleasure such as we get from drinking a glass of whiskey or smoking a cigarette then these painters have succeeded splendidly. But if the purpose of art is to project man imaginatively into the Other World, to discover in clay symbols the divine pattern, the Secret, then the exhibition has failed. And if a secondary purpose of art is to hold the mirror up to life, to be a document as well as a symbol, then we may well leave the show to the children of the gombeen men.

[The Editor takes no responsibility for Mr. Kavanagh's opinions. — Ed., I.T.]

Chapter Nine

The Lay of the Crooked Knight

In December 1944 I received my Ph.D. from Trinity. Patrick was at the ceremony dancing with delight. Now he had a weapon against those who dismissed him as an uneducated ploughman — *Talk to Peter about that*! In fact it was to achieve this end that I went through the labour of getting a Ph.D. We were both so broke on the day of my graduation that I had to borrow the price of my lunch from George Leitch, *The Irish Times* photographer. But it was a great day: I had a passport out of poverty, from having to teach under slavish conditions in a Dublin school. Now I was in a position to leave and if the worst came to the worst I could take Patrick after me.

Patrick was no help with my thesis — that kind of writing revolted him — but he did help in other ways. He it was who in the first place got me permission to do the Ph.D. And when a rebellious rump in the College Gaelic Society caused trouble he lent me his strongest support.

In May 1945 the war in Europe came to an end. The excitement it engendered mattered nothing much to either of us. Our war continued.

One of my visible means of support, Patrick relates, *was as a professional writer of verse. When Roosevelt died I rushed home and came back in a couple of hours with an elegy on his death which appeared in The Irish Times the next day (14 April 1945). His widow Eleanor was very pleased with my effort.* Here it is:

Roosevelt

He did not wear the cruel mask of will
That little men put on to terrify
Poor human children climbing someone's hill;
These were not trespassers fearful of the eye
Of a policeman or the Lord God of Law.
He had the innocence of heart that's found
Not in the mighty husk, but in the awe
Of a spirit conscious of the Original Wound —
Original Sin, the gap through which Love passes
And Pity and Humility; that gap that leads
Through the wilderness to the summit of Parnassus
Was open wide to all misfortune's needs.
He was a man and not a mask of power,
Upon whose grave I lay this simple flower.

After being out in the familiar darkness of poverty for more than a year (February 1944 to July 1945) the miracle happened — Patrick was appointed as Editorial and Feature writer for The Standard; a momentous event, the culmination of a long struggle. We held no celebration to mark the occasion — so immune had we become to the batterings of fate. Even the date disappeared from my memory and had to be recalled by an informant: July 1945. The appointment was made by Peter Curry, the editor. He had spent several years in Maynooth before turning to journalism.

Peter Kavanagh, New York 1950 [Photo. Paul Radkai].

133

Towards the end of his life Patrick paid this tribute to Curry:

He was the only man who ever gave me a regular job. He was also the only editor who would and did give me complete freedom to say what I liked without fearing that the remarks of a 'genius' would cause scandal, widespread sinfulness and — worse than all — loss of advertising revenue.

It turned out that this was to be the only steady job Patrick was ever given. The salary was six pounds a week. He held on to the job for three years and was a most reliable member of the staff. He stuck it out even though Miss Kneafsey, business manager, didn't fancy him much. He told me that she ruined the job for him.

On a morning in November 1945 Patrick came searching for me at Trinity. He had received word that Mother had just died. We were both distressed. Only recently both of us had been to see her and she was then in good health. We buried her in Inniskeen.

I urged Patrick to write a verse in tribute to her. He wrote two very good pieces (both published in my edition of *Complete Poems*). Together we wrote her obituary for *The Dundalk Democrat* and here it is:

KAVANAGH: 10th November 1945, at her residence Inniskeen, Mrs. Bridget Kavanagh, R.I.P.
Her family for which she had worked so hard are sad because of her death. She was a loving mother and a simple, wise and practical Christian. Her neighbours and friends also feel sorrowful that she can no longer be in their midst to brighten their lives by her intimate and sympathetic conversation. The large number that attended her burial at Inniskeen graveyard on 12th November was a great tribute to her own popularity. Those who knew her cannot help indulging in the sublime belief that her soul went straight to heaven . . . .

In later years it has been claimed that Patrick had an exceptional attachment to Mother. Not so. Not more than was normal. He was also deeply attached to Father and wrote a poem in his memory too. A year after Father's death, Patrick was still affected and wrote in a notebook:

26th August 1930. Tuesday: Sunny morning. Harvest in after long spell of wet weather. Going to Peter Hamill's of Dromore today to tie corn. This day twelve months Father was very bad — died next day. R.I.P.

In a letter to *The Irish Times* 8th November 1978 Mairéad Byrne correctly assesses Patrick's relation to his mother:

Patrick grew up — and left mumbling, How will she carry on? How will she carry on? Yet he had to go. The only reason why it is possible for someone today to refer to Mrs. Kavanagh is not that for thirty years she slaved to keep a family fed but because her son who had the supreme selfishness to get away wrote a poem about her.

On 22nd February 1946 Patrick took on the additional assignment of Film Critic for *The Standard* and continued the feature until 8th July 1949. It was an entertaining column in which he treated the films casually, almost as an aside. Here was his opening statement:

On my first appearance as a film critic I should perhaps make a generalized statement on what my attitude is likely to be. A critic should have an attitude, a bias, for as some writer has said, scales which are evenly held may contain nothing.

There is no writer more liable to deceive — and perhaps none more biased — than the one who gives the impression of being impartial.

Letting the facts speak for themselves is an immoral

135

principle when we all know that facts and figures can be selected to prove anything.

I am fully aware of how embarrassing self-relevation can be. In my head there is the woefullest anthology of bad poetry, and for years I have been terrified lest this mangy cur of my youth's bad taste might escape from the bag. So when I announce that my taste in films runs to comic stuff — Popeye, Laurel and Hardy, Abbot and Costello, the Marx Brothers, etc., the prospect is terrible to contemplate.

I used to like gangster pictures, but since nowadays the gangsters are always enemies of democracy they have become a bit of a bore.

I cannot abide musicals or films in which large numbers of airplanes continuously roar, and above all, I am allergic to hospital pictures in which crowds of young handsome doctors and nurses with masks on are rushing through long corridors to the operating theatre.

The handsome young surgeon is in love with the beautiful nurse, but in spite of this defect in his reason, he will save the life of the rival on the table.

Finally, I remember with real pleasure, and would return again to see them, only three films — Pygmalion, The Petrified Forest and The Cheat. Perhaps it is significant that two of these were originally plays, and in them appeared the imcomparable Leslie Howard, whose loss must forever be lamented.

Thus to the Irish cinema world which has a higher percentage-to-the-population of filmgoers and no film factory, or studio of its own — I make my bow.

Some film critics handle this industry as a very precious art medium but from what I have seen this week the medium is empty of any kind of intelligence.

Patrick did not sit through the films he reviewed. A glance was usually enough. He would not take a seat but would stand at the back of the Pit for perhaps ten minutes and as soon as boredom struck he would leave.

Here is an extract showing his style of reviewing from the issue of 12th April 1946:

Tomorrow The World is interesting in that it is the first piece of open bare-faced propaganda to appear here. It is a head-on assault on our commonsense and sense of politics as well as religion. The young actor, Skippy Homeier, carries on his undeveloped shoulders the whole weight of the Nazi ideology . . . .

My question would be, What do you do with people who have set about re-educating him? They never mention the word religion, and it never occurs to them that the excesses of the concentration camps and all the other crimes alleged against the Nazis are evil only if you believe in absolute Good and Evil. Since they began to make films the people in Hollywood have implicitly and explicitly denied these fundamental principles, and when they talk about crime now or false philosophy they have no redress because within their own philosophy there is no absolute court with jurisdiction to decide what is bad and what is good . . . .

Apparently they think they have a duty to perform in the 're-education' of the Germans, and they are pulling their weight. I can only say, God help tomorrow's world if it is going to be anything like the chaos, the jungle of sex-appeal, without literature, without art, or without religion which is being created for the simple uneducated by Hollywood.

Occasionally he turned up for a Press Conference called to publicise a visiting film star. His questions always created more interest than the principal as when he asked Paulette Goddard *Do you want to have, or have you had, any children?*

I ghosted for him once or twice when he was out of town. He paid me in abuse. He pretended to be horrified at what I wrote under his name. I recall one of my columns was a review of *The*

137

Spectre of the Rose which had incidental music by George Antheil.

Frequently Hollywood's trade magazine picked up his comments. He once commented on an Irish-made movie:

> .... *A woman backs into a grand piano and sings Mother Macree .... To say this is the worst movie ever made is not enough: it is worse than that ....*

The Hollywood magazine commented that here at least was one occasion they could prove that he was exaggerating.

In a short story to *The Irish Press* 10th January 1946 entitled *The Lay of the Crooked Knight* Patrick summarised his emotional position. Here it is:

The Lay of the Crooked Knight

Once upon a time there was a knight who was loved by a very beautiful lady. How she ever could have fallen in love with him was an astonishment not only to the town but to himself: for this knight was neither handsome nor what most people would call wellmannered. Not without reason was he nicknamed the Crooked Knight.

He had it is true an interesting, lively mind, could compose sonnets and verses that were above average, but women — he believed — did not fall in love with minds nor with verses but with flesh and blood and the qualities that derive therefrom. He was six feet tall but angular, of graceless movement and eccentric mien. How could he fail to be astonished when this lady who was supremely beautiful and wealthy and who had the pick of all the gallant knights — the sons of rich shopkeepers who frequented that university town — should have chosen him? She did choose him, not he her, for he had a faint heart due chiefly to his having it dinned into his head by his relations during his whole boyhood that he was the ugliest thing and the stupidest thing within the four walls of the country. To make his chances worse he dressed badly — execrably. Some days he was too lazy to shave, or comb his hair or put on a clean shirt or polish his shoes or have the hole in the heel of his sock darned.

It was on such a day as this he met her for the first time. Gazing in rapture at this divine creature he checked his emotions. She had all those lovely qualities of softness and sense and sympathy which established her in his mind as another of what he always called 'poet's girls' — whom to love was so dangerous. He had seen her kind before — though nothing at all so enchanting. They always married big businessmen or noted doctors.

He had the opportunity of speaking to her on the first occasion but he hardened his heart and did not speak. He met her again the next day and this time she looked still more enchanting, still kindlier, more the 'poet's girl' but he did not speak. On the third day she spoke.

She said as she sat with another girl dangling her legs from the wall of a bridge:

'I knew quite well that you were mad to speak these last two days. You were acting.'

'Are you sure of that?' said he.

'Of course,' she said with a laugh that sounded to the Crooked Knight so free from all feminine malice — which indeed it was.

When they met the next day she called him by his Christian name. The day after that he kissed her. Afterwards he invited her to his derelict castle, making all sorts of excuses for its appalling condition. The ruin that she saw was not the result of poverty but due to the fact that he was in the course of having the place remodelled. The thought of his derelict, squalid castle had a bad effect on his love-making. He was unable to concentrate. The damp walls and the rotten furniture kept coming between him and the

c. 1950: Patrick Kavanagh by Larry Morrow.

girl. He wished that he had invited her to some restaurant in the town and kept her as long as possible from knowing his real condition.

The result of his first evasion of the truth resulted, as was to be expected, in a whole series of evasions. But the lady loved him and did not mind small things like that. She already had taken him in hand.

She told him that he had a nice voice 'but at the same time you ought to make it a little less natural.'

He took her advice and put on an artificial accent as he had heard young students at the old university doing. It was a great strain but he stuck it out and in a short time only small pieces of the original voice could be heard through the chinks in the veneer. He had been fond of his bottle of stout or small whiskey; the lady advised him to take sherry because it would not make him drunk. It ruined his digestion. She told him not to smoke cigarettes except with a holder, which of course was as good as not smoking at all. She went with him to the shop and chose new clothes for him.

'Bedad, I ought to plaze you now,' he said in his excitement, showing the old vulgar tongue in all its grossness.

She sighed but made no reference to his uncouth speech. 'You are middling'.

. . . . How happy he was. How he tried to concentrate on the moment as it passed. Such happiness could not last. He said to himself: I'm not going to be sorry in years to come, as I have been about other things, that I didn't know I was so happy at a particular time.

Although the lady only grudgingly admitted that he was getting 'more presentable' it was becoming obvious enough to his own companions.

He no longer reacted violently when someone said something with which he disagreed. She had advised him to be calm, not to get excited, for insults were really due to excitement.

For all this he sometimes did revert to his old self. One day he came in and in a fit of bravado or because he wanted to come to her with a sensational story such as he always tried to bring home to his mother — he boasted how he had told a great patroness of poetic knights that she was an ignorant old fool who knew nothing about art.

The knight's lady almost wept. She was less vexed than sorrowful. She shook her head and turned her large dark eyes upon her gallant and, dumb as he was, he knew that he was forgiven.

'I'll never, never do it again,' he declared vehemently.

'Don't say 'never'. Just try to be a little calmer.'

Time went by. The knight and his lady grew more in love with each other. The knight, abandoning his native prudence, knowing as he now did that he really was an improved person, let his passionate heart take flight wherever imagination winged it. He let himself fall helplessly in love. No more as they went out together rushed to his frightened mind the notion of running fast in an opposite direction. Yet he did in the back of his mind remember — like most of his countrymen — a small exit of escape. Was it completely closed? In his most ecstatic moment he reasoned that his countrymen fail in the great things of love because they are afraid of letting themselves go.

By the end of three months a very remarkable change had come over the Crooked Knight. He was no longer crooked. As he sauntered along the fashionable avenues of the town he was almost indistinguishable in his suavity, poise and speech from one of those rich young men who are generally, in the popular mind, believed to be writers or artists or something of that sort but in fact whose only art is as exponents of the profession of arty, slightly decadent, slightly feminine living. Not being burdened with anything in the shape of a vocation or even a strong impulse for ordinary life they were able to

142

handle themselves with superb ease.

The Crooked Knight always had a vocation — to fight against the infidels, Untruth and Charlatanism — to create a great estate and build a fine castle in place of his present habitation. That done he would then set to work to express his poetic soul.

Now he was losing interest. His rough edges which were actually the grips on the wheels of his destiny were now smoothed out. Along with all, his lady had taught him how to be politic in a commercial way.

All the rich men with an interest of a sentimental kind in the projects of knights of art and literature, as well as knights of more common kind, used to fight shy of the Crooked Knight — when he was crude and crooked. His reaction was too genuine for their fancy. He was a dangerous man, a man to discredit. They were changed now. The knight had begun to take part in harmless parties where odd notions such as table rappings and fraudulent hypnotism were practised.

Although the fellows who frequented these parties were very fond of the arts, they had no money for them. The Crooked Knight was amazed that money was so easily come by if one were a humbug of any breed.

He got rich, or at least fairly well off. He was no longer at all interested in his derelict castle or in his wild fields. He took a beautiful furnished flat in one of the fashionable squares. He had a radiogram and hundreds of classical records. He had a piano. A modernist painter decorated his walls.

And he was still in love.

It was for this moment he had striven, for this moment when he would be able to offer his lady all the things that are worthwhile in the modern world. He had asked her to marry him before but he should not have done so until he was in a position to support her as she was accustomed.

For some time before this he had been too busy to see her

as often as he would have wished but he knew her well enough to know that she would only be glad that he was progressing as she had designed.

He rang her on the phone. She was out. He was a bit puzzled. Later that evening he rang again. Still not in. In something like the desperation of which his former self had been capable he went down the town, thinking out in his mind all the places where she was liable to be.

He could hardly believe his eyes. A man could easily make a mistake at that distance. He followed the pair who had come out of the cinema together. It was indeed she walking with a man whom the knight placed as the type of active young country solicitor who would be better informed on city dances and social functions than any city dweller.

'Good God?'

He was in despair. He went further down the town and entered a polite cafe. Around him there were all the smooth feminine men and the wives and daughters of rich men sipping their tea or eating richly flavoured ices. He heard sweet affected talk. He listened to a few words of his own sweet affected talk. And then he rose from the table and gave one huge roar. He cursed everything and everybody. He spat on the floor. The crowd stared at him. And he knew that they were wishing that they could do the same, rise out of their futility.

He saw with horror the emptiness that had been scooped out of his heart to make a smooth outside. Now the thin walls were crashing in. He was real again. He felt like a man who had saved himself from damnation at the very gates of hell. Hell was that great emptiness, the place of no purpose where damned souls spent their time dancing, or looking at race-horses or gossiping in tea-shops — planning, planning to no purpose.

Returning in all his crooked angularity to his derelict castle he was filled with the joy of a man who once more feels himself going forwards to deeds of high adventure.

144

Chapter Ten

This is the past the poet recovers

In November 1946 I left to seek my fortune in America, Patrick tearfully seeing me off at the boat and urging me on. I had only a visitor's visa because at this time, immediately after the war, American officials in Dublin hated the Irish for their neutrality and wished to be as nasty as they could. But no matter, Patrick told me, he would take care of the home front and supply me with any documentation I might need when changing over from visitor to permanent status in the U.S. Furthermore, I was going to the United States entirely on spec. and was anxious to hold onto the job in Dublin, bad as it was, in case I failed and had to return. Patrick would take care of this aspect of things also, he assured me. I left pretending to be seriously ill and Patrick promised to put my cheques in the bank for me — no problem since his signature even in Gaelic was identical to mine. As it turned out, he put the money 'accidentally' in his own account and wondered in a letter of explanation if perhaps the bank-clerk had stolen the money. I was upset for a while but I am gradually getting over it.

I had no demanding ties to keep me in Ireland. Mother had

died and Patrick was now floating on his own with a regular salary; even though meagre it at least was guaranteed. Except in matters of petty cash Patrick was most reliable — he cheered me on, sent me a cable in mid-Atlantic and even phoned me in New York. When I needed documentation he got it and provided me with strength, hope and confidence in a very difficult situation. I never doubted that he would.

He wrote frequently giving helpful advice, especially valuable in those early months when my position was precarious. I had only three hundred dollars and was forbidden by law to earn money on my visitor's visa; a big worry. I didn't like the idea of being deported but it was earn money or fail so I picked up a few dollars here and there. Padraic Colum gave me twenty-five dollars to introduce a stage-Irish movie he had just made for Pan American Airways. The next month I got a teaching job at a college in Brooklyn. With this job as a base I left the country — going to Canada — and returned with a permanent visa. Using my job once again I moved to Chicago where in September 1947 I became Professor at Loyola University.

Here I suspend my commentary so that Patrick may be observed as I saw him at this time through his correspondence with me. The letters which follow are extracts only and are selected from *Lapped Furrows* (New York 1969). With almost every letter came a press cutting.

62 Pembroke Road, Dublin. 28th December 1946
Had a good time in Lond. Met everyone. May go to B.B.C. in a couple of months. Department of Education here very contrary on account of your job but I am still working on them through Dr. Ryan. They may declare the job vacant unless I drive hard, as I am doing. Doesn't matter a whole lot. God forbid you'd have to return to teaching. The Herald blurb was good publicity. I think you'll get good reviews. Sold a short story in London to John O'London's 'The Cobbler & the Football Team'. Eight guineas, cash on the spot. La

146

France Libre also paid up ten guineas. Was in Inniskeen for Christmas Day. No news.

. . . . Interview with Spellman would be fine. The film with dialogue by Colum was shown here. I cut it up. Stage-Irish dialogue. Hope Colum doesn't see my notice. It is a Travelogue made for Pan American Airways showing the beauties of Erin. You praise it anyway, praise the ideal Catholic life of romantic Ireland.

Let me give you some points about the Colum film which I saw.

The dialogue is Synge-like. We are shown a typical American family arriving at Shannon. They visit the East, the Corrib Country, Cong, and see old Irish mothers at spinning wheels, a man, either Harry Brogan or Mick Dolan, thatching a cottage and saying some grand Irish sayings. There is also a jarvey.

Praise this way of life, is my idea for you. You know all this country. Talk about your experiences and the good sayings you heard. Praise the Catholic simple life. Quote poetry, Colum, Higgins, Yeats, even myself. The beautiful Irish colleens come into it. Praise them for their simple virtue and beauty.

Keep away from the low Irish quarters.

Keep out of that section and do not let them know your movements is my advice.

* * *

62 Pembroke Road, Dublin, 12th January 1947
Dear Peter,

Got your latest letter. Glad book has arrived. Hope you get a job soon. Without book is like being a soldier without a gun. I am doing my best to look after your interests here — publicity, photographs to press etc. The Department of Education very uncivil about the job. Not sanctioned, are ordering the Manager to declare the job vacant. I discussed the matter with Arthur Wright who doesn't think the matter worth fighting about. I feel that you would always get as good a job. The only thing is the profit on the sub. I spoke to Dr. Ryan. I could go a lot harder, write to DeValera himself and knowing the phoney he is on Higher Studies expect a good reply. But hardly worth the trouble.

* * *

. . . . Will go harder to hold school — for spite. I am glad you are getting fixed up in a job. That is the big thing. I am sure you'll do well. Once again you have broken away and the probability is you'll break me away as before. No future in Ireland — U.S.A. will give no wheat, and bread is rationed. My poems are listed in this month's Macmillan Spring List. I'll write again after Saturday.

* * *

62 Pembroke Road, 2nd February 1947
. . . . well-known people took a poor view of Smyllie over letting Woods write that notice about your book The Irish Theatre. Desmond Ryan, Peadar O'Donnell, Frank O'Connor saying it was unfair and rotten criticism that could be used against any book. These bitter barren minds are poison. May I point out to you something you may not have known that Smyllie disliked you, and I am beginning to guess that he didn't exactly love myself, never gave me a job. A gasbag of no ability.

* * *

. . . . My book is out (A Soul For Sale). Smyllie is raging because I did not acknowledge The Irish Times. Bugger him. I will send you a copy of the book today.

* * *

62 Pembroke Road, 8th March 1947
My book is out and getting good notices of course.
Are you not also a humbug? The idea of claiming everyone else a fraud is very insincere and bad business too. I gave the 'works' to Smyllie, told him the attack on your book was engineered in the office, and more. Told him I wanted no review. Bruce Williamson did my poems fairly well.

148

1951: Interview in a Dublin Doorway [Photo. *Illustrated*, 1951].

The Standard, Dublin, April 8th 1947

To say that I am pleased and at ease over your visa is to put it mildly. I don't care now what you do. It is really a wonderful chance but you worked for it for seven or eight hard years. Besides this all other things sink into insignificance. Frank O'Connor reviewed you in a column length in The New Statesman. Haven't got the cutting on me but will forward. He went for you but to be noticed in the N.S. & N. is far better than to be ignored.

I am getting sick of this dirty job here and will probably leave it soon. What have I to lose? No wife or cares and I can always get enough.

* * *

62 Pembroke Road, April 14th 1947

Now that you have got your permanent visa I do not care a hoot. In fact it has made me terribly impudent, as the fella said. It is most unlikely that I will remain with The Standard much longer. In fact I may scram this week. I can get on without their lousy job. I am promised a fiver a week from two sources. However we shall see.

You were lucky indeed. You were not merely lucky in getting to the U.S.A., that was on the merit of your five years' hard labour in that big room. By the way I hardly ever look in there. Thank God the winter is over and the weather like summer. It was awful. The Bell is publishing an 8,000 word chunk of my novel (a version of Tarry Flynn) which you have with you. Do nothing about that as I am making a new novel of it.

* * *

. . . . I don't think I'll go to the U.S. now. Have retired from The Standard but still do films. Four guineas a week.

Since you got the visa I am inclined not to care.

I am no longer on the staff of The Standard. I left. I am retained by them to do the films and other occasional specials at four guineas a week. I have a fiver from another

*source. I am writing a new novel based on the one you took
with you.*

* * *

62 Pembroke Road, May 6th 1947
*Since you became imdependent I am careless about writing.
You are lucky, for in this country there is a mean streak — a
great hatred, little room. I am so glad you are in a university
because I was a bit ashamed answering questions. I do not
think you should let everyone know your business.*

* * *

*I am not enthusiastic about going to America for while as
you say it has great possibilities, on the level salaries are
rather poor there. 750 pounds a year as you are offered. On
the other hand you can go far. I am quite sure you would
never get a break here, always be an N.T.*

*. . . . I have nine guineas a week since I left The Standard.
Perhaps ten. I am retained at Standard at four guineas and
I have five writing a novel, the one I have been writing for
several years. Four pieces of 10,000 words each are
appearing in The Bell as a serial.*

* * *

*I am not too badly off and can make money. No sign of me
getting a woman at all.*

* * *

*I had that bad, (a love affair) but am about cured, I believe.
More chronic than your disease but bad enough, remember. I
feel very impudent with you in America knowing that I can
tell everyone to kiss my arse.*

* * *

62 Pembroke Road, Dublin, 31st May 1947
*I have no news. I agree with you about the novel but am
experimenting. When it is being published in book form
which I hope will be in the autumn, late autumn, I can
change it. People dislike grossness. I applied in an insulting
way for one of the Script Writers jobs on Radio Eireann,
750 per annum and was not even asked for an interview.*

151

Incidentally, I would not have accepted the job for, like you, but so much later, I have discovered that 'futures' are illusions filled with misery. Hilda wanted a man with a future, the sure sign of a shallow mind — or in the words of Shaw 'middle class blasphemy'.

Sissie's letter to E. Kerr was born out of her imagination. I never mentioned going with the football to New York and the idea of going over never occurred to me; and I would rather swim over than go with a crowd of louts of that kind. What a joke! The sisters of ours on the outside are trying to guess what goes on in the temples of our minds.

* * *

62 Pembroke Road, Dublin, 20th June 1947 Frank O'Connor reviewed me for the Evening News, mentioned Kathleen Hoagland's book about my being now in the front rank of Irish poets and he said that I must have the capacity of forming fours on my own. Not bad.

I am not too badly off for women these days. Hope you Pick up someone. I don't agree on your theory of a mistress — your work alone. And most marriages are a success! I do hope you'll fall in with someone interesting and nice. And I don't like your idea that you'd come back to see me. To blazes with me. The world is small nowadays.

When you send the poems to the next publisher do not be so naïve as to say my brother's poems. Send them in saying: I have been asked by the author, who is Ireland's most distinguished poet, etc., to send you these poems.

* * *

In the meantime realize that you have got a great job and that you should avoid getting into an attitude which would produces the impasse with the bosses similar to what happened here. Life is the same everywhere.

* * *

Regarding my getting to the U.S. I think I'll be able to manage the fare and if I go, I'll go on a lecture agency with which Peadar O'Donnell is mixed up. They would pay fare etc. Everything depends on successful finishing of novel which is going rather well these days. An entirely new plot and details different. In fact a different novel with the same characters.

I have little to say. As I say, everything comes to him who works and I must work at the novel and then the walls come tumbling down and I'll see you in Chicago. Please God. I don't need to say more. I'll write if I think of anything later.

* * *

7th August 1947

By the way, I read a good article in an old Reader's Digest for 1942 on peptic ulcers. There is 'the disease of the twentieth century'. Might interest you to know that it is caused not by indigestion proper but by having too much digestive juices. Nerves and smoking induce a flow of the digestive juice and when all the food in the stomach is digested the juice that is over starts to work its way through the lining of the stomach and begins to digest the walls of the stomach. Only cure is bicarb. That is what I've had, and you too, I think. Purely mental. I hope you are well as this leaves me. I have the novel well under control.

* * *

62 Pembroke Road, Dublin, September 10th 1947
Dear Peter,

Glad you got fixed in Chicago. I appreciate all you say about the U.S. but I think that for all that, there is not much future in this country — except for a writer who can sell his work outside without leaving. A mean gang run the show — possibly a mean gang run it everywhere, but here the small opportunity makes them more obvious and more menacing. I finished the novel yesterday (Tarry Flynn) and Peadar O'Donnell brings it to London today by air. It is a lively story and a remarkable improvement on the foolish original.

* * *

Some of these appointees on Radio Eireann like Larry Morrow are very gelt of themselves when they meet me as my name has been going up and I sneer at Radio Eireann. My never being on the radio is becoming obvious to the public — and I never will be on it, please God.

Wrote a damn good article on Fred Higgins for Irish Writing. I'll send you a proof when I get it.

Now that I have the novel complete I'll be free to make a few bob on the side. It is rather likely that I'll take a holiday now for a week, for though I have been away the fact that the novel was not complete did me no good and I came back more tired. It is also likely that my sojourn at 62 Pembroke Road is near its end. I'll let you know my plans in advance. I have no intention of burning my boats and if I go to the States I'll try to continue my attachment to the Standard.

* * *

62 Pembroke Road, Dublin, 3rd October 1947
I have no news so far. I am writing to get my passport sent to the Consul.

Whatever money I put in the bank I took none out — could not. I am quite certain I put in more that sixteen pounds but as I got no receipt, you having documents, I have forgotten. I should not be surprised if the fellow who took it in, seeing he was supplying no proof, stuck some of the dough in his pocket. There was nothing to stop him.

I kind of think I put in about thirty pounds, but as I say I'm not sure yet. When I have news — on this as on other things — I'll write.

I am engaged on another novel which I want to have sold to Macmillan's before going to the U.S. I expect they may advance me a couple of hundred pounds but it will take time. Work is the way to America.

* * *

62 Pembroke Road, Dublin, 11th October 1947
I had better explain the position as it is at present. I sent in

my passport for visas and was told I'd get them when I produced a few rather simple documents: a document showing I won't be a burden on the States while away, a note from a shipping company saying they can take me. On the form sent me by the American Consul I said I was going over for a holiday on your invitation and this is enough. All I want, I think, is a letter from you preferably with a University heading inviting me out for a holiday and guaranteeing to keep me while in the United States.

Regarding my ability to get away, I am hard at work on a new novel. When I have three chapters and the synopsis complete I am sending it to a London publisher and according to O'Donnell I'll easily get an advance on it, of 200 pounds. With this I can safely travel by a decent ship. O'Donnell doesn't believe in me travelling on the lower deck as a steward or on the cheap on one of the Irish boats. Bad for my reputation and I'd meet important guys aboard a good ship. It will take me a week to get the three chapters ready and then 'twill be a further three weeks or so till I get the money. But everything is going fine and, faring well, I hope to be over there in about two months. If I want an affidavit from you I'll let you know. I hope you are well and I am looking forward to seeing you in America.

I am just correcting the proofs of an article on Higgins for Irish writing. I got a good review in Voices, the Yankee Literary Mag. You may have seen it. I'll send you on the Higgins article when it appears or I may get an extra pull of the proofs. I have also a good verse play in the next Bell — The Wake of the Banned Books.

* * *

62 Pembroke Road, Dublin, 25th October 1947
Dear Peter,
You'll be expecting to hear the news. I got all you sent me and I'll get the visa no doubt easy enough but I am doubtful about a permanent one. Everything depends on whether

Macmillans come clean with the dough. If I get that I'll be sailing from Southampton on the Queen Mary December 4th. I have a berth booked and fifteen quid deposited. If that comes all is well enough though, like you, I am nervous of America. Yet I have little to lose. You couldn't call the lousy four quid from the Standard a job. I always could get better; in fact I'd be better down the country digging a ditch than working for them. Still — .

You took a chance and were lucky. I read Horizon. I am waiting for Macmillans decision on the 20,000 words of a new novel I sent them. Be here any day. I am really sick of The Standard though I am hoping I can interest them in my American visit to the tune of a few pounds. Think I might be able to write a book on my adventures for them — people I met in the U.S. I have nothing to say for I am waiting on Macmillans. Soon as I hear I'll give you the buzz. All my papers are in order. I'll sublet the flat for six months or maybe only three — rent in advance. I ought to get three a week for it as it is 'furnished'. No need for you to write till you hear from me.

I have done a smashing essay on Frank O'Connor and the other on Fred Higgins. Would make a pair of good lectures for the U.S. I'll send you copies. On O'Connor is for The Bell, 3,000 words. Four of those would be good in the U.S. I'll write as soon as news comes through.

All the best, PATRICK

P.S.: If I can't get money for U.S. I'll go to London, I think. The money is the sole problem.

* * *

62 Pembroke Road, Dublin, 23rd November 1947
Dear Peter,

Macmillans offered me a retainer of 300 pounds a year provided I did not go to America but stayed here as a 'creative writer'. The retainer is provisionally for two years but will continue as long as I like provided I keep writing seriously. Now, with a proposition like this what would you

1954: Patrick with Myles na gCopaleen (Brian O'Nolan). [Photo. *The Irish Times*].

do? I have decided to wait a while before going to America now. Tarry Flynn is coming out from the Pilot Press in Spring and also will be published in New York; so I think I will have a better chance if I wait. If I went now I'd be at the mercy of Chance. You may be disappointed but I think you will agree with my decision. I am also assistant Editor of The Bell and with the three items I'll have sixteen pounds a week for practically no work. I'd like to hear your view on this. I hope you are well and I'd like to hear how you are getting along. I have my papers right and can go to America when I decide. No bother getting a visa now.

Nothing else worth writing about until I hear from you.

* * *

62 Pembroke Road, Dublin, 2nd December 1947
Glad you thought my decision right. I fear however that I overpraised the situation here, for the Income Tax will hole badly the Macmillan bounty and Peadar O'Donnell is trying to diddle me out of The Bell job. Wants nobody bigger than himself. Still, I am safe and will try to get to America in the Spring for a short holiday. I had a letter from John Fischer of Harpers, New York, asking for the novel which I have written so when I get the proofs from the Pilot Press I'll send them on and may get 1,000 dollars advance which would take me to the U.S.

I am sending you on two articles which may be of use to you. Austin Clarke is spitting bile over the Higgins one and he is right, for it devastates his life's work.

* * *

62 Pembroke Road, Dublin, 8th April 1948
I hope you will be able to get a boat. You probably will. I agree completely with your idea of what makes a novel Worthwhile. It is another thing putting it into practice. That is the way to write enduring literature. A novel's story is of no consequence unless it illustrates a theory of life. There is O'Connor's weakness. I am doing my best.

158

A propos the novel, have we, have I, a theory of life? I used to have, and I think I still have. I will fail till I get at the truth and then the thing will write itself.

I'm sending you bits from the final number of The Bell — it is finished. One on me by Larry Morrow, 'The Bellman', and one by myself on 'Poetry in Ireland'. You'll like them I imagine.

* * *

62 Pembroke Road, Dublin, 18th June 1948
So glad to hear you are probably coming. I don't think I want anything from U.S. that isn't to be had here. Needless to say it is not a question of my putting you up; just resume occupation. You won't be starved I think.

* * *

62 Pembroke Road, Dublin, 1st November 1948
Nothing much new. T. Flynn is out and I am sending you a copy. It is what I have believed a delightful job, a good novel. Of course I agree that there is another me hardly seen in it. But in the next — .

I do hope that Tarry Flynn brings me a rich wife; it could do that, you know. A man needs to be rich to tell these hures to f— themselves, and to give him a relaxed mind to do his best work. I know a beautiful woman, but, alas, no dough.

* * *

I forgot to tell you that the landlady of this house got contrary. I told those tramps above me to mind their own business and not to intrude on my guests so they informed on me — that I do be making noise, etc., and be the holy fly didn't she send me a solicitor's letter. But my solicitor tells me I am secure. There are only about two ways a man can be evicted — non-payment of rent, conviction for keeping a brothel. Still one doesn't like this. The lodging house man must be giving her an extra rent. The two flats would make a fine lodging house! P —.

* * *

159

62 Pembroke Road, Dublin, 17th November 1948
I couldn't agree more, the proper attitude. I read it somewhere, in Horizon, I think, for a writer to hold a job until he has established himself in it and then to shunt. You have established yourself as a university professor. Nothing like moving; you are giving your destiny a chance. Of course America is a tough spot. One needs constantly to glance behind to see who is coming. Teaching is the last. They are just as frustrated here. Bunch of unfortunate nobodies who know it. They become nasty, too. I am sure there is a terrible lot of frustration in the world, it is the disease of our time.

* * *

17th November 1948
Met Roisin Walsh the other day and she says Tarry Flynn is the best novel of country life ever written. I think I told you it was banned, but it was expected the Appeal Board would lift the ban. I saw where the Press Association sent out the story of the ban in a sensational way. That means that it went to every newpaper in the world almost. Good advert. I'm in middling form. Health alright but depressed. No woman. A country in which a writer as good as me cannot get a wife is not a civilized country, is it? I need one, I really think you have the proper outlook and will go far. Actually I didn't send you on the novel yet, knowing you weren't too enthusiastic. I myself am not too enthusiastic — between ourselves. At the same time it is easier saying than writing a better book. Even an Ave & Salve book.

We are being declared a Republic today by the Dáil. No difference to me or to you.

* * *

Christmas 1948
Ban on book revoked. Poorish reviews. Between ourselves I agree with you about it.

* * *

160

Chapter Eleven

Stretching out hands
To Seraphim

The New Statesman & Nation, February 1949, referred to the banning of *Tarry Flynn*. Patrick didn't appreciate being defended by a Left Wing periodical and replied as follows in the issue of 5th February, 1949:

Sir, — It will seem ungracious of me not to feel flattered by Critic's puff in his Irish diary. I am not a bit touchy yet I found his remarks about me as a person extremely familiar — and stupid. How awful! Critic will no doubt say; when I try to give the man's book a boost, bring his name to the notice of the readers of The New Statesman & Nation he takes offence. How perverse, stage-Irish, natural and ploughmanish! No publicity can compensate for familiarity; and I should much prefer, as hitherto, to be ignored by your journal than exhibited as a strange animal discovered by a visiting journalist. I am sorry for, possibly Critic meant well, but he achieved ill as we all do when we talk idly. If any of your reviewers should write of a natural poet, sack him. Articles like Critic's Irish Diary are powerful stimulants to wavering Catholics. Is this hysterical, non-thinking representative of the pagan outlook? The best thing to be said for prejudice is that it is insincere. Surely no sincere thinker holds that contraception is an ideal?

What is weakening my resolution as I write is that there was some truth in Critic's article. About the un-official censorship, the whisper over the phone or dinner table which blacklists a man. Catholics in Ireland are aware of these sinister manifestations of frustrated mediocrity. Mediocrity in power, that is our problem and we are hardly alone in our misfortune.

The fallacy in Critic's article is that like all journalists he accepts the melodramatic heresy of national distinctiveness as a spiritual reality. The universality of Catholicism (as of literature) is that it deals with people as people. Journalism, politics and other forms of immorality deal with people as regional phenomena. So newspapers and politicians are full of clamorous superficialities which seem important. Apparently not even a weekly review such as yours could afford to postulate true values – even if you knew them.

The politician who told Critic that he was 'Anti-British' was a real stage-Irishman if Critic had but known. The opposite numbers to this self-deceiving mentality in England and elsewhere love these declarations of national dislikes; they have the unsubtle, irrational quality which appeals to vulgar emotion, upon which mass-circulation newspapers and wars thrive.

PATRICK KAVANAGH

The Gallivanting Poet

Irish Writing November 1947

Extract:

Writing about F. R. Higgins is a problem – the problem of exploring a labyrinth that leads nowhere. There is also the

162

problem of keeping oneself from accepting the fraudulent premises and invalid symbols established by the subject. The work of F. R. Higgins is based on an illusion — on a myth in which he pretended to believe.

The myth and illusion was 'Ireland'.

One must try to get some things straight about the man: He was a Protestant.

He most desperately wanted to be what mystically, or poetically, does not exist, an 'Irishman'.

He wanted to be a droll, gallivanting 'Irishman'.

Nearly everything about Higgins would need to be put in inverted commas. All this was the essence of insincerity, for sincerity means giving all oneself to one's work, being absolutely real. For all his pleasant verse Higgins was a dabbler. It is not an easy thing being sincere; it takes courage, intelligence, and integrity. It is difficult to take seriously a man who could so consistently deceive himself.

The word 'gallivanting' appears throughout his verse. The last thing you find in this Ireland is gallivanters. No doubt Synge made the gallivanter his theme, but for me Synge's characters and language are offensive and humbuggish. The quality in Synge which excites has nothing to do with Irish peasants, and it survives in spite of their silliness.

It is well known that the sure way of making ourselves imcapable of true feeling is by pretending that we have it. A true lover doesn't have to pretend being in love; on the contrary he is always pretending that he isn't in love, hoping thereby to auto-suggest the pain away. So by Higgins and his Irishness.

Somebody writing recently in the press described Higgins as a 'noble Protestant gentleman' — and I am not inclined to disagree about the final two words. The most valid aspect of the man was his Protestantism and, for all his gallivanting, his un-Irishness.

Their Protestantism has been a great tribulation to Irish writers of that persuasion. Alone of modern Irish writers

163

Yeats got there merely by being himself, by being a sincere poet. He dug deep beneath the variegated surface to where the Spirit of Poetry is one with Truth. I say this with reservations, but none the less it is largely true. O'Casey turned Communist which is the real Protestantism of our time.

Another development of the Protestant writer's dilemma is to be found in his attempt to build up the idea of Dublin as a spiritual entity — the Dublin of Swift, Berkeley, Gogarty, Joyce, and 'Larry-the-night-before-he-was-stretched'. This was really gerrymandering the constituencies of the soul so as to segregate disagreeable elements and to provide one's own narrow outlook with a safe seat.

Most of us at one time or another have allowed ourselves to pretend that we believed in the mystique of the Nation or the City State. It is not an adult attitude though it can be amusing.

Higgins is full of this nonsense.

It is not very easy to base a critical argument on the work of a man when it is so unreal, so unrelated to any values we know.

What is getting me down as I write these words is the futility of all this verse, its meaninglessness. We have reached a point where we cannot continue this pleasant dabbling. A poet must be going somewhere. He must be vitalising the spirit of man in some way. He must have dug deep beneath the poverty-stricked crust of our time and uncovered new veins of — uranium, the uranium of faith and hope, a transcendent purpose.

Now is the time for silent prayer and long fasting. Literature as we have known it has come to the end of its tether.

It can be said for Higgins that he wrote before the final disillusionment. In his day it was still possible to believe that pleasant dabbling in verse, word-weaving, white-magic, was enough.

By finding ourselves prostrate before God and admitting our dire distress we may be admitted to a new dispensation. The best poets are those who lie prostrate before God. But poets like Higgins keep on pretending that the futile decoration on the walls is enough for the day.

Oh for the kick of Reality.

On the hysteria of nationalistic charlatanism we can shout away our pain no longer. We must dig. Many Irish writers came into being on the wings of this hysteria, but when the day of reckoning came they were found without a penny in their pockets, the pennies of experience.

NOTE: The editors suggest that my thesis gives the impression that I think a Protestant cannot be an Irish writer, and have asked if I would disclaim such a theory.

My immediate reaction would be: Who wants to be an Irish writer?

A man is what he is, and if there is some mystical quality in the Nation or the race it will ooze through his skin. Many Protestants, doubting that their Irishism would ooze, have put it on from the outside. National characteristics are superficial qualities and are not the stuff with which the poet deals. The subject matter of the poet is the Universal and in this he is one with Catholicism. By a peculiar paradox the pursuit of the Universal and fundamental produces the most exciting local colour as well. In desiring to be 'Irish' a man is pursuing the non-essential local colour. 'Seek first the Kingdom of God and its justice and all things will be added'.

Coloured Balloons

A Study of Frank O'Connor (Extract)

The Bell, December 1947

O'Connor is poised on the ridge-tiles of a literary house of cards — above ordinary life.

'He has his roots in the soil', is a well-known phrase and people who say it generally mean that the man was born and reared in a country place. But the real soil in which a man's roots are is the soil of common experience. You can follow the tracks of the writer whose feet are in that soil — Blake, Wordsworth, Milton, Shelley or Yeats their clay trail is the trail we can follow. However high they raised their mystical heads they all had their feet on the clay earth. That is why they felt the electric shock. Can one say the same of O'Connor?

This very fact that he began as a translator is somewhat of a key to his work — that his technical and imaginative machinery is greater than his material. For, like a great actor who is useless without a theme, O'Connor is inclined to be futile when left with only his own experience. Surely nobody has ever done such exciting translations as he has.

He seems to me to fall between two stools. He is neither on the safe earth nor among the stars. What makes his work deceptive is the fact that he is very nearly on the earth. He is — as it were — about one inch from the top of the grass.

In some of these stories there is a charming poetic atmosphere, but even it is always half and half. You cannot damn it without being wrong and you cannot praise without being equally wrong.

He was under the influence of Yeats at this time; one man's integrity is another man's compromise; and so it was with O'Connor.

He is an outsider even more than Synge was in this thing. It is the prudent mind carefully spreading the material thin.

You cannot satirise fraudulent piety unless you stand on some dogmatic centre of truth. This is necessary even as a hypothesis. In so far as O'Connor has a centre it is in his unholy laughter which is fairly constant.

Passing an interim judgement of O'Connor I find that he is a purveyor of emotional entertainment, and that he has surrendered to this minor role. There is tension in his mind

1954: Bloomsday (opposite *The Bailey*). [Photo: *The Irish Times*].

but most of this tension is expended on the construction of the container so that there is little left for the contents. He is like a powerful engine drawing a light load. The same is true of many writers who have achieved great contemporary fame — Joyce is a good example. Every generation produces fine technicians, designers, entertainers. But time destroys the tension of the wrapping paper, which their contemporaries mistook for inner excitement, leaving the dusty contents to be blown by the wind.

* * *

The Gaelic Language

The Bell, January 1948

Sir,

In every country inarticulate frustration uses whatever weapons are handiest against the creative writer. For a quarter of a century the most potent weapon against the writer in this country has been the 'revival' of Gaelic as a written language. Men with such Irish names as De Valera, and Blythe talk of it as the 'badge of nationhood' and have the audacity to speak of writers named O'Connor, O'Faolain, O'Donnell, O'Flaherty as 'Anglo-Irish' writers. Another weapon is also being used — the weapon of the safe arts of painting and music.

None of these attacks would be so very dangerous if the writers themselves did not fail to see the position as it is. The position is: The Gaelic language is no longer the native language; it is dead, yet food is being brought to the graveyard. The attempt to provide a safe alternative culture in the shape of painting and music is nothing more than the old nineteenth century Dublin of silly opera expressing its emptiness again.

Therefore, let me put down a few uncultured peasant facts

about the language: It can never be revived as a spoken language not to mention a writing language. However much we have loved the creature when it was alive we must be realists and accept that it is dead when it is dead. Let the frustrated and inarticulate continue to lay food beside the corpse.

Drive your cart and your plough over the bones of the dead.

End this inability to make up our minds whether we are to keep the corpse of a language propped up with pillows, bring it food, accepting its authority or to bury it decently. Every decision, as Chesterton says, is a desperate decision. Now, although the old language is dead so far as speaking or writing goes something of its spirit could without compromise be saved.

It could be taught for half an hour in the schools every day so that children might find the poetry in the names of places, in their own townlands. This is as much as can be hoped for without injury to the cause of reality.

Two or three events have recently given me new hope in the essential soundness of the native heart.

Speaking to a priest who teaches in a secondary school he told me that the change of attitude on the part of parents to the teaching of Gaelic was amazing. He did not like it. Through the children he could learn that the parents of these boys were simply sick of the humbug revival of Gaelic. They had endured the farce long enough. This is the solid sense which must delight the heart of the creative writer.

Another story which shows the return to realism is the story that a prominent ecclesiastic wrote to the Head of a Catholic school where Christian doctrine was being taught through the medium of Gaelic and ordered that the children be taught through their mother-tongue. What, he asked — and he was right — could children know of Christian doctrine taught through a language with which they were only vaguely acquainted?

169

These two things have cheered me immensely as they must cheer all sensible people. The core of reason is asserting itself. I think a political party which had the courage to lead this new — and old — commonsense would have a great future. Or must politics here be forever based on sentiment?

One often hears people saying that if Carleton had written in Gaelic — which he knew even better that English — or if Dan O'Connell had used it as he might, the language would have been saved. In our own day too, Liam O'Flaherty, a native speaker of the tongue, wrote in English. Did these deliberately let down the language? Those who say so do not understand that the creative writer has in him a feminine passivity. He is not so much a positive thing as an instrument played upon by the vital consciousness of the people. There is a kind of amoralism about him which accepts the force of life without question. Anyone who has written seriously knows that one of the supreme tests of the vitality of a subject is to try to write it down. It is the same with a language. If the subject or the language is dead or dying it will come to pieces in the writer's hands. Therefore it is not to be wondered at that all the movements, literary and political, which have had a vital impact on the people of this country used English as their medium.

What the writers must realise and express is the fact that language is not particularly a badge of nationhood. The language a man speaks has very little to do with his outlook and character. What do words matter to a lone ploughman in a field?

The extracts just quoted from the essays on Higgins and O'Connor — even the essay on the Gaelic language — are of such importance that they must be commented-on immediately. Patrick claimed somewhat dramatically that he was born as a poet on the banks of the Grand Canal in 1955. It is however in the nature of a genius that he be constantly reborn:

I have known the delight
Of being reborn each morning
And dying each night.

(Complete Poems, p. 63)

Patrick was re-born many times. One of those occasions was
when he wrote these two essays. With the publication of *A Soul
For Sale* he threw out the old leaven and began anew. There
were a few good poems in the book but for the most part they
were thin. Nor would he a year later have permitted the
publishers, Macmillans of London, to include a bowdlerised
version of *The Great Hunger*. It was one of the few books he
did not dedicate to me. He put the name of O'Curry, Editor of
The Standard, who had given him his first job, on the fly-leaf;
in Gaelic to disguise it somewhat. He would have pulled it out
entirely but by then the book had gone to the binders. On the
presentation copy he sent me he scratched the name out. And
in scratching out that name he was scratching out a life that
had passed. As a further gesture of rebirth he resigned his job
on *The Standard*, though retaining the position of film critic.

Before 1947 was ended he had demolished completely the
literature of the Celtic Twilight and whatever tangential
influence it might have had on him. He opened up in the
November issue of *The Bell* with a mummery called *The Wake
of The Books*. The editor of *The Bell*, a liberal who loved to
attack windmills, the Censorship of Books being one, suggested
in an editorial that a wake be held each year for all the books
that had been banned. Here is how it opened:

This little drama that I introduce
Is no great lecher to excite my muse,
For howsoever I try I can't but feel
The censorship of books is not a real
Problem for the writers of this land:
There's much that's insincere in what is banned —
And time if left the corpse would bury it deeper
In ten years than our bitterest conscience-keeper.

Yet as I have been asked to undertake
Master of Ceremonies at this comic wake
As I lead the characters in I'll try
To show the kernel of the tragedy —
The reality of bank and bake-house
Screeching unheeded round the writer's wake-house,
The inarticulate envy and the spleen
Echoing in the incidental scene
We call the Censorship . . . .

It all adds up to native cultural life,
The whore's honoured as the chastest wife;
The journalists cheer loudly for all
The noblest verse and the stupidest doggerel . . . .

(*Complete Poems*, p. 190)

The Wake of the Books was not taken too seriously mainly because it was written in verse. Putting similar ideas into prose is a different matter — and Patrick was as great a writer in prose as he was in verse. From 1947 to 1951 and beyond, through the medium of prose he publicly dismantled and destroyed what passed for Irish literature, leaving only himself standing in the field with Yeats and Joyce. All the others were on the distant horizon. One result of this assault was that he undermined and destroyed his own economic base and drove himself into isolation and poverty.

With the battle long won it is difficult to understand why Patrick's views should have been considered iconoclastic. His analysis of F. R. Higgins's work is reasonable and even understated. His report on Frank O'Connor seems friendly and generous. Yet such is the nature of what is called the simple truth that when it is uttered it causes an explosion. A controversy followed but not of the usual flamboyant and witty kind. Patrick had delivered a thrust to the heart. There was quiet seething and then the death rattle. *Very low, to attack a dead man* (Higgins) *who cannot defend himself*. Even Frank O'Connor was furious and stopped talking to Patrick. In an open letter in *The Irish Times* 8th December 1947 to Patrick, Ewart Milne writes:

. . . . But first let us recall that F. R. Higgins is dead. I am not quite sure what this conveys to you . . . . you were concerned with the fact of his Protestantism. It is against this sort of thing that I protest . . . . Was it really necessary to dwell on F. R. Higgins's un-Irishness, on what you call his desperate wish to be a droll gallivanting Irishman when by so doing it is quite possible you may give needless pain to those of his relatives still living and to his friends . . . . Truly you may well add that you hate being cruel to his memory for what you have written must surely hurt you now and in time to come.

Patrick replied as follows (*The Irish Times*, 19th December):

Mr. Ewart Milne demands a reply from me and himself supplies it: Protestant poetry is un-Irish poetry. It was against the silliness expressed in this phrase that I wrote in my essay on Higgins. Poetry is not Irish or any other nationality; and when writers such as Messrs. Clarke, Farren and the late F. R. Higgins pursue Irishness as a poetic end they are merely exploiting incidental local colour. Strip their writings of this local colour and see what remains. Their outlook is similar to the sentimental patriotism which takes pride — or pretends to take pride — in the Irishness of a horse that has won the Grand National — with the emphasis on the beast's Irishness instead of on his horsiness. A great many Protestants seeking roots in this country have attempted to build the national myth into a spiritual reality — Irish horses, Irish soldiers, Irish dogs, Irish poets. There is no poetic merit in the adjective Irish though mediocrity tries to put itself across on this fortuitous and empty distinction. Mr. Milne spoke of a common religion, the poet's religion. He was right. There is a common religion, a man being simply and sincerely his unique self. This is genius.

Chapter Twelve

I am fenced,
The light, the laugh, the dance, against

The problems connected with the publication of *Tarry Flynn* may not be sufficiently apparent from his letters and it may be best if I add here some further information. He had begun the writing of *Tarry Flynn* around the year 1941 and had been re-writing it up to this time. There was something fundamentally wrong with it which neither of us could put a finger on. I never really liked it: it was not the Patrick Kavanagh that I knew, not really the poet. He was out of his element writing something that bordered on social science. Hence there were at least ten full length versions of the novel, all of which I listened to and one version of which I still have. I even contributed a section myself, the part where the father is fighting with his sons and replies to each with some such remark as: *Smoke horsedung, yeh hure yeh!* It was published in *The Bell* of July 1944 but excluded from the final version.

I made several suggestions while he was writing it. One was that he should dismiss the idea of prose and write it in verse. He tried this and gave up. It was also my belief that part of his problem in the writing was that he was too close to his subject;

1954: The Law Case, Peter and Patrick. [Top photo: *Irish Press*; left: *Independent*].

he needed more detachment. To this end I suggested the name Eusebius for his main character. This suggestion was accepted.

It seemed there was no chance that anyone would publish it. He tried it on Methuens in 1942 under the title *Stony Grey Soil* but it was rejected. Eventually in 1947 while I was in America an outfit called The Pilot Press set up for business. They saw possibilities in *Tarry Flynn* and contracted to publish it. Patrick was not given a copy of the contract he signed and shortly after it was published The Pilot Press, without showing what he signed, claimed all sorts of options on his future work.

At this point we must back-track a year or so.

In November 1947 just before he had exposed his new level of integrity, Patrick managed to persuade Macmillans to give him a subsidy of six pounds a week if he would stay in Ireland and write a book for them. He had been threatening to go and live in the United States or even in South America. He was serious about it too and I had filled out all the necessary affidavits for the visa when the Macmillan offer came through.

He began a novel for Macmillans, or said he had. In fact he had several novels under construction for years and it is difficult to know which of them he had earmarked for Macmillans. He himself wrote about his novel writing at this time:

In those dear dead days beyond recall from the time of the Hitler War till about 1952 I was engaged on at least three major works, all still unpublished, and during the writing of which no one asked me if I were writing anything. And today I am taking these works down to have a look at them and to see if they can do something for me.

And they do.

With my cup of tea beside the typewriter I bang away. It is a summer's morning. I am working on this novel, not for the present generation or for posterity but simply if I do not I'll be lost. I did not know then the whiskey alternative or alleviate.

176

The novel belonged to my anti-clerical period. I had been brought up on the Celtic myth and no great masterpiece existed outside it. Anti-clericalism was part of the jag. I'm not saying I'm pro-clerical now, and I must point out that the anti-clericalism of the Celtic school — literary and political — was very much admired by the clerics themselves. They expected it from you. If you didn't care you were dangerous. The revolutionists of the Celtic school were not real; there might have been a smattering of genuine Orangeade in some of them like O'Casey but they all subscribed heavily to Mother Ireland. That covered every sin. It was an invention.

My principal novel had an agrarian-clerical plot.

On the main road-end of the townland of Miskish there was a three hundred acre farm with a large house on it. This farm was the only level land in the townland of Miskish; the remainder of it ran sharply in triangular divisions disguised as fields. Worse than that, unless when given permission by the owners of the large farm to use their private road the hill natives had to get in and out by a long narrow, rocky, boggy lane.

But those natives had hopes: the last of the Mullins (I kept changing the names of people and places as often as in a Russian novel, because I forgot and sometimes because a new name gives me a fresh stimulus) in the big farm were two old sisters and as soon as they were gone, which couldn't be long, and maybe before, the land would be divided among the natives by the Land Commission. An outfit like the Land Commission was very close to my imagination in those years.

The two old ladies hadn't gone to church, chapel or meeting house for years so nobody was worried too much that the old pair would leave their property to the priests and nuns.

I find on looking up my old ms. that that was not quite the case, though what eventually was the case is hard to say, for I kept repeating myself and changing names and characters and the point of view, so that apparently nothing came out *clear in the end. Here where the rats and mice stopped nibbling the ms. runs:*

'The last of the Mullins to own the farm, an eccentric named Jane, had died three months previously. For the last thirty years of her life this woman had gone to neither church, Chapel nor meeting house. On Sunday mornings when the rest of Miskish would be away at Mass she would be seen in the orchard cutting thistles under the trees with a scythe, or in the winter, inside playing jigs and reels on an old piano.'

Tarry Flynn wasn't long published when word reached Macmillans that The Pilot Press had an option on his next two books! They stopped their subsidy immediately and though Patrick wangled as best he could that was the end of the subsidy.

Further trouble came his way. *Tarry Flynn* was banned by the Irish censorship. The ban was lifted but the damage had been done. He was ruined with most readers of *The Standard* and in July 1949 he was more or less fired as film critic. In America a Catholic magazine called *Tarry Flynn the Tobacco Road of Cavan.*

As usual in a crisis like this he appealed to his friend the Catholic Archbishop of Dublin, John Charles McQuaid, and as usual he was given charity. But better charity than nothing. John Charles didn't trust Patrick and possibly didn't even like him.

A year or so later I begged Patrick that at all costs he must write the story of his life in Dublin during the 1940s. He was hesitant but took me at my word just the same. He gave up in the middle of the work but he left sufficient behind that I was able to finish it in 1978 and publish it under the title *By Night Unstarred.** Here is an extract. He had given the name of Michael to his chief character but I changed it to Patrick to make it more personal.

* By Night Unstarred, an autobiographical novel (Ireland and New York, 1978).

One of the men was slightly older than the other and he also seemed to be the more troubled, the more nervous. He kept turning round to get a better seat but did not remain long in any one position; he shrugged his shoulders like a man who had the itch — nerves, a habit he had taken with him from the handles of a plough, perhaps, when he had left the country some years before. This habit was more his undoing — for undone he had been many times — than many more important things. But he was not aware of this: he imagined that men are judged by their main principles and not by the little things. He scratched his head: he yawned. Sometimes he would sit up straight as if he had sighted something extraordinary passing on the sea-road below.

Except for these peculiar habits he was a normal man, fairly good-looking and far more attractive than his looks would appear to deserve. He was aged over thirty but looked fantastically younger — the poetic streak, being itself a native of the Land of Perpetual Youth, keeps its possessors young. And keeps them virtuous-looking too even when they may have been less than saints. Perhaps he was truly virtuous. Perhaps what looked out of his eyes was the judgement of the gods. Virtue is often confused with what is narrow of heart, bitter. Patrick was not bitter or narrow-hearted. Nothing seemed to make him bitter or a pessimist.

Though for over six years he had been engaged in the only valid war — the war to which there is no armistice — the war of life, and had been seriously wounded, he came up again and again to continue the battle. And where he had been wounded before, he was wounded again — the same error, the same weakness. Why was that? He was still trying to find out.

For every man the battle of life has a different meaning but for all men the getting of money is a large part of the incidental background. With Patrick the getting of money — otherwise, a job — appeared to be practically all that battle. For six years he had tried everything — everything that in his

179

foolish heart he imagined to be wires, he pulled. He met a new influential acquaintance and he flattered him for a while and the man promised to do the necessary for him. But nothing ever came of it. He was one of those futile labourers whose only permanent job is pulling the devil by the tail. He had no background, no family, no formal education. He was self-educated.

While the callouses of the plough-handles were still tender on his palms he had read through the literatures of Europe. He was not a profound scholar but just the same he knew a great deal more than the average writer. He had written a novel but had made no money out of it. His three published books of verse had brought him a reputation — but in addition it brought all the jealousy of mean, pub-crawling Dublin where the chief pastime consists in sneering at serious men who stay home and work.

He was praised by these public-house critics and he liked the praise for a time — until he discovered that something poisonous lay at the bottom of it all. That little versifier with the narrow eyes who knew all the gossip of the town had praised him to his face and Patrick was shocked and puzzled when he heard that this same person was giving quite a different opinion behind his back. But Patrick kept no spite. Why should he keep up spite? The injury is all to oneself when one hates or is bitter. Love your enemies is a sound doctrine for in loving one's enemies a man vanquishes them, while in hating them he vanquishes himself.

Patrick loved simply, though not deeply, because that is what gave him pleasure. Sometimes he deliberately set out to hate people, and though hating by all the rules of warfare seemed the proper thing to do, it was always a failure with him. A friend had put him up to these hates on some occasions and, in despair, seeking the secret of life, he experimented. Little by little he was getting terrified of hating.

He was weak, easily led. He knew that his will was weak

but could do nothing about it. From his mother he had inherited this weakness of character. In one way Patrick was thankful to her because, had it not been for this weakness of his mother's will he would probably never have been born. And it was a good thing to be born.

He had a hard struggle but he had also happiness. He had known the love of beautiful women. This day, the love of a beautiful girl coming into his thoughts, made the scene about him and the sea below him insignificant, not worth a thought. He could love the scenery and the sea too but only as an aside. The light of the intangible Truth had flashed across the hills to him and that, he knew, was something to be grateful for, something worth being born to misery for.

He had seen that light flash on the hills: it might be the sun going down or it might be nothing at all. It was just the hint of of the miracle of Creation that makes poets gasp. He had seen it in streams and in ploughed fields and on roads to fairs in country towns, in among the open gaps of the morning where the ash-plants of drovers were swinging. Yet in all that beauty there was something that made a man unhappy. There was a price that had to be paid. And the price for such visions was a high price.

Natural life, lived naturally as it is lived in the countryside has in it none of that progress which is the base of happiness. Men and women in rural communities can be compared to a spring that rises out of the rock and spreads and spreads in irregular ever-widening circles. But the general principle is static. Rural life is all background. Life in cities is not a spring but a river, or rather a watermain. It progresses like a novel, artificially. There is no progression in art; there is none in life. And a man coming from a circular static mood to the forward hurry of city life is at a disadvantage. He must learn to pose. Patrick had not learned to pose. He did not want to pose. He wanted to apply natural laws to an unnatural situation. He was conscious of this at times, but being conscious of a fact is not the same thing as knowing how to act on that consciousness.

The happiness he had know in the country was an unconscious yet superb happiness. Since coming to live in the city six years ago he was beginning to wonder if that happiness he had known was any different from the happiness of a cow or of a vegetable in the sunlight. The people with whom he had to deal had awakened early to life. They had escaped the unconscious of the creative soul at an early age — by education, by worldliness, by being perhaps superficial.

Patrick wanted more than anything else in the world the means to get married and to keep a wife. He had found a beautiful and sensitive girl named Margaret O'Carroll and the thought of his inability to marry her drove him to desperation.

For one man to succeed in life or in love — which is the same thing — another man must fail.

Patrick did not realise the extent of the jealousy raised by his success with Margaret. He did not realise that he was surrounded by hundreds of men who required only a little more heat to be raving lunatics with jealousy. Life is a madhouse and a battlefield combined.

As a poet, too, he had those who hated him because they thought that being a poet was a free gift of Heaven not something for which a high price must be paid. And yet there were all these people who were all optimism with Christian charity towards all. These were the most poisonous. He sensed these things in a vague way, but when it was a question of survival, ethics did not count. Bit by bit he was learning how the wheels go round.

One of the biggest hopes in his life had been the Bishop of Dublin. This man had taken an interest in him because he thought that he would be able to get inside information about the pagan writers from him. He suspected the bishop of being a slippery customer but saw that he had nothing to lose *except his self-respect and stood to gain a lot if the deal went through.*

He visited the Bishop regularly and kow-towed humbly. For hours he listened to this man trying to impress a poet with his immense learning and piety. Patrick bowed to the profound wisdom of the bishop while he waited for the money that once again was only a temporary expedient 'till a job turns up'. Patrick saw the fun of it sufficiently to be cynical and when he was out of the shadow of the bishop's palace he would relieve his feeling by remarks like 'Son of a bitch, I wonder will he come across with a job'.

No job came at that time or after, but Patrick did not fall out with the Bishop when the Bishop gave him the hint that he would not be at home for a few months. A man should never fall out with a Bishop. Patrick deliberately chose to fall out with many of his supposed friends when after a reasonable trial they proved useless to his purpose. But even in this throwing-over of friends there was something of a method, a sacrifice to the gods, as it were. He had been severely tempted to write a scorching letter to the Bishop telling him what he thought, but restrained himself.

At this moment the Bishop swept into the room like a hostess in evening dress. To look at, but without undue emphasis on the man's character, his entry had the speed, the determination of a hangman calling to the condemned prisoner's cell at five minutes to eight in the morning. He had his head down, he was smiling at the floor. He had a habit of looking at a visitor's boots first. Patrick remembered how when he first met the man he was wearing a pair of broken shoes and the Bishop, looking as it seemed at the shoes, embarrassed him. The fact is that the Bishop hardly saw the shoes at all. It was a habit of his born out of some far hidden spiritual defeat of his ancestors.

The Bishop of Dublin was not the typical bishop at all. He was spare of flesh and slight of build, about five feet seven or eight in height. His face was hard and his mouth tight. There were three large furrows in his brow; his head was bald. A man looking at him with the objectivity of one who had nothing to lose or gain by knowing the man would say that here was a man of deep cunning. Not a pernicious cunning perhaps but a sharp knowledge of the world. His grey long face was the face of an ascetic, or of a dealing man from some mountainy district in the county Leitrim.

Patrick had too much to lose if he lost the Bishop to be able to see the man in an objective way. None the less he was not deceived, for out of the Bishop's presence, in the days when he had first known him he could discard the man quickly and effectively. 'Son of a bitch'. He should have more respect for a bishop of the church. As a bishop he had respect but he was not a respecter of persons, except as a pretence, when as now he wanted to get something out of a man. But his pretence was of no avail. The Bishop saw through the mask. It is useless pretending to be something one is not in some degree fundamentally at heart. The Bishop was no fool though he was not the kind of wise man he ambitioned.

By the beginning of 1949 Patrick's economic situation had so deteriorated that he was starving and being threatened with eviction. He resolved the situation by selling Reynold's Farm for four hundred pounds — you might almost say, for nothing. He sold it without even consulting me. It was one of those mean acts of which he was capable. He was the owner of record but only in a formal sense. I had as much right to the place as he had. Had he asked my permission I would very likely not have protested or I might have somehow borrowed the money and bought the title from him so as to retain the farm for sentiment. Patrick knew that he had acted unfairly and had wounded me. How did he explain himself?

With five or six hundred I might get in with a rich widow . . .
I intend using the money as deposit on a house . . . .

184

Reference : A/N. 155813 C

25 - 8 - 58 19

~~installing~~

A visit was made to your premises to-day for the purpose of removing ~~testing~~

your telephone, but access could not be gained.

Will you kindly telephone to the District Engineer (Dublin 45651) (Advice Note Control) or return this card stating a convenient time for carrying out the work, and giving as much notice as possible.

The work may be carried out at 2 A.M. — 3 A.M. (time) on the ~~any date except Christmas night~~ (date).

Signature ...... P. Kavanagh

Address ...... 62 Pembroke Rd. — Ballsbridge

I.2641.

13066B:1,000.6/57.Fleet.28B.

August 1958: Patrick's reply to the Post Office (Distillery Rd., Drumcondra) states that the most convenient time for removing his telephone is between 2 a.m. and 3 a.m. any date except Christmas night.

185

— completely dishonest, but it saw him through a difficult situation with me. I am still annoyed with him over that act though I never said a word about it. No need to. He knew well enough.

In a manuscript in my possession he writes with more honesty about this transaction:

My black hills have never seen the sun rising
Eternally they look north towards Armagh.

Recently I sold a small farm which as a literary background has served me well.

Many years ago after I had done a series of radio talks, numerous newspaper articles and part of a book about this farm a neighbour of mine put one foot up on a stone in the fence and peering through the bushes said to me:

'Kavanagh! Do you know what it is, you're the only bleddy man that ever made money out of that farm'.

I smiled a large learned smile and wandered up those hills of Shancoduff which overlooked the Border across the valley.

It was suggested to me that I should write an epic poem on the sale of that farm. Perhaps it would be a true epic, the epic of the sense of loss, the loss of the boats that all heroes burn. It is only by burning the past that we are free of the future, and a man must not regret.

Yet, I am surprised at my present mood, for I had intended a humorous mood, and now it seems that the mood is in danger of being pensive.

There were good Gaelic names to those fields too: Páirc an Ceóltóra, Páirc Mhárcuis, Cúl an tSiopa.

* * *

62 Pembroke Road, Dublin, 19th January 1949
I have decided to sell Reynolds if I can get six or seven hundred for it. What to do with the money? I intend using it as a deposit on a house. The Buildings Societies advance the

rest, if you have the deposit on a house. In that way I'd eventually have my own house. As it is the landlady, Mrs. Beauchamp, has been troublesome, has been trying to evict me and has refused my rent so that at the moment I owe her four months. If I can get a house quickly I'll leave her without her rent — six months at least. It is a nuisance living in a flat. However, I have another plan; spreading one's bread on the water is not a bad idea. With five or six hundred I might get in with a rich widow. Possibilities are good. I am about the most talked of man in Dublin. I'm enclosing poem from last Saturday's Irish Times. These things and the novel give a man a great lift with the women.

Am in trouble with the Macmillan subsidy. The Pilot Press claim a lieu on my next novel. I may fix it but anyway the annuity is only for the next eleven months and I'll have to find some way of living. Tarry Flynn as I probably told you was un-banned. I sold four pieces to Reynold's News for thirty pounds. The Pilot Press is dishonest. I may have to denounce them to the Authors' Society.

* * *

62 Pembroke Road, Dublin, 27th February 1949
You'll be expecting to hear from me, and I have been waiting on more news. Here is all to date. You know that the Pilot Press done me out of the Macmillan subsidy — for the present at any rate. They claim an option but I don't think an option exists and they have refused all my demands to see a photostat of the contract. I am quite sure by this time that none exists. Macmillan has promised to renew the agreement if the Pilot trouble is settled. I have sold Reynolds and may well need the money — 450 to Paddy Fitzsimons of Lannat. I am sure I did right. My main aim must be to get a rich woman — and that soon. The Pilot Press affair upset my work for a while but I am getting on again.

Cities are the only place for anyone but a peasant. It really is living in the mentality of a slum, the women who would place you or me on a lower level that that of a dancer

187

or a footballer. The country is awful except to write about. As you may observe, I am giving you back your own views at a delayed action distance. I have learned slowly.

I have been wondering if I shouldn't try to get to America for a short lecture tour. I am thinking it over. There is a Government Cultural Committee formed though they would hardly back me. Bunch of ignoramuses.

The novel lies in much the same condition but I am progressing on other fronts.

* * *

62 Pembroke Road, Dublin, 30th May 1949
Yes, Carruth told me it was you arranged it. You are a good agent. I am sending you on two cuttings, the one by Joyce's brother is interesting. My review of Contemporary Irish Poets which is from the Standard caused, you'll be glad to know, Farren to have an apoplectic fit, so Larry Morrow told me and suggested I lay off the man before he bursts a blood vessel. Larry was serious, said Farren was in a terrible state of helpless hate. That is why he went for you, I suppose. I wrote a satire in verse which I think is rather good and sent in to Carruth, so you might be able to read it if you get this letter before you leave Chicago. Farren, Clarke, M. J. McManus are the chief characters in it which I have titled The Paddiad, from the Dunciad. That's good news.

I am beginning to note you have the same sort of sensibility as myself and know about the same time* — that the less you have me as a brother the better. One should build up oneself and not one's brother. Going over on a brother's fame lessens oneself in the mind of the audience. I often do it about you and I suppose one does get an amount of boasting out of it. But I don't think it wise. Things like that should be heard as an aside, unless one wants of course to get an introduction. In that case I'd claim the pope as my father. However, as I say, I have noted that you

* *Sic.*

188

appreciate these matters about the same moment as I do. Good luck till I hear from you.

* * *

17th June 1949

Your sketch has great merit. You have a real lyrical touch, a touch of Borrow in your feeling for character and characters and it would be a pity if you fell for the enormous idea of writing for a particular public. You are good and could do a smashing fine book, provided you remember that it is your personality filtering the experience which has the merit.

I felt in this article a kow-towing to the newspaper idea of news — Standard copy. There is real sensibility in your writing, in that old Bible preacher for example. What a character you could make of such men. It is for this purpose I am writing to convince you of the importance of your point of view. Don't be corrupted by a public in your mind.

Enjoy yourself and your observing. You have a touch, I'm telling you, and may well find the material you require in this journey. What I find in your writing is the best thing in all writing — a love and an enthusiasm for life and people.

* * *

12th July 1949

I am no longer a film critic — they as good as fired me, though I was about to leave. Petty Curry's ego is small.

By the way, Horizon is publishing that satire (The Paddiad) which the Poetry Chicago bollocks couldn't see the merit of. A shit.

189

Chapter Thirteen

Not beyond the ring
Of inner truth . . .

With money from the sale of the farm now in his pocket, Patrick was in the mood to renew the attack on literary immorality. In May 1949 he sent me *The Paddiad* so that I might submit it to the editor of *Poetry Chicago* who was an acquaintance of mine. He turned it down but *Horizon* which first published *The Great Hunger* was glad to get it and publish it in August. Over the years it has been popular for those who call themselves critics to lament the fact that Patrick spent his energies writing *The Paddiad* yet it is a marvellous piece, hilarious and as good as anything he ever wrote. It describes those with pretensions to literature who used to assemble in The Palace Bar. It begins:

> *In the corner of a Dublin pub*
> *This party opens — blub-a-blub —*
> *Paddy Whiskey, Rum and Gin*
> *Paddy three Sheets in the wind;*
> *Paddy of the Celtic Mist,*
> *Paddy Connemara West,*

Chestertonian Paddy Frog
Croaking nightly in the bog.
All the Paddies having fun
Since Yeats handed in his gun,
Every man completely blind
To the truth about his mind.

The four hundred pounds he got for the farm didn't last long. After he had paid his major debts he hadn't much left. Once again he owed rent to the landlady. The E.S.B. was demanding entrance to his flat so it could disconnect the utilities. I did my part here by installing a *busybody* mirror outside his window so he could see who was knocking without himself being observed. Once again he found temporary relief — he managed to persuade Hollis & Carter to advance him one hundred pounds on a book he promised to write for them on Irish pilgrimages. The book was not written though he made a start. Here is his account of Croagh Patrick:

Croagh Patrick

Each year, on the last Sunday in July, is held the Croagh Patrick Pilgrimage. Although newspapers report the event little is known about the actuality of the Pilgrimage. It is just another small mountain which people climb. There is a lot more to it than that.

One of the reasons why so little is known about this Pilgrimage is that it imposes too much hardship on the usual reporter. Just as on Lough Derg he has got to take full part, not be a mere observer.

There is a good deal of spiritual value to be gained from being forced into the mill where experience is ground; you will not like it at the time but afterwards you feel richer.

The Croagh Patrick Pilgrimage is based on Westport and is primarily a west of Ireland religious festival. There is a lot of laughter and open-heartedness about the west (as there is about every other part for that matter) but the one great impression that one brings away from Croagh Patrick is that amid all the laughter, singing in the all-night pubs, is the tremendous Catholic piety of the people. This is the traditional piety which has remained undisturbed by the Age of Reason.

We arrived at Westport on Saturday evening. When we came to within thirty miles of the town we began to catch up with pilgrims on bicycles with the necessary stick tied to the cross-bar, the over-coat on the carrier. These men were strong young farmers, or farmers' sons, and as we watched them we felt that this was the true pilgrim idea and that if one could only join in with them one would be at the source of material for literature as well as of grace: something seeps through. The same feeling that there is something which deserves the superimposed order of art touches us as we wander through the streets of the town.

All the shops, not only the pubs and restaurants, were open till near midnight. There were a few tinker women and I was interested to observe that they were dressed in gaily-embroidered skirts like true gypsies.

I talked to a shopkeeper about the tinkers and he told me the interesting thing that the tinkers have become so rich, most of them have become so comfortable, that the roaring fighting tinker looks like disappearing.

The weather was terrible; cold rain poured down and I heard a man in great good humour say that 'it was only a misht'.

During the rain we were able to sit in a cocktail bar that would out-flash anything in Dublin. A man came in to buy a bottle of wine and he was very choosy in his vintage.

From twelve o'clock onwards the cars began to race through the town on their way out to 'the Reek', as the mountain is called. Thousands of cars passed through in a couple of hours while we waited for the rain to stop and with

192

hopes to begin the climb near daybreak. So at three o'clock we began to drive out to the Reek which is only five miles from the town. But when we got out about three miles we caught up with a traffic jam something like (something worse) what I have experienced going to Fairyhouse Races at Easter. There was an accident, too; a big car behind us mistook the glint of rain on a low fence for the road and somersaulted into the waste-land by the sea where it came to rest upside-down. Luckily no one was injured much.

The misty rain still poured down and it was dark as a mid-winter night. A large force of Civic Guards tried to get the traffic moving. Eventually we were diverted off the main road towards a car park. The car park we got into was part of a potato field, the headland deep in mud but at last we got parked in what turned out to be a little meadow with a cock of hay in it.

A group of amusing fellows from Galway were there changing into mountaineering clothes and one of them with a very good voice was singing about a Mary from Cork.

Still the rain slanted down from the mountain up the slopes of which in the distance we could discern the flickering of little lights. My companion with his camera said we should make a start but I said nobody in his senses could face the mountain in that weather.

We moved off about four when the dawn was breaking with difficulty through the sleet and mist. We had to walk more than a mile to the start of the Pilgrim's Path. Here along the lane that led to the foot of the Path were rows of stalls selling all sorts of medals, rosaries and pious pictures. Plenty of tea-stalls too. Everything was on a plentiful scale including the pilgrims of whom there were thousands. From where we stood ankle-deep in perishing gutter to the top of the mountain there was a two-mile line of pilgrims twenty or more deep, a slow tortuous snake of humanity that made me think this must be something like what happens to refugees fleeing from war. Weak enough people entered that stream

193

*and were carried on by the mass will, the crowd emotion. Of
our own individual strength we would never be able to do it,
especially those of us who had not the Faith which climbs
mountains, never mind move them.*

*The rain kept coming down and it remained dark. The
Path which is a narrow furrow winding up the mountain got
even muddier as we went up, and there were big shifting
stones in the mud which when you stepped on them you were
liable to slip and smash an ankle.*

*There were old men and young women and all were
cheerful. The weakness of will and of stomach which attacks
mountaineers attacked our party, but there was little we
could do. We stepped aside from the stream now and then to
draw our breath. There was no shelter and no place dry
enough to sit down. Now, half-way up another torture was
added: a stream of pilgrims which had already made the
climb began to come down and when the two streams met in
the narrow muddy stony gorge it was awful.*

*And yet the pilgrims managed to stop at the various
stations on the route and say the prayers that are part of the
pilgrimage. Somebody mentioned the Sherpa Tensing and
this drew an amused response from the crowd. We asked the
down-coming pilgrims how far we had to climb and the
answers were encouraging. Still we climbed, and our
resolution became weaker. The ambulance men of the Order
of Malta appeared with a casualty carried on a stretcher on
their shoulders. This didn't encourage us. Shortly
afterwards another such funeral procession met us. The
horror that assailed us here was not the thought of the bit of
mountain we still had to climb but the thought that we would
have to go back down it again.*

*The cone of the mountain was invisible as we reached its
base. The throng became more entangled. Here the mud ends
and the sharp stones do duty for self-denial. The path here as
nearly elsewhere is V-shaped like a potato drill. The heavy
mist penetrated to our bones. On the top of the cone were at*

194

Patrick by *John Ryan*, **1950.**

least five thousand people either in the process of going up or the process of coming down, or hearing Mass in the crude stone oratory which is built on top.

It was after six o'clock when we reached the top and the mist was heavy; we could see nothing of Clew Bay. I was so weary, so horrified at the prospect of having to go down that I could not remember a day twelve years ago (1940) when I had once before climbed Croagh Patrick and in bright sunshine gazed at the exhilarating scene.

My friend with the camera took a few pictures but the mist on the summit was too deep on the lense.

Then back down again, an ordeal not much better than the climb.

I fell in with a Galwayman who was a pleasant fellow but I felt somewhat abashed and felt the need to dissemble when he asked me to wait for him while he said 'a few prayers' at a Station.

I was in the midst of a Faith of a most powerful simplicity and this thought struck hard into me beneath the local colour.

You realise that it is no superficial romantic impulse that is behind this mountain climb. You are at the raw sensitive heart of the active Faith; too raw and sensitive perhaps for poetic exploitation.

Patrick's Dublin friends were exclusively women. Men in general resented his genius and were rude to him. No doubt later in life there were men, some with homosexual tendencies who were attracted to him, fascinated by his apparent abandon; but as far as I know he remained to the end exclusively a woman's man. He kept repeating the theme:

Now I must search till I have found my God —
Not in an orphanage. He hides
In no humanitarian disguise,
A derelict upon a barren bog,

196

But in some fantastically ordinary incog.
Behind a well-bred convent girl's eyes,
Or wrapped in middle-class felicities
Among the women in a coffee shop.
Surely my God is feminine, for Heaven
Is the generous impulse, is contented
With feeding praise to the good. And all
Of these that I have known have come from women.
While men the poet's tragic light resented,
The spirit that is Woman caressed his soul.

(Complete Poems, p. 237)

Towards the end of his life he repeated this theme:

. . . . I am brooding, I am breaking my heart
And that is why I must turn forward and thus positioned
Observe the past un-lost: Nuala and Sheila, Mary and
Deirdre
And the time itself beautifully composed
And the moral-brake sickness in me from some lie
Believed by my mother before I was born.
No, I was always anything but queer, abnormally normal
And I probably had more women who loved me than Byron
And pure ones all. The wild, wild explosions of the innocent
Most of the famous women-men one hears of
Were very easy to please; it was all the same
The second-hand or the fiftieth-hand.
But I was the true romantic,
Too far in that direction perhaps.

(Complete Poems, p. 340)

Neither Patrick nor I discussed our girl-friends: that would be
a betrayal of the love secret, would be gross and lacking in
honour. I was acquainted with most of his women friends and

197

in compiling this book I wrote to each of them for a memoir. I received no reply: they too prefer to retain their secret. Nor will I speculate except in a general way on Patrick's relationship with them, as far as I have any information.

Those familiar with the Catholic doctrine on marriage and relations between man and woman will understand me when I say that Patrick had great sexual virtue. He was not a libertine. He needed a girl not just for sex but for all the more important feminine attributes. The light that emanated from an attractive girl was a dancing flame that attracted him almost as much as the poetic thing. He loved the ideal of the female more than the reality. It kept him in a state of near constant excitement. Here he is again:

> She waved her body in the circle sign
> Of love purely born without side,
> The earth's contour, she orbited to my pride, Sin and unsin.
> But the critic asking questions ran
> From the fright of the dawn
> To weep later on an urban lawn
> For the undone
> God-gifted man.
> O the river flowed round and round
> The low meadows filled with buttercups
> In a place called Topras.
> I was born on high ground.

(Complete Poems, p. 289)

The women he mentioned and who were known to me were not really the important women in his life. They often, it is true, rescued him from starvation:

> Seeing through the comic veil
> The poet's spirit in travail.

— but it was the fleeting female caress that mattered, that really lighted up his spirit. In a manuscript I have before me he gives an illustration:

I made it. I made it. I made it.
What are you saying? What did you make?
I am. I am here. I am alive.
I was speaking to a beautiful young girl, a barmaid,
today. She was interested in me. She was asking me leading
questions to find out about my financial condition. I had
mentioned that I did a lot of flying and that I had squatters
rights in London airport. She quietly asked how far was
London airport from London. Her eyes were the thrillingly
gay eyes of a young virgin.
'When will you be in again?'
'Tomorrow, more than likely'.
'Tomorrow's my half day'.
'I see, I see. I wo—nder . . .' (No, no, no. It wouldn't work
that soon). 'I'll be in on Friday anyhow'.
I looked at myself in the mirror that was the window as I
went out and (as newspapers say of brides) I looked radiant.
. . .

This was written towards the end of his life but it is true of the earlier part.

I found Patrick very conservative, religious, and even straightlaced. He was my godfather and never forgot this obligation. He explained himself thoroughly in a poem which he wrote in 1951 entitled *Auditors In:*

The problem that confronts me here
Is to be eloquent yet sincere
Let myself go rip and not go phoney
In an inflated testimony.
Is verse an entertainment only
Or is it a profound and holy

Faith that cries the inner history
Of the failure of man's mission?
Should it be my job to mention
Precisely how I chanced to fail
Through a cursed ideal.
Write down here: he knew what he wanted
Evilest knowledge ever haunted
Man when he can picture clear
Just what he is searching for.
A car, a big suburban house,
Half secret that he might not lose
The wild attraction of the poor
But proud, the fanatic lure
For women of the poet's way
And diabolic underlay;

The gun of pride can bring them down
At twenty paces in the town —
For what? the tragedy is this
Pride's gunman hesitates to kiss:
A romantic Rasputin
Praying at the heart of sin.

He cannot differentiate
Say if he does not want to take
From moral motives or because
Nature has idea in her laws.

But to get down to the factual
You are not homosexual.
And yet you live without a wife,
A most disorganized sort of life.
You've not even bred illegitimates,
A lonely lecher whom the fates
By a financial trick castrates.

(*Complete Poems*, p. 242, Extract)

I gave him what money I could afford but it was too little to be of much help. Then he did what is common to many people on the verge of starvation: he turned to gambling. He himself describes the experience.

One Derby Day in 1949 I entered a bookie's office for the first time. I went up to the girl at the hole in the partition and shoved in a pound — 'On Nimbus'. I said. She told me I'd have to write it out on a slip. While I was writing it out a porter out of a local pub sneered:

'Well, he'll not be in the first three anyway.'

I started to tear up the slip: 'Are you sure?' I asked. He made a contemptuous snarl out of the corner of his mouth. Then it began to dawn on me that I wouldn't give any heed to a chap like this on any other subject so I doubled my stake.

Nimbus duly won in a photo-finish at seven to one. The girl who paid me said I'd be sorry for my win. I'm not sure she was right. I don't think I ever became truly addicted to betting.

Previous to that win on Nimbus I had a terrible horror of Bookies' shops. I used to step wide and warily past the groups of what I considered degenerate derelicts who lounged around the doors of such places . . . .

The world of the punter or the gambler is not a rich imaginative field and the reason for this is that it is a form of disease or of sin. I'm not sure which. The orgy is followed by remorse. Sickness whether of the soul or of the body is not a funny subject. It is only in normalcy that you can have originality. Anyone who has ever looked at those newspapers which devote themselves to crime and sin will realise how drearily they repeat the same boring story. The real immorality of gambling does not consist as certain puritans suggest in the getting of easy money but in the way that gambling is lived by the sensations.

Patrick had no hard business sense and on almost every

occasion he signed a contract he left himself open. Those who called themselves his friends whould shrug and say the contract didn't matter and order another drink. Because of this kind of carelessness Patrick had difficulty collecting the miserable few pounds owed him by the publishers of *Tarry Flynn*. He had to appeal to me for help.

Chapter Fourteen

For most have died the day before
The opening of that holy door

In December 1949 a new literary monthly called *Envoy* began publication in Dublin and continued for a year-and-a-half. Patrick was given a section in the back of the magazine to expound his views and this he did, infuriating still further the literary set. Payment was negligible but having the forum was important. He called his piece *Diary*.

By the time *Envoy* closed Patrick was hated not merely by the pretenders to literature but also by the Government. There existed for propaganda purposes a Government group called The Cultural Relations Committee which sent Irish people abroad at Government expense to spread the word of Ireland's devotion to the arts. One of Patrick's acquaintences was a member of this Committee and Patrick saw a chance of cutting in on this junket. All he needed, he wrote me, was an invitation on university-headed paper to lecture in America and he felt sure he would be on his way. I obtained that formal invitation for him. When he applied to the Committee, submitting the letter of invitation, his application was vetoed by the government Minister — Mr. Frank Aiken, a notoriously illiterate politician. Even Patrick's picture which was to appear on the cover of a magazine called *The Irish Digest* was withdrawn. Patrick was out in the cold for good.

* * *

62 Pembroke Road, Dublin, 9th August 1949
I hate having to try to explain the position about the Pilot Press. First I must congratulate you on having your Abbey Theatre book published and I am sure there is in it the makings of a fine book. What worried me about it was the lot of good stuff which was lost in the bad. However, with editing it ought to create a bit of a storm here. Madness will be no name for some of the chancers.

About the Pilot Press: I signed as you know a contract in The Bell offices. I never received the duplicate of the contract. Expected Peadar O'Donnell to have it. On that contract was an Agreement to let them act as my agents and when I saw it I objected. But when they explained they were ordinary agents taking the bare 10% I agreed. Next thing they interpolated in the contract, when they guessed I had no copy, a clause giving them an option on my next two novels. They wrote to Macmillans who needless to say stopped the monthly payment to me. Every time I demanded my American payment through David Charles, solicitor, who had been acting for me for months in vain, they said: not till the matter of the option has been cleared up. At the same time one never knows what option. They just won't pay. They sent me a check for my English royalties and it bounced. Advised by Charles who is a bags I think, I did not prosecute. They sent me a new check. Everything that legality can do from this side has been done. Macmillans suggested that I send them my next book and they will deal with the Pilot Press. In the meantime I would like to know what contract the P.P. has, or tried to make, for me with Devin Adair. I have never seen any such document. There is the position. I sold the Ms. of The Great Hunger to the Nat. Lib. for fifty pounds. Had to write The Great Hunger out.

On Pembroke Road look out for my ghost.

The Pilot Press has not paid and I need the money rather badly. I wrote to them yesterday threatening the police on Lantos for embezzlement. According to current exchange I have ninety five pounds coming not counting what they made off the the book. I believe they are very poor.

* * *

8th November 1949

The Pilot paid when I threatened them — police! I discovered that to convert money entrusted to you as agent is a serious criminal offence — a felony in fact. It will just put me over the winter. I should have said I got your letter this morning and was pleased about Frank O'Connor; he doesn't speak to me. I cannot tell how much I look forward to seeing your Abbey Theatre for if you managed to get the bad stuff out and pull the ironic witty parts together it will be one of the great books of entertainment ever to appear.

Nobody struck me over the Paddiad. There is a new magazine called Envoy coming out in December. I am close to the so-called Editor, a young chap called Ryan (Monument Creamery). I am doing a nasty diary at the back of the magazine each month, and it occurs to me that you might express your nastiness there, too, now and then.

* * *

I am thinking of going to London by plane today to see if I can pick up any ready-money job such as a column on a Sunday paper. It is now half-eight in the morning and if I go I'll go on the 9.30 plane and I haven't shaved yet.

I've had sinus and a bad cold* lately. You had sinus trouble, I think. The doctor said mine was minor.

* * *

I am continuing this 'Diary' every month and should succeed in maddening plenty of mediocrities. Horizon is closing this

---

* NOTE: The early symptoms of cancer.

month. Just got in in time. Connolly thought a lot of my poem. It is good to know you are well, and that you are making a mark over there. At a distance you look like being important. You know how people are impressed.

* * *

62 Pembroke Road, Dublin, 30th December 1949
I didn't bother writing for Christmas. Boring time, as usual. Sat in alone. My writing is about going now and I may have something ready soon.

* * *

62 Pembroke Road, Dublin, 25th February 1950
I am writing but with indifferent success. Novel did not go well. However, I think it will eventually do alright. Needless to say I am as broke as bedamned but I have the rent paid in advance and have no bills. Nothing you could do about it so don't mind. I'll manage.

* * *

62 Pembroke Road, Dublin, April 12th, 1950
Am enclosing a play which I wrote in Envoy. Hope you like it. I am in a bad financial position at the moment. There is just the possibility that something will turn up within the next six weeks though I am not sure. There is the News Agency which the Government has set up. I have been more or less promised but. . . . How I have lived for the past few months without an income is a miracle. My novel has not come off well at all. There is some false note, something in this story which my imagination rejects. However, I am trying my best. Without a permanent job no writer can survive long, and I have infuriated and will continue to, all the hateful people. If it hadn't been for a few quid I won on horses I'd be on the rocks utterly. I have been very lucky. Last Saturday I had only a quid and I had three pressing debts of over ten pounds. I paid them with my one bet. But there is no future in that and no guarantee. It really is desperate.

207

I don't like to say it and it is on the cards that before it could come I mightn't need it but it would be perhaps good if you could manage a few quid. I have exhausted every source here but I may hold out. The last straw might break the camel's back. I have the rent paid up but . . . . I know this will annoy you but there is the position, a bad one just now.

*   *   *

c/o The Irish Press, Fleet Street, London, 10th October 1950
So far, I have not got any job though I have a large number of friends. I haven't yet explored all the openings. I am going this evening to meet a publisher who may possibly offer me a contract. I believe that if I succeed in hanging on I may click.

*   *   *

62 Pembroke Road, Dublin, 15th October 1950
I got a 100 pounds advance from a publisher which will help me pay some of my debts. I may sublet part of the flat.

*   *   *

c/o Legation d'Irlanda, Rome, 28th October 1950
I must congratulate you on O'Casey review. Wonderful to get it. As you see, I am here in Rome. Happened to get offer of free ticket which I took. Am staying as a guest at the Legation. I came by plane yesterday and am in good form. All is well in Dublin and what harm if they were all wrong.

*   *   *

62 Pembroke Road, Dublin, 1st December 1950
Rome was a bit of a bore. No thought there. All spectacle, empty. Some people were wondering how I got the money to fly to Rome. A woman it was to be sure.

*   *   *

December 1950
I have been asked by the B.B.C. to do a series of talks on the Third. They said they 'were ready and anxious' to have me so I am preparing the talks. I have a free hand.

208

I am in London preparing those talks. The first is on the 20th February mainly about myself. The B.B.C. is a very constricted field, all the staff afraid of their jobs.

* * *

62 Pembroke Road, Dublin, March 1951
I am still in Dublin waiting for a certain man to invite me to a job in London. I did a twenty-five minute talk on the Third Programme which went down very well. I am a very pleasant speaker, they tell me.

I am replying in my 'Diary' next month. The truth is that Ireland hates your book because you destroyed the mediocre legend by which they survive. It got no reviews which ought to be a lesson to you though you didn't need it. They were furious and they kept silent. But you must have wrecked the Abbey in America.

* * *

62 Pembroke Road, Dublin, Good Friday 1951
I am less broke than have been for some time. My third talk went down well. They want more.

* * *

62 Pembroke Road, Dublin, 18th March 1951
This is another letter or note. John Ryan, Editor of Envoy, has been telling me that the Cultural Committee of which he is a member, sends people abroad to lecture etc. Roger McHugh to Iceland, Ria Mooney to Salzburg. He says that if I get an American university to invite me to lecture on Irish Life or poetry etc., they will pay my fare and expenses.

* * *

I have had a letter from Burns & Oates. I asked him for some money. I don't suppose Envoy will go on much longer and so I want to have the 'Diary' published — as a book of course — before it folds. I'll do that book for Burns & Oates.
I am doubtful about the Cultural Committee giving me

money to go to the U.S. seeing they wouldn't send my photograph.

* * *

62 Pembroke Road, Dublin, 29th June 1951
I shall probably be in the U.S. this autumn. The Cultural Committee have agreed to pay my fare over and back and maybe something more. I have been a long time without writing — laziness. Envoy is closing down with July issue. I am doing a talk on Carleton on the Third next month, July.

* * *

62 Pembroke Road, Dublin, 5th August 1951
Frank Aiken vetoed the Cultural Committee's offer to me, and there may be a row over it. I always knew instinctively that Fianna Fáil was the dirtiest, lowest crowd we ever had. I didn't vote for the bastards. So that puts America out for the present. I may try the British Council. I am even considering starting a Hands Off Ulster movement here!

The B.B.C. is my best friend. I did a talk on Carleton last week; it was repeated yesterday, Sunday. I discovered from my talk that Carleton is no good.* They want me to do a Personal Anthology of Irish Poetry but I find on going through the anthologies that it is very poor. Even Mangan is second or third rate. Yeats is the only one and Tom Moore and neither lend themselves to talk. I am supposed to be a very fine verse reader. B.B.C. view.

The sooner I get out of Dublin the better. I must have been a fool to stay here so long. Belfast is much better. I could be on Belfast radio.

I am not really over-worried over Aiken's act and am looking forward to making him look what he is and all the crowd — loutish enemies etc.

* * *

I hope you are well and I will be glad to hear from you. This is the August Bank Holiday and it is spilling rain, most beautifully.

---

* An interim judgement. Carleton has the effect of disillusioning the reader at times.

210

Wasn't it great about the Abbey Theatre? I am wondering if you were able to cash in on the fire. You know I foretold its burning in the Envoy two months before. I kept all the cuttings for you. I doubt if the Abbey ever will be rebuilt or a new theatre till Blythe & Co. are gone.

I have little news. Envoy closed down. I saw your piece in the Mercury. It was very good. A little forced but it came over in the end as a very vicious satire. I didn't see the Shillelagh article.

All the best till later PATRICK

P.S: Reading back this letter I find an astonishing resemblance to your point of view.

I got your letter and cutting. Good article and very effective to injure the friends who will be looking to U.S.A. for money (Abbey fire). By the way a member of External Affairs said re. my going to U.S. that it would take twenty Patrick Kavanaghs to undo the damage you have done. I am broke as usual. The Abbey is playing in Guinness's Brewery Hall. They are really finished.

* * *

62 Pembroke Road, Dublin, 31st August 1951 I have learned a great deal about the Cultural Relations Committee from John Ryan. He told me it was incredible the hate that was for me among people who are all over me in the street.

As for Aiken, not only did he veto the U.S. matter but Cronin and myself have been invited to attend some International Congress of writers in Belgium next week. He gave directions to the Cultural Relations Committee with Ryan dissenting that they should send instead Austin Clarke and R. Farren as Farren could read Gaelic poems to the assembly — we who had been invited through External Affairs Department! But the upshot of it all is that we are going in any case and will raise hell and put Ireland and its politicians and poetasters on the carpet.

* * *

62 Pembroke Road, Dublin, October 1951
I am not such a villain as to wish to take your hard-earned money. You need it all for yourself and more. As a fact, I seem to be able to manage to get money easy enough, easier than you, maybe. I am alright, and if I want, can get to the U.S. There is a strong chance that I might go to South America for the British Council. They don't cover the U.S.

I have really no news except that I am well and am always excited at getting letters from you though not at sending them.

* * *

62 Pembroke Road, Dublin, 11 January 1952
I don't suppose I'll be in America before you come, so you may take it for granted I'll meet you here and I am looking forward to seeing you.

Chapter Fifteen

Knowledge does not take the stage
At the prompting of an age

Envoy
December 1949 / July 1951 —

There is health in the barbaric simplicity of the ballad; it compels one to say something. Most of the verse written in this land suffers from only one thing — the writers have nothing to say. Having something to say is largely a mood. A man sits back in the arrogant humility of his certainty that about those things which are worth knowing he knows as much and as little as any man who has ever lived. This produces a calm mood, a still centre, which is the key to whatever heavens of the imagination there are.

Poets are not only born, they are also made. The nature of the true poet is such that it produces around itself an antagonism through which he must fight. Some men create this antagonism artificially, but they do not become great poets. I would say that the great poet flies from his destiny, but cannot escape it.

I have seen young men with poetic ambitions making grand gestures, throwing over jobs, living the 'simple life',

213

but the genuine artist is running the other way, like Stephen Dedalus in Ulysses.

There is an instinct in mankind which recognises the priestly nature of the poet's function. This instinct has never been strong in Ireland, for Ireland is a particularly cynical and materialistic country — for all its boastings about religion.

Yeats wrote at a consistently high level but one single scream of the heart that pierces heavens he could never reach. For this reason he leaves me cold and leaves me in much doubt about his ultimate survival.

* * *

What would my diary for to-day be?

Day in June, 1950:

It is almost midnight and I am sitting alone before my typewriter in my room wondering whether I should surrender to my natural and sinful sloth and go to bed.

I have been reflecting on my friendlessness in a society where everyone gives the impression of wanting to be friendly. I am sure that no one has ever been more sympathised-with than myself. Yet it is a case of 'water, water everywhere nor any drop to drink'.

Who has ever sympathised less with his suffering fellows than yourself, Patrick Kavanagh? Yet you think the neighbours should be worried as to whether or not you die of loneliness and hunger. nobody has ever invited you out although they know you are constrained to live alone. Why should they care? Some of them claim to be interested in art and letters, are to be seen at all sorts of Exhibitions and Openings, but they really don't care for these things. You should wake up to the fact that your death would be no more to the majority of your acquaintances than a further sensation. Tell me of anyone's death which would be more to you.

You are as selfish as a cat.

214

Lines Written on a Seat on the Grand Canal
Dublin
" Erected to Memory of Mrs. Dermot O'Brien "

---

mmemorate me where there is water
nal water preferably, so stilly
eeny at the heart of summer. Brother
mmemorate me thus beautifully.
here by a lock niagariously roars
; falls for those who sit in the tremendous silence
f mid-july. No one will speak in prose
o finds his way to these Parnassian islands
; swan goes by, head low with many apologies
ntastic light looks through the eyes of bridges
d look! a barge comes bringing from Athy
d other far-flung towns mythologies
! ~~commemorate~~ memorial me with no
      hero · courageous
mb, but just a canal-bank seat for the
     Passer-by.

Patrick Kavanagh
Dublin · 1956.

1956: Manuscript of poem: the final version contained a few changes from this.

215

Yes, I agree with you. But why do they want a man to go on writing? Why do they blame me for letting them down by writing so little? The other day a woman lamented to me and said: 'Terrible pity the way you are throwing your life away'. But why should I not be happy this evening, out swimming, or at the Pheonix Park Races instead of sitting here hammering the typewriter?

How do you know they are happy? You know that Thoreau was right when he said that the masses of men lead lives of quiet desperation. Most of these 'happy' people would give a good deal to possess the pleasures of the mind which are open to you.

My view on that is that the pleasures of the mind are there for anyone who will pay the price. The price is loneliness and poverty.

You have endured much less of either than you pretend. You have never been hungry in your life — and everyone is lonely. See the millions of lonely women in the world. What about that woman who keeps writing you the passionate anonymous letters twice a week? I tell you, you are the luckiest man I know.

Lend me ten bob.

If you wanted to make money you could make it, as Ethel Mannin has told you. You have a touch which can make you the most popular writer this country has produced.

I partly agree, but something always prevents me realising it.

A defect of character, my friend; you've had it since you were not (as country phrase has it) 'two hands over a hen'. It is hard to define this defect of yours, which is actually the source of your attraction. It produces pride, covetousness, lust, gluttony, envy, anger and sloth.

It is a great pity.

Yes, but in arguing with me you seem to suggest that this defect can be cured. Can it be cured? I have tried but it is always there bleeding my life away.

216

Actually I find the defect less than it was before you began to talk.

That is because for the first time in about two weeks you have sat down and used your mind and not gone to bed to luxuriate in wicked dreams.

Work, that's the cure for your disorder.

You are a proper bourgeois. I heard one speaking the very same things to me a few days ago. He said I should be glad of my state, and not be constantly running away from it, into pubs or wherever I could find distractions to make me forget.

Good on you, as the fella said to the ballad singer; you're showing a fine improvement. A little more of that tension and you'd have less time to criticise a sincere man like Clarke who has written many verses of excellent merit and who as a critic is far less sycophantic than many of your so-called friends. He is a sharp critic and writes nice prose too.

But how am I to get immediate money?

Didn't I say, work? If you work all the other things will fall into your lap. You needn't tell me that you couldn't have married on account of poverty. Several women to my own knowledge have quite recently been most approachable. None of them had a great deal of money but all had character or they wouldn't attempt to approach you. Any of them would have helped you through for the next two years and if after that you couldn't keep her you deserve to be in the state you are, O idle monster! There is also the B.B.C. which is quite friendly to you, and there are scores of journals in America if you weren't too damned lazy. Ah, Kavanagh, I'll never make a man of you. Stick to your typewriter. Don't mind that call at the door asking you out to the Pub to waste your time and his money.

You're a slave-driver.

Nothing to what I will be if I get half a chance. This is the first time you've listened to your conscience since — I can't help using country expressions — since God was a gossan.

I'm tired; I want to go out.

Stay in; there's just the chance that your hard work will earn you something you've been hoping for. Everything comes to him who works.

This is terrible.

Another June day:

I have been returning to the writing of verse. It has been a long time since I last wrote verse.

Ante-Natal Dream

I only know that I was there
With hayseed in my hair
Lying on the shady side
Of a haycock in July.

A crowd was pressing round
My body on the ground
Prising the lids of my eyes.
Open and you'll be wise.

The sky that roared with bees,
The row of poplar trees
Along the stream struck deep
And would not let me sleep.

A boortree tried hard to
Let me see it grow;
Mere notice was enough —
She would take care of love

A clump of nettles cried:
We'll saturate your pride
Until you're oozing with
The riches of our myth

For we are all you'll know
No matter where you go —
Every insect weed
Kept singing in my head.

Thistle, ragworth, bluebottle,
Cleg that maddens cattle
Were crowding round me there
With hayseed in my hair.

Now for bed:
That was a harmless sort of a day's writing you did
yesterday.

I was writing other things.

You were not; you spent an hour studying the racing page
of the paper, and time and again I have told you that this
behaviour is a terrible waster of time. Didn't Mr. Leopold
Bloom whom you mentioned earlier come to the conclusion
having listened all day to punters' talk that guess-work it
came to in the long run? Give it up whatever you do. As a
result of your betting you can't pay for lunch, but the loss of
time and nervous wearing is worst.

I am not quite satisfied with this diary.

It is excellent. You have managed to reveal yourself at
many points without self-pity or loss of dignity. You have
succeeded in looking at yourself from the outside.

I haven't lacked discretion, have I?

Well, the mask has been thin in spots, but generally no.
And you've told no lies to yourself or to your readers.

* * *

The real reason why Joyce and O'Casey and others have left
Ireland is because they were exiles there. How could they be
other where publicans, race-track touts and dispensers of
trivia are in authority?

What is truly moral about English intellectual life is that here judgements are pronounced. In Ireland we never come to a last judgement. There are always a score of great poets, painters, novelists.

To praise everybody is to blame everybody.

* * *

It seems to me that God through the agency of society manages to breed a race of artists by the process of starvation and all kinds of indignity due to poverty. Is it not on the cards that an artist can be bred artificially in this way? Or must he have the kink in him originally?

He has got to hate society, that is nearly certain.

* * *

Art is life squeezed through a repression.

* * *

The poet is born-not-made to the extent that no one by taking thought can produce in himself this synthesising nature. I learned, or was made aware, from reading Auden that the great poets never teach us anything. The great poets are those who burn in the smithy of their souls the raw material of life and produce from it this erotic-creative essence. Shakespeare, Homer, Cervantes, Dickens, Swift and Joyce provide us with an orgy of sensation and nothing else or more.

There is wisdom in Shakespeare but it is incidental. Almost any kind of the crude material of life can be burned to give us this intoxicating thing. Wtih the great writers we are in a constant state of excitement, like gamblers waiting for the result of a race.

* * *

A university cannot give a man the unlearnable quality which makes a great writer — and no one should be interested in anything else. The Auditor in his references to journalism and schools of writing had sinned but not wittingly, so there was no sin actually. He had been a coward and all lies are

220

due to cowardice. He had kow-towed to convention. 'Dare to be true, nothing can need a lie', said George Herbert.

To have the courage of being yourself is to be truthful. You will be an iconclast and considered a maker of wild statements but every true personality in movement is iconoclastic. The usual iconoclasm you get among undergraduates is not the true article which springs from a man expressing the only thing he has in him to express — his unique personality; but it could be good practice.

To want, as so many do in a superficial way, to express themselves is quite a different thing from true expression of their true personality. They rush off to become actors or things like that, hoping or believing that the beat of publicity releases their true selves.

How the essential personality is released is a mystery really, but by going to a university and stumbling on some remarkable mind the way might be pointed out.

A good man cannot tell you the right way; he can only tell you the ways that are not right. He can tell you what is dead or was never alive and that you are to bring no conventional offerings to the graveyard. He might even meet some experienced man who could tell him to deal with the sneering enemies of promise.

By one brave gesture a man may be saved.

One of the things it would be necessary to teach in this country is that the pygmy literature which was produced by the so-called Irish literary renaissance is quite worthless.

But it would be a mistake to concentrate on the negative too much.

It is essential as I said at the start to consider nothing but genius; for anything less is no good. The aim of a good deal of literary and academic criticism is to raise up the mediocre, to get people to believe that the tenth-rate is in someway the respectable. It takes courage not to praise the tenth rate, for as soon as it is known by society that you are one of these mediocrity-admirers they know that you're 'all *right' — a serious traditional man deserving of a stake in the country.*

There are few geniuses in the world at any time, for the world could not stand more than a few, for though they do in a remarkable way ennoble they are at the same time a destructive element. They have a voracious appetite for living and the ordinary man who comes into contact with one of these monsters will find himself, and his personality, getting thinner and thinner.

Unless he accepts. Society as a rule hates the great poet because he eats up all the emotion; he is the cuckoo bird in the nest. But society in behaving like this is immoral. The bees make a queen at the expense of thousands of sterile workers.

That is the apparently sad position. If there is a genius or two at large in society the moral thing to do is accept him and to accept your own sterile fate.

But immorality is something you cannot eliminate.

To have the fortitude and the faith to be willing to be nothing is one of the best ways of being something . . . . for if a man has the original appetite his sense of smell will lead him to experience.

I might even illustrate my theme with views of my own life. I may say that I have never been to school, but I have never felt that I was in any way hindered from doing what was mine to do, or saying my say; and I have never, as some people say un-universitied men of genius feel, had nay discomfort or inferiority-complex because of it. And I would say that any man who felt such a puerile emotion could not possibly have that detachment which sees both the grandeur and the significance of man in the world which is the most important quality of poetic genius.

If a man has the poetic nature in him he will take the universal view which is ultimately so personal, and so gay.

The rest of the world should be satisfied by loving God by praising His works, and the greatest work of God on this earth is the dancing flame of the poet's imagination.

The wickedest thing, and the universities might teach this, is to try to deny it, to try to pretend that what is dead is alive.

To bring food to the graveyard, that is the artistic sin.

Genius is the only thing worth considering. The next best thing to being a genius is to recognise him and praise him and ignore everything else, and to do our best to cut down the nets which mediocrity flings to hold back the soul from flight.

Every organ of opinion in Ireland to-day is in the hands of the enemies of the imagination. The most pernicious enemies are those which have pretensions to culture, such as The Irish Times which has a large weekly 'literary' page in which the dead and damned to dullness express themselves. Poor Mr. Smyllie, the editor, is not to blame entirely; it is generally believed that he has little power. The tendency in the newspaper world of the Board to make its editors mere yes-men and to curb their personalities — if they have any — has spread to all the Irish papers. Perhaps this is just as well.

What is most appalling here is that the Government-controlled radio station, supported out of the taxes, is in the hands of mean little men who are partial to their own pathetic points of view. They haven't the morality to admit large viewpoints which would destroy their own — and that is what morality consists of.

* * *

Comparative criticism is criticism without standards. A true creative critic is a sweeping critic who violently hates certain things because they are seeds which choke the field against the crop which he wants to sow. Truth is personality and no genuine writer as a critic was ever anything but absolute in his destructiveness. If a piece of writing is good there is nothing one can or should say except the words, 'It is good'. If it is bad there is not much necessity to say anything either, as time will do the job of destruction.

223

Everyone wants to express himself. Bowelless they press at stool and not finding a catharsis are very miserable and frustrated. Large numbers of them go to the Ballet, music, acting or criticism. This is a most unhappy world for, as I suggested, the creative writer is a selfish brutal creature who can never conceal his contempt and whose only interest in these people is what he can get out of them.

* * *

There are probably not more than twenty creative writers of first-class merit in the contemporary world, a fact which might be borne in mind by those readers who would call my criticism niggling or carping. In a rather poverty-stricken world, anything less than the whole world is not worth considering.

Judged by these, by no means Olympian, standards, few in Ireland exist.

The first falseness is in this ideal of Ireland as a spiritual entity. No good poet was ever a patriot — as a poet. Only minor poets, such as Kipling, Thomas Campbell and Rupert Brooke, cared about their country. Neither do they possess that most hypocritical of appendages, a 'social conscience'. The poet may be human and humane, but he is not humanitarian, which is another way of saying that he isn't a fraud. The poet is in many ways like a woman. Unspoiled women, who have not been introduced to actors, fiddlers and schools of bad painting, have no nationality in the nude. The poet has this same simplicity, this indifference to the babble of journalists and politicians.

* * *

The more I argue on these matters, the more I regret that Frank O'Connor should have fled the controversial field, for at one time he had the truest instinct in the country. To-day he sits high on the heap of weeds that grew in the garden where everything is lovely, a comical king of a comical castle,

62 Pembroke Road, Dublin

who with fatherly affection looks down on bad poets and novelists whom he praises generously.

It would be worse than useless to organise those people — and there are many who feel as I do — into some sort of academy or school. The essence of integrity and unity is to remain diverse. That is why academics always become the thing they set out to oppose. See the Abbey Theatre, and the Irish Academy of Letters, to-day indistinguishable from that old women's bridge party, the Dublin P.E.N.

* * *

Chapter Sixteen

The Momentum

Bohemianism as a way of life can be quite satisfactory because the level of expectation controlling happiness can be plotted in advance. Patrick was not a bohemian. He hated being poor and dependent. He sought wealth and dreamed of being rich. Consequently on the numerous occasions he was forced to seek a hand-out he did so with resentment and never provided the giver with that happy glow which comes from giving charity. He was just as likely to abuse the giver instead of offering thanks — for Patrick was a moralist and no hand-out was likely to affect his views.

I myself never *gave* to Patrick: rather, I shared with him in the sacrifice he was making. He was well aware of my attitude. From my salary during the early forties of eleven pounds a month I paid the rent, bought the food and paid for the utilities. I had no money in the bank and very little in my pocket. What hurt most — and I still feel the pain — was giving him money for cigarettes, I might have no more than, say, thirty-six pence in my purse and I would have to fork out over twenty of that for a dangerous luxury. His response always was that without the cigarettes he could not write. I had no answer to that argument. He was a heavy smoker from he was a teenager. He didn't drink then — not until after his operation for cancer. Or if he did drink then it was very lightly.

To be a giver demands great skill, great love and great fortitude. I wasn't much good at it and I don't blame Patrick if he felt resentment later on because of my style of giving. Just the same we remained friends until the last and even retained our conspiratorial association.

Having to beg from friends left Patrick open to all kinds of indignities and insults. As a consequence he became an object of ridicule and the butt of many tall tales.

In an essay in *The Bell*, April 1948, Larry Morrow under the pseudonym *The Bellman* produced a word-caricature of Patrick which though highly amusing reflects something of the general disrespect in which he was held:

Meet Patrick Kavanagh

We all — even mild men like little elderly bank-clerks and civil servants, book-keepers in Guinness's brewery, and frayed-edged shopwalkers in Sweeney's Stores — enjoy posthumously brief apocrypha in which we are charitably credited, by both friend and foe, with feats physically, mentally and even morally beyond our earthly achievement. But of only one man in Ireland today can it truthfully be said that he enjoys his apocrypha — though apocrypha with a difference — while still very much alive. For, whether you like or dislike him, Mr. Patrick Kavanagh, poet, novelist, autobiographer, film-critic and (to some) Stage-Irishman-about-Town, has become so fabulous as to be almost a figment of his own imagination. If anyone were to assure me that Mr. Kavanagh wrote anonymous letters to himself and believed them to come from someone else I shouldn't be surprised.

Where Mr. Kavanagh is concerned, indifference is impossible. He shares with Mr. Frank Sinatra, Mr. Dylan Thomas, Picasso and the Marx Brothers the capacity for rousing the emotions to screaming-point. You either scream for him or against him. Even Mr. Kavanagh himself is in a state of almost chronic hoarseness, screaming at himself — be it said both for and against. And — let it also be said — he seems vastly to enjoy it, neither boastfully nor bashfully. Yet, however often or forcibly he may try to impress his listeners to the contrary, one suspects that he is about as neurotic and nerve-ridden as the average Mooney's manager — as like a character in Chekhov as any of the late Miss Annie M. P. Smithson's.

Mr. Kavanagh has been described, by those who pretend to dislike him, as a Consommé of a Boy; by others (who don't pretend so hard, perhaps) as The Last of Lever's Gossoons. And (it must be confessed) he himself does little to dispel that illusion — if illusion it be. There can be hardly a film-star's publicity agent who would not give a considerable 'cut' off his fees for the secret of the 'build-up' with which, in a few short years, Mr. Kavanagh has become surrounded. Mr. Kavanagh, from time to time, lunges violently at the whole vile business which is Publicity: it is only when he has subsided into his cup (be careful with your s's, Mr. Printer) that one notices that he is wearing a tartan-pattern shirt, with a Paisley tie not quite to match, and a Josephan sports-jacket which would throw any self-respecting chameleon into convulsions. And that surmounting all, perched on his equine head, is a check-pattern cloth cap in the cycling mode of circa 1895. Surely one might be forgiven for suspecting that such a tenue so reminiscent of a pre-war seedsman's catalogue — was devised by design rather than by accident. Clearly (one is forced to conjecture), Mr. Kavanagh is determined not to be caught napping if and when Technicolour Television comes to town.

Like all who wilt under the fierce beams of Publicity, Mr.

Kavanagh never runs to form — good, bad or indifferent. He has a form all to himself. Make a date with him, hinting at such-and-such a pub (low-ceilinged, sawdusty and still with memories of Joyce clinging to) and he'll say he has no time for such places — that he prefers the 'homely' atmosphere of the Shelbourne palm-lounge. Suggest the Gresham or the Hibernian and he'll plump for a faded chintzy tea-room off Grafton Street. And so it was that he and I compromised — and met, by solemn appointment, in one of those Dublin restaurants in which only the bravest (or the most insensitive) would dare demand high tea for fear of being thought low.

Eating or drinking with Mr. Kavanagh — both mentally and physically as well as vocally — is constructed on what the sculptors call the 'heroic' scale, which is to say, rather a little larger than life. Rodin would have adored him as a model — a 'companion-piece' to Le Penseur, with title to match. Or as one of the burghers — or whatever they were — of Calais. There is always something faintly frightening about the heroic scale — in conventional surroundings it is forever hinting that everything else is out of focus, out of proportion: that you yourself and the other normal objects have shrunk suddenly, nightmare-fashion, like poor Gulliver in Brobdignag.

And so, seated at the same café table as Mr. Kavanagh, one is constantly conscious of what women novelists used to call The Elemental. A great root-like hand shoots across the table to the toast-dish, casting a thunder-cloud shadow on the cloth. P. K. without warning, suddenly crosses his legs, jerks the table a good two feet in the air, cups and dishes a-jingle-jangling, and continues the conversation as if no earthquake had occurred. Or he as suddenly hunches the enormous, mountainous shoulders, and chairs, table, walls even, seem to shiver with him. Nuclear fission (one reflects) is a ripple in a teacup compared to Mr. Kavanagh in a tea-shop.

230

Mr. Kavanagh's policy in conversation is frankly one of Disarmament — by force. 'I reserve the right to tell whatever lies come into my head,' he warns you in a stevedore's whisper. 'I've been telling lies all my life. I invented so many stories about myself in The Green Fool to illustrate my own unique character that I don't know myself what's true about me and what isn't'. To enquiries about his age, Mr. Kavanagh is equally equivocal. 'I'm like a woman, when it comes to my age', he says with a shivering neigh. 'Any answer I'd give you would be bound to be a lie'. It's only when he comes to his birthplace that Mr. Kavanagh descends to the factual. 'The ferocious fact', he says, 'is that I was born in County Monaghan — in a place called MUCKER! What a name!!'

The family background was that of a small farm — the father a shoe-maker, 'and a good one'. Mr. Kavanagh himself claims to have inherited his parent's craftsmanship — specialising, he claims, in ladies' footwear. There were eleven children in the family — 'roughly', he adds, somewhat enigmatically. For details of his early life he would refer readers to Tarry Flynn which, he claims, is 'nearer the truth', than The Green Fool. His early reading seems to have consisted of Old Moore's Almanac and The Messenger. At eighteen he came fourth in a poetry competition (first prize half-a-sovereign) in the Weekly Independent. The first-prize-winner on that occasion, as on many subsequent occasions, was Mr. Paul Vincent Carroll. An extract from Mr. Kavanagh's also-ran poem would indicate that even at eighteen he had begun to trail his coat:

> *Now I am freed from first-love pain:*
> *She's back with them that sent her—*
> *My love who will not come again.*
> *But why should I lament her . . . .?*

'As soon as that poem appeared I at once went up in the estimation of the neighbours', confides Mr. Kavanagh to the

young couple at the next table but four. 'We were thrashing on a neighbour's farm when my brother rushed up with the paper'. He sighs heavily in reminiscence and one notices — though not for the first time — the extraordinary equine head, the scobed nostrils, the great eyes of Man's Second Best Friend. The heavy tortoiseshell spectacles — with their suggestion of blinkers — curiously contribute to the horsey impression. There is, too, more than a hint of the gargoyle about it. One suddenly has a vision of Charles Méryon's fierce etching of 'Le Stryge' on Notre Dame de Paris. God's Gift to Epstein — or any worker in bronze or granite.

But Mr. Kavanagh's career as a poet began long before he was eighteen, he'll tell you. When he was 'about twelve' he wrote a ballad — about a dance held to celebrate the building of a loft by a local worthy of Mucker. He heard that same ballad recited while on a visit to Monaghan. It had only been 'slightly changed', which is not bad for a thirty-year-old ballad. Or for Monaghan. Or for both. Other ballads of his — written during this period of juvenilia — are still to be heard at dances, whenever Mucker makes merry — a subject for folklore research which I heartily commend to the notice of Messrs. Seumas Delargy and Seán O'Sullivan.

'It was A.E. found me', Mr. Kavanagh continues his confidence in a voice one imagines to be causing serious traffic dislocations as far off as College Green. 'I was out selling a load of hayseed in Dundalk one day. I couldn't get Tit-Bits so I bought the Irish Statesman. I sent them a poem and A.E. wrote to me, offering to pay ME! I thought it a great thing not to pay for its publication myself'. And so (as he says), he never looked back! He left the Weekly Independent to the author of Shadow and Substance.

A fierce toss of the head, a wave of the hand that all but sends the waitress and her trayload flying, and Mr. Kavanagh suddenly slumps into the depths of introspection. The great head, hung over his plate, shows a wispy nimbus: oily-black fleece of a sheep caught on the barbs of a fence.

232

Suddenly the head jerks back again — one almost hears the jingle of harness — the eyes cock at me, showing the whites. The nostrils flicker. The broad-sculptured lips peel back, revealing two rows of teeth so strong and even-topped that he'd be a poor vet. who couldn't tell Mr. Kavanagh's exact age from them. Over his specs he peers at me, the enormous forehead corrugated like a warped washboard. The voice booms again: Tenebrae in a Gothic cathedral.

'No one ever stayed as long in the chrysalis stage as I did. At twenty I was still a baby. Spiritually, I'm only twelve years old. But talent is a road — a road that will let you out eventually. I was on the farm — digging the ditch — till the year 1939. And then I went for three months to London. It was there I wrote The Green Fool — wrote it twice over. My hair fell out as I was writing it. I had a pain in the stomach all the time I was writing it. Still — a pain in the stomach's not a bad thing — it keeps you from going to sleep!'

And he heaves the great shoulders again before going on.

'Ay — The Green Fool business — the libel action over the head of it — did me a lot of damage. It destroyed — The Momentum.'

'Would that explain what I might describe as your comparatively — your extremely small output?'

'It would — though output's a word I abhor. That — The Green Fool affair — and laziness. I'm the laziest person in the whole world — bar none. I hate work. I want to get rich. Writing makes me ill. I'm fed up — lonely . . . . alone. I want a beautiful, sympathetic and rich wife. I'm very fond of women — beautiful women. I hate men. They bore me. Talk about poetry I abhor. I never discussed it with anybody. I hate praise, too — and publicity. A man wants to be alone. Publicity's a cancer. It eats out a man — till there's nothing but the shell left.'

'But who — if I may ask — is your publicity agent, Mr. Kavanagh?

'Nobody — except Frank O'Connor and Seán O'Faoláin.

233

*They were the only ones who ever did publicity for me. I hate
— I abhor — publicity I tell you!'*

'And the future — your future as a writer?'

*Mr. Kavanagh cocks the horse-eye at me again.
Anticipating another earthquake, I grip the table with two
hands and knees. But I'm disappointed. Mr. Kavanagh
lowers both head and voice.*

*'The future? I'd hate to talk about it. I feel there's a tabu
about it — tempting the Gods. If I were to say anything about
the future I'd have to tell you lies — complete lies — to protect
the tabu or whatever it is. That's why all the time I'm
hedging — afraid to talk . . . . Anyhow — what's output, as
you call it? What about Gerard Manley Hopkins? Would
you judge him by — output? Two or three books will say
all a writing man has to say. Anyone can turn out books, but
they're still-born. That don't mean a thing.'*

'Balzac?'

'Maybe'.

'Dickens?'

*'Dickens wrote one book — the same book, over and over
again. And Scott wrote no book.' The head is lifted now, one
almost hears the harness jingle.*

*'The next six or seven years will see great changes in me',
resumes Mr. Kavanagh a little tangentially. 'I hope to write
millions of words — novels — good ones. I'm the only man
who has written in our time about rural Ireland from the
inside. I'm willing to boast about it. It's a fact. And when I
go back to the country nobody ever takes me for a literary
man. They just treat me and talk to me as if I were one of
themselves. Which, of course, I am. Millions of words I'm
going to write — now I've started, after ten years in the
wilderness, suffering frustration and great hunger. It was
only by accident that I was born — spiritually, that's to say.
My own father died without waking . . . . It's a frightful pain
to be born — spiritually. I was once happy all the time. Then
I was born — spiritually. It was like coming out of darkness*

234

Miss Mae O'Flaherty (with Japanese visitor), Parson's Bookshop, Dublin.

into the light — a terrible pain. I'm one of the few who appreciate what Rimbaud did when he gave up writing at nineteen. I'd rather sink back and be forgotten.'

Mr. Kavanagh may sink back — one reflects gratefully — but he will never be forgotten. He is already with the Irish Immortals — from Goldsmith to 'Zozimus'.

Chapter Seventeen

The Northern Contingent

During the same period 1946-1949 another view of Patrick is to be found in the following memoir written by a small group of North of Ireland enthusiasts — four young people who met every evening in a house on the Kashmir Road to discuss books and inform each other on what they were currently reading. The four were John Kilfeather, Renée Dougherty, Gerard Keenan and Peggy Dougan. The North's 'literary' set met in Campbell's coffee rooms but these four, not having produced a 'work' did not have visas for admittance.

It was not long before they discovered Patrick Kavanagh. They read *The Green Fool* and from it got the picture of a bearded old man, consumptive, who travelled the roads of Ireland, sat in ditches and wrote poems. They were ecstatic about their discovery and soon they were referring to him famililiary as *Yer Man Kavanagh* just as they had been referring to *Yer Man Stendhal, Yer Man Goethe,* and risibly *Yer Man Mann.* It was at this moment that Renée Dougherty joined the group and hearing of Patrick being spoken of so familiarly wrote to him through his publisher saying she would like to meet him. She was at this time considering the possibility of finding a job in Dublin. Patrick replied:

> *62 Pembroke Road, Dublin, 2nd February 1948*
> *Dear Miss Dougherty,*
> *While I think it would be very foolish of you to come to Dublin merely to see me I do not think there would be any difficulty from my side. All you'd have to do was to say you were coming and take a 6, 7 or 8 tram to Landsdowne Road or a 9 or 10 bus to Baggot St. Bridge as this would prevent the danger of you missing me. I might however point out that you have the advantage of me in that I have no idea what you look like etc. I wonder would you give me some information about yourself so that I'll know what I am meeting. Are you young, middle-aged or old. I presume you must be rather young having been to Dublin only once. I would be glad of this information and anything else you might be glad to tell.*
> *All good wishes, P. KAVANAGH*

Renée Dougherty was twenty at this time. She replied by return as did Patrick in the following letter:

> *5th February 1948*
> *My Dear Girl,*
> *Will you write by return post and tell me what train you are coming on and I'll meet you. You must not think I'd be ashamed of being seen with you however you look or are dressed. You will recognize me at the station gate as you know me by sight.*
> *Yours, Patrick Kavanagh.*

Renée came to Dublin on a special excursion fare. She now takes up the story:

> *As the train came nearer to Dublin I bought a glass of sherry in the dining car to give me courage. I was not used to*

drinking and I took it fast like water. It hit me when I stepped on to the platform and for the next half hour everything took on an air of unreality. I floated up to a man who sat on a pile of newspapers and stood in front of him and simply stared. 'Is it you?', he asked. Sixteen years later when he came to read his work at Queen's University Festival, the last time I was to see him, he greeted me with the same words, 'Is it you?'.

Patrick Kavanagh was not the old man of the roads, but a young looking man of about forty, quite handsome, who peered at me through thick glasses. He was tall and well-built and I noticed that his nails were carefully manicured. His navy gaberdine coat was serviceable rather than stylish and he carried a brief-case. A cloth check cap gave a sporting look to the otherwise sombre attire.

For myself, I was wearing knee-length socks, a new fashion, to relieve the drabness of utility clothing in which we in the North were still clad. He kept glancing furtively at my socks. 'Do all the girls in Belfast wear socks?' he asked. I could see that he was a very conservative man, indeed rather shy. We kept meeting people who greeted him and were both so embarrassed that a perfectly innocent occasion took on the appearance of an illicit affair. We skulked along side-streets and because of the surprise on the faces of his acquaintances we arrived at Pembroke Road hysterical with laughter. 'They will all think you are a relative up from the country,' he said. He flung his arm around me and ushered me along with his nose high in the air as though he were following a scent.

We were both broke, so we searched his flat for money. When in funds he scattered a handful of money over the place and it rolled under furniture and stayed there waiting for a rainy day. We found half-crowns and sixpences and were able to buy cigarettes. He was a film critic for The Standard then, so we got into the cinema free. We had boiled eggs, soda farls and mugs of tea for lunch. We spent several hours reading his poetry and he sang in a weird voice some ballads he had written. He allowed me to read a couple of chapters of a novel called Tarry Flynn that he was completing and showed me the proof of an advertisement from the Irish Times. There was Kavanagh flying through the air on an O'Dearest mattress with the caption saying 'Let him go and let him Tarry'. This delighted him.

He loved to laugh at himself. If he said something exceptionally funny a look of shock would cross his face and he would twist about on the chair shaking his head in surprise as if he had been stung by an insect. He was always quite astonished at his own wit and he would peer at you as if to say, 'Well, what did you think of that for a remarkable thing?'

I had brought a book for him, Hunger, by Knut Hamsun. 'How did you know?' he said, 'I love this man'. We met next day at a basement restaurant where we had stew for lunch. Kavanagh delivered a sermon on the virtues of stew and mashes even for Sunday dinner. He was a man who had trained himself to make the best of everything. When we were served with thin custard and stewed apples we could not contain ourselves and almost choked with giggling. To make up for a stew on Sunday he said I could draw a picture of him if I cared to. I had no talent at all. He straightened himself up in the chair and posed for me. I thought there was a great air of nobility about him. He pretended to be horrified at the result. 'Was it necessary to give a fellow such a big nose?' he commented. But he was far from vain; he did not believe he was a lovable man. He was not aware of his own charm. I like to remember him as he was that day. Although he could be formidable and rude, he always regretted this because he was a soft-hearted and gentle person underneath.

He came to Belfast to see me. We went for a tram ride to Cavehill on a wet, dark evening. We stood on the steps of Bellevue overlooking Belfast. He was depressed. He wanted *to go to America where he would be taken by the hand. He longed to be esteemed. Too many people wanted him to play the clown and did not want to take his work seriously so that he began to think of himself as a failure. He was proud and sensitive to a high degree. His most dominant characteristic was his dread of scandal. There were jealous men, he said, who sneered at his origins and who would welcome his downfall. They would not accept that a poor country farmer could emerge as a great writer. 'Wait till they read Tarry Flynn', I assured him.*

Patrick told me of his new-found admirers and spoke of them as his Northern Contingent. He was pleased, amused and surprised that he should be so admired. It was too much for him fully to accept so he spoke of them with bemused hyperbole. Most of all, he was impressed by Renée's courage and sophistication in writing to him. *Your courage in writing,* he informed her in a letter, *is something I often wanted to do myself and which on a few occasions I did do though often it ends in disappointment.*

Patrick arranged to pay a visit to his Northern Contingent for a weekend. The rendezvous was to be the house of Peggy Dougan a teacher who lived in the Kashmir Road with her widowed mother. Renée and Patrick first went out sight-seeing and while they were gone John Kilfeather and associates clubbed together to have a bottle of whiskey for Patrick when he returned. Patrick was in great form when he returned with Renée. He praised the meal they had prepared and professed to be overpowered by the sight of a full bottle of whiskey. After dinner they all sat together into the wee hours of the morning in a marathon Question & Answer session. They wanted all the information he could give them. Nothing was unimportant. They discussed *Tarry Flynn*, excerpts of which had appeared in *The Bell:*

I have closed the door on that class of novel — no one for a generation will attempt to write about the Irish countryside.

241

No, I didn't enjoy writing it. I write reams of what is to me boring stuff in order that I can slip in maybe a paragraph, maybe only a sentence, under the reader's guard. The 'Tarry Flynn' I have in my head is a good book — I attempt to write best sellers but apparently I cannot compromise enough to pull it off — alas! When I am deeply moved I write awkwardly and I never revise these portions of my work because the uncouth expression is part of the writing. It often signals to the reader that the writing is clotted and hard to read because I am involved and feel strongly about these passages. Only clichés come easily: that which is original is hard to express elegantly with style.

John Kilfeather continues with his account of that evening and subsequent meetings:

He told us that he admired 'Gil Blas', 'Moby Dick' and, surprisingly, William Saroyan's 'The Human Comedy'. On another occasion when Renée gave him a Hamsun novel as a gift from me he was astonished that I had guessed that he read Knut Hamsun. He told us that he admired Brian O'Nolan. He has kept himself in virtual beggary educating and financing, helping his large number of sisters and brothers.

He told a yarn that Myles had told him about P. V. Carroll's visit to Dublin. Myles and his pals had determined to put the cocky Carroll out of countenance and when they couldn't get him stone drunk as a desperate resort they pretended that now was the time to visit a brothel. Carroll (who was playing along up to this) recoiled visibly and pleaded a variety of excuses which were howled down. In desperation he craved their indulgence as he 'was going to the rails' in the morning. Patrick roared at Myles's bon mot. At this time he seemed to adore Myles — 'He is a saint', he assured us.

Every time we attempted to give him whiskey he recoiled

in mock horror (we kept the bottle exclusive to him) and he said 'Boys o'boys, you'll destroy me', and 'This is a terror'. We were all greatly gratified as he gave this flawless performance of a man being wined and dined to excess. Of course he was being kind but I like to think that he was also enjoying our admiration. We literally worshipped him. He told us how happy we should be to have one another as five friends and told us that if we could describe that little kitchen and fireplace with truth that in the words of Thoreau the world would beat a path to our door to share in our happiness. Whatever it meant to him, it was a day in our life.

I was never in Patrick's company for a comparable length of time again. He was no longer the bearded dark tramping man of our imaginings but a man of the highest gifts under the common contemporary stress. He was tortured by the fact that the world put more regard on a bank manager or civil servant than on any poet. He couldn't believe that those who professed friendship for him would not do one tenth for him what he would have done for them if the positions were reversed. He joked that he was looking for a rich widow woman. He that was so extraordinary was bewitched by dreams of ordinary safe life. In Dublin he seemed to eschew the picturesque — he was to be found in cinema restaurants and the milk parlours of Grafton Street. And these places underlined the incongruity of the huge personality he embodied, and he was out of his element there but apparently derived some nourishment from these places.

With us Patrick never used a coarse expression and seemed most particular not to give scandal to young people. His manners were old-fashioned and punctilious, even to the extent of once saying your Queen is . . . .'.

After his Belfast visit I spoke to him only twice again . Renée (my wife by then) and I met him in Grafton Street one morning and he looked very poorly. His shirt was stained with dried vomit and he had cut himself shaving. He was warm and pleasant as ever and asked us to meet him later *for a drink but he didn't show up. I got the fixed impression he was broke and too proud to say so.*

I was posted to Cookstown, Co. Tyrone and each weekend I carried a dozen copies of Kavanagh's Weekly to distribute among the Civil Servants in the office there. Renée wrote a little article for the Weekly and Gerard Keenan wrote quite a few. However, I regret that I was too diffident to attempt one myself. These were heady days for us as we believed Patrick was on the brink of being afforded the recognition which we knew was long overdue. When he made his appeal for a pound per copy for No. 13 copy of Kavanagh's Weekly we were thunderstruck. We had not believed things were so bad. Keenan and I sent a pound apiece only to have the money refunded and the sorrowful news that K.'s Weekly was now defunct. I can only dimly apprehend how bad you and Patrick must have felt.

In Dublin along the quays I bought for 10/- the Cuala Press edition of The Great Hunger personally inscribed by Patrick to Lord Dunsany with a poem 'Aladdin's Cave' holographed on the fly-leaf. My wife has an inscribed copy of The Great Hunger and we have all his books with the exception of a paperback selection of his stories of William Carleton for which he wrote an introduction. We have copies of The Bell and Envoy and X Magazine and Non-Plus and I have twice visited his grave.

We took no joy from the trial. From the outset I believed that Patrick had made a mistake — creative people cannot seek redress in courts of law, that's for bank managers and the like. I have a framed photograph of Patrick from The Irish Times as he entered the court with his briefcase. It is a very sad one.

I last met Patrick on the Quadrangle of Queen's University on 27th November 1964. I had known he had a disease of the throat and Renée and I had phoned him in Dublin after we read the notice of discharge from hospital in The Irish Times. His voice on the phone had sounded odd

c. 1959: Patrick at the Grand Canal (top) and at Parson's Bookshop.
[Photos courtesy Miss O'Flaherty].

but we had taken this as the usual telephone trunk-call distortion.

I approached him and he greeted me as 'Mr. Keenan', a mistake which was understandable and he corrected by saying, 'You're Renée's man'. He asked me if I had attended many of these Queen's Festival Lectures and said in his husky tones fearfully: 'I suppose they're full of the nouvelle vague'. I re-assured him on this point and he laughed sardonically and stated firmly: 'They are not getting any of that from me'. His voice was thickening with phlegm and there was no welcoming body in evidence so he asked me to direct him to the toilets. I did so, and a collection of stout female dwarfs with mops berated us for attempting to use the cubicles 'when the cleaners were in'. Unabashed Patrick growled: 'I'm not for sitting down, madam'. He proceeded to hawk and spit into the toilet bowl.

He commanded the biggest crowd of any at the reading. He kissed Renée publicly when she arrived a few minutes before the start. He sang: 'From a Munster vale they brought her . . . .'. He reaffirmed that poetry was a pagan thing. Despite his failing voice I have never seen him more noble looking. He was lionized.

We asked him deferentially if he would like to come home for a meal but he muttered that he 'had commitments'. Renée and I were saddened and elated by seeing him again. We never saw him afterwards.

This year in Dublin we bought another copy of his splendid Self Portrait as a present for Renée's seventeen year old English niece and were made happy by hearing her chuckle whilst reading it on the train back to Belfast.

My Patrick Kavanagh was a highly cultured mind with a lot of innocence in it. Not since Burns has a great figure emerged from the people who has left such a faithful record of what it is to be of the people and yet apart from them. His life was not the least of his works of art.

246

Chapter Eighteen

Here wait I on the world's rim

When I returned to Ireland in the spring of 1952 I found Patrick on the verge of starvation and totally isolated. Since *Envoy* closed a year before he had nowhere to publish his views. No newspaper or magazine would touch him. Yet he was bursting with ideas. *What I need*, he said to me, *is a newspaper of my own where I can say what I like without a hint of editorial control.* Even *Envoy* did not supply this latitude.

Through long experience of borrowing money Patrick had developed to a high degree of accuracy the ability to tell how much money you had in your pocket. I had about $2,500 in savings and he guessed it. *Why don't we start a newspaper together*, he urged; *I have many friends who will be willing to share the expenses with you.* I too was not without my own capacity to sum up a situation, especially the worth of Patrick's friends. After some anguish of mind I came to a decision: I would sink whatever money I had in the venture. If Patrick's friends contributed money I would accept it gladly but my plan was to go it alone until my savings were spent. After all, what better use could I put the money to? If only for a brief moment it would give an outlet to genius. Very well, I told Patrick abruptly, we will begin as from next Saturday 12th April. *Start writing the editorial*, I ordered, *while I go off to find a printer.* Patrick was astounded and delighted. The situation had fairytale qualities. He laughed in part uncomprehending but went straight to the typewriter.

I went off to find a printer and when I came home I found that Patrick already had his editorial written, *Victory of Mediocrity*, and was engaged on another piece. I began working on a dummy and then did a cast-off. To my amazement I discovered we would need about ten thousand words. When I told Patrick, he brushed the information aside. He had enough unpublished stuff, he said to fill ten issues. But to be on the safe side, says he, you'd better start writing also.

No problem for me: I was already an experienced magazine writer and had published a popular book on the Abbey Theatre. My first piece was an exposé of the Irish Foreign Service. I wrote several other pieces as well.

When Friday afternoon rolled around Patrick and I stood by as the first issue of *Kavanagh's Weekly* came off the press. It was a very exciting moment for both of us. We took the first two copies and double autographed them. I still own them. Our press run was 3,000. We carried the copies home on the bus to 62 Pembroke Road and sat down to gloat over our success. Patrick was especially pleased with himself. Here is how his editorial opened:

Thirty odd years ago the southern section of this country won what was called freedom. Yet from that Independence Day there has been a decline in vitality throughout the country. It is possible that political liberty is a superficial thing and that it always produces the apotheosis of the mediocrity. For thirty years thinking has been more and more looked upon as wickedness — in a quiet way of course.

All the mouthpieces of public opinion are controlled by men whose only qualification is their inability to think.

248

Being stupid and illiterate is the mark of respectability and responsibility.

The basis of this point of view is a fundamental lack of belief in God. In a somewhat subtle way it is materialism. Nothing matters but the job and the salary it brings. Does anyone really believe in anything? Can any of these people who presume to be our leaders and voices be hurt in any way except through the pocket? It is very doubtful.

There is no central passion.

. . . . This country is dead or dying from its false materialism. Where the mistake is made is seeing life as a purely material thing. Life itself is a sort of madness, something out of a transcendent imagination.

Why are people leaving the countryside in their thousands? They go to England where conditions are extremely bad. What they are seeking is the enthusiasm for life . . . .

As with sin, mediocrity is never pernicious until we begin to call it statesmanship and sound sense . . . .

Other articles in the first issue dealt with the Budget (by myself, of course) Tourism, Literature, Exhibitions and several other subjects.

After gloating over our success for some time we had to think of distribution. We had 3,000 copies on our hands. Most magazines are distributed by some central firm that specializes in this facet of the business. In Dublin this meant Easons. But old Bob Eason didn't like what he saw and refused to distribute it until he had thoroughly read the issue and had a lawyer pass it as being free of libel. While Eason was thinking over the matter I went off with a bundle on my bicycle distributing it to any newsagent who would take it. It was marked as sixpence and we wholesaled it at fourpence.

One or two of the national newspapers noted our existence and in this way the public became immediately aware of *Kavanagh's Weekly*. There seemed to be an immediate surge of curiosity. Certainly there was much talk. The Foreign Affairs Department was in a state of fury at my article which was entitled *Diplomatic Whiskey*. Professional journalists shook their heads and said this was a very low attack. Patrick was bad, they said, but I was worse. My piece was gutter journalism. Even Patrick shook his head and shivered when he read my piece, for though he approved of the article at first he began to have doubts that it should have been published. Yet twenty-six years later a conservative Dublin journal featured a similar article and entitled it *Diplomatic Whiskey II*. What seemed revolutionary in 1952 had become ordinary and commonplace in 1978 because that battle had been won. And so it was with other articles. One wonders today why they created such a hubbub, the criticism seems so mild. They stand merely as tombstones to battles won.

Our gloating turned to dismay when we suddenly realised that we had to prepare immediately the second issue. Another ten thousand words to be produced in a day to two; it was back to the typewriter for both of us. Fortunately I had brought my typewriter to Ireland with me.

When after twenty five years I read Patrick's editorial in the second issue I begin to wonder how he could accuse me of being the violent one and he the conservative. Here is Patrick:

The editor of The Sunday Press is a military man with a deep devotion to his Fuehrer. We have seen him on a political platform kiss the edge of an imaginary sword as he named — The Chief! . . . . The lads who had been telling us about the mentally deficient stars of the screen, giving us football players with genitals that hardly conformed to the modest Greek canon, and Nietzschean heroes who have a pane of glass for a diaphragm were called into council . . . .

As Oscar Wilde has pointed out there is only one thing worse than injustice, and that is Justice without her sword. That has been the position in this country — until our arrival.

250

So that the reader may judge who was the more conservative of this twosome, I append a section of an article in the same issue written by myself on the Cultural Relations Committee:

More than 20,000 pounds has been spent by this committee. Members of the committee were the usual mixture of ex-politicians and frustrated pedants. One or two of taste found their way by accident onto the committee but they soon resigned or bowed in desperation to the mediocre majority. Much of the 20,000 was spent on making a documentary film about the life of Yeats. It was shown in a small cinema (100 seats) in New York and was viewed by some two or three hundred Irish-American charwomen. The conversation in the foyer was interesting:

'Well, Maggie, how are the legs?'

'Ah, sure I'm all bet up; even the knee is at me again'.

Another sum of money was spent on sending a hundred or more photographs of dull people to America to be exhibited there. No gallery of any standing would let the photos inside its doors, so the pictures were exhibited for a week in a room in a small town in Massachusetts. More money was spent on sending various students and lecturers abroad; one went to Los Angeles to study oceanography, another to the polar regions to lecture the Esquimaux on Irish literature. A group of folk singers went to Venice to sing Mother Macree; dancers and pipers went to Wales and a schoolboys' choir went on a tour to Rome. A thousand was paid to the Dublin Grand Opera Society to finance the visit of a fellow torturer — the opera company from Hamburg.

The 20,000 appears to have been rationed out very skilfully, everyone who could guarantee that he couldn't think, getting the cut that was due to him. But there was still some left when all the expenses were paid. How they asked, could the change be spent. The answer was simple: they would have Mr. MacLiammóir, the actor, write a booklet on the Irish Theatre, and Mr. Austin Clarke, the reviewer, write

251

another booklet, this one to be on Ireland's numerous poets (1,400 of them — the quota established at Druim Ceat in the 6th century A.D.). The books were duly written and the problem now was what to do with them. No use sending them to London or Paris. Ireland's book-reading public would be served but that still left the original tonnage more or less unchanged . . . .

I wrote similar essays on the Irish Radio, the Hospital Sweepstakes, Puck Fair and many other topics.

We carried on for thirteen issues until my money ran out. As I had guessed, Patrick's friend who was to go halves in the cost disappeared — not, I would say, because of the money but from a malice which was part of a larger aberration. This is true also of a number who still claim his friendship.

But even if we had the money it is doubtful that we could have continued. By the thirteenth week we were utterly exhausted. We had no one around who could help us with the writing and keep up our standard.

Patrick wrote the last issue. Here is an abstract:

The keynote to Irish thinking is summed up in the phrase 'And where will that get him?' Undoubtedly it will get him nowhere if you don't believe in the God of Life, of the grass, of the sun. What kind of world would it be if there was no hope, if we all felt with the average Gael: Where will that get him? There would be no Shakespeare, no Homer, nor a St. Thomas Aquinas. There would only be as here men swilling themselves into forgetfulness . . . .

For more than ten years this editor suffered from the delusion that he had in Dublin a large body of friends of a special kind. These friends were friends of his genius. They feel that he deserved to be supported.

They were all 'cultural', they were all engaged in various liberal works — good Samaritans, defenders of liberty, helpers of the poor, some succesful commercial writers. The keynote to all their character was kindliness. These gave the editor to understand that they were working for his canonization as eager as the supporters of the cause of Matt Talbot are working, and that they were only waiting the opportunity to do something to advance the ideas in which he believed. True it is, he caught whiffs of a humanitarian stench on many occasions; he got an inkling that these people loved the poor and defeated, so that they might steep their stinking hearts in the precious ointment of poverty. They wanted something over which they could exercise power. It was for this reason that these people were pleased to do all in their ability for the editor so long as he would guarantee always to remain poor and ineffectual, never to enter into competition with the world on any serious level. How right Oscar Wilde was when he remarked that anyone can sympathise with failure but that only a great saint can sympathise with success.

They kept telling him to stick to ballads, to what he knew of country life, but not to start talking about such abstruse matters as money and politics.

Then the editor who for so long provided these people with a potential subject for the exercise of filthy power began to take a hand in the game and the venom that was openly exuded by his cultural friends would be impossible to describe. It is no mere melodramatic, persecution-maniacal delusion; it is very real, so real that as the same editor sits at his typewriter on this hot summer's day in 1952 he is finding it hard not to splutter with ironic laughter over his machine. He will always remember with gratitude the ultimate goodness of these friends of his for at last fully exposing their hands. He called their bluff and is a wiser man today than he was three months ago. The only power that is worthwhile is knowledge, knowledge of oneself and of other people in relation to that self . . . .

Patrick learned his lesson — but he forgot it quickly and, until the year he died, kept falling into the same trap. That was his way. It was a weakness, perhaps even a virtue. But it ruined him for living, in the way the world knows living.

After *Kavanagh's Weekly* closed we thought it advisable to leave town. Patrick took off for London and I returned to America. I foresaw no difficulty in succeeding as a freelance writer in New York. My first assignment was to write an account of *Kavanagh's Weekly*. The piece captioned by the editor, *My Wild Irish Weekly*, so offended Patrick that during a dispute twelve years later he commented in a letter that I had written a piece *that was very familiar and which wounded me — and my women friends — a lot*. It was published in *The American Mercury*, September 1952 and I give it here in full so the reader may judge for himself:

Six months ago I returned to Ireland to complete a book I had been writing. When I had finished this work and was about to depart Patrick Kavanagh, the Irish poet, entreated me to help him establish a weekly newspaper which he had been contemplating for some time. It was to be an intelligent paper, lively and full of ideas. He pointed out that there was a great need in Ireland for such a paper, and that he had among his friends men who were only waiting for the opportunity to support such a paper with contributions in cash. I was less enthusiastic for the proposal. I remembered the manner in which Yeats was treated when he attempted to establish the Abbey Theatre; I remembered that Joyce described Ireland as an old sow that eats her farrow, that every writer of real talent had to leave Ireland.

But though I was conscious of all this and much more I was willing to be persuaded that Ireland had changed for the better; in any event it would be well worth the expense and energy involved to establish clearly if Ireland were becoming more enlightened or — as I believed — more barbarous. Furthermore the opportunity of examining Irish political and social life while I stood at its very centre appealed to me —

Patrick in Dublin (Mc Daid's Bar) [Photo courtesy Miss O'Flaherty]. Original photograph in poor condition but we felt it was worth reproducing.

why Ireland, noted for its dairy farming, had to import butter from New Zealand; why no one was getting married; why Irishmen were fleeing the land for the English factories at the rate of 40,000 a year; why we needed an army costing seven million pounds a year; why so many vague institutions were set up, like the Cultural Relations Committee, the Irish News Agency, and so on? Why had a labouring Irishman to pay when he entered a hospital in spite of the fact that the Irish Hospitals Sweepstakes were making millions a year? All these and more were interesting problems.

'Very well,' I said; 'start writing the editorial — we will begin publishing next week'. And so began Kavanagh's Weekly, a paper which The Manchester Guardian recently described as the brightest bit of journalism to come out of Ireland for a long time . . . . 'a paper from which some English Weeklies might have learned a thing or two'.

Patrick Kavanagh then brought me to a pub to meet a wealthy shopkeeper who, it was claimed, was interested in literature and who already had published a literary magazine. There was general enthusiasm when the plan was outlined and the shopkeeper offered to back the magazine financially if I would remain in Ireland and manage it. I was delighted and proposed that I would share equally in the expenses and furthermore would do all the technical and business work involved. Within a week Kavanagh's Weekly was on sale. But the shopkeeper departed and stayed away until the printer's bill was paid.

Then another fellow with more cash than brians called me up; he was a writer, of course, and begged to be allowed to share the expenses. Contributions from this gentleman came quickly but none had the name of a bank on it.

In the meantime the second and third issues were published and were receiving enthusiastic praise from the ordinary reader but not from the political grafters. The government paper through its 'Night Reporter' had the presumption to attack me. Was I not that dreadful man who had written for that notorious magazine *The American Mercury*? Then followed a garbled quotation from *The Mercury*. The reaction of the public was interesting; all copies of *The Mercury* sold out the next morning. We replied to *The Sunday Press* pointing out that it was yellower than the yellowest Hearst paper, that on one page it had an essay on purity and on the next the picture of a many-times divorced film slut, that it was attempting to impose on Irish society an alien vulgarity. Furthermore that the ordinary reporter was an anonymous nonentity whose name or works would interest no one, that he was buried in the hack work of the daily muck heap, and except in very obscene societies seldom forgot his place.

Our reply rocked *The Sunday Press*, got the Night Reporter fired, lost them advertising and almost drove the editor, Mat Feehan, into another political job.

The editor of *Kavanagh's Weekly* was on the phone daily to his 'friends'. Were they willing to support the paper with cash. Some were very vague in their replies while others pretended not to be at home. There was the wealthy 'writer' of about fifty stage-Irish novels. He was one of the editor's good friends and admirers. Would he help? He had not brought his cheque book along; besides, he had to send some money to a poor woman in Kerry who had lost her only cow. But he would send money when a cheque for a story in *The Saturday Evening Post* came through.

So far, I was paying all the bills and though we were selling about 2,000 copies a week it would be almost two months before any returns came in. Our readers were mostly professional men, civil servants, the hierarchy (searching for heresy), and a few farmers. I drew the editor's attention to our financial position. 'Hold on', he told me, 'I haven't looked really hard for support from my friends'. And so we leave him there sitting on the edge of the bed as he turned the names of his friends over in his mind.

Our paper had a wholesale distributor whose terms were

forty percent discount, all copies to be given to him on a sale or return basis, while he, as I learned later, would sell to his customers only on order. Furthermore, he demanded an advance 'censorship' copy each week. This I accepted as part of the indignity which I must endure for going into commerce:

The distributor wrote to our printer demanding that the latter put up a large amount of cash in case of a libel action. This was too much for me — business instinct or no business instinct . I pointed out to him that he had libelled me by writing to my printer instead of to me as publisher and so creating the impression that I was a man of no financial or moral responsibility. I agreed to settle for an apology. But though the apology was quickly given, the distributor continued to demand a weekly censorship copy.

Even this I was willing to bear. After all what mattered was the response of our readers to the paper. Our circulation was going up no matter how distribution might be jammed. Our readers were delighted with the satirical articles and the articles exposing political grafters. Our census report on the number of asses in Ireland was very popular. The exposé of the Irish Hospital Sweepstakes as a racket was considered very daring and everyone waited expectantly to see if the publisher was going to be shot. It was well known that the Government was searching for some excuse to put the publisher in jail for sedition, but there was no law which could jail a man for enquiring as to who in the Government stole the forty-million E.C.A. funds.

As I said the public was delighted with these articles. That was all very well, but those articles were not intended as the important part of the paper. It seemed to us that the original ideas expressed elsewhere in the Weekly were being ignored. This, of course, would not do. We were getting popular. To our surprise, we found that although our readers were very enthusiastic for the paper, scarcely one of them ever wrote us a letter. I then began to write Letters to the Editor to encourage our readers to write similar letters on matters that moved them, but even then there was no response. I was beginning to suspect that our readers only bought the *Weekly* so that they might have something to talk about. We were selling 2,000 a week which meant an estimated reading public of 10,000; how could this be when I knew well that there were no more than 500 intelligent people in the whole country? But though I was suspicious of our readers' reaction I decided to continue; getting rid of our undiscriminating readers and training an intelligent group could be accomplished later.

We were receiving manuscripts from well-known 'writers', but they were all so dull that we were compelled to reject them and continue writing the paper ourselves.

We now return to the editor out on the trail of financial support. Although he was writing about 6,000 words a week for the paper, he managed to have enough time to call all those numerous 'friends' which he had, and also to pay visits to the advertising agencies and company directors. The business people of Dublin (per square foot the richest city in the world) would surely lend support to our altruistic venture. He was certain he would get an advertisement from Pye Radio because the manager of this company was a culture-lover. All he got was a sweet smile. From the monopoly, Dunlop Rubber Co., he got a similar smile, from Aer Lingus a snarl, from McConnell's and Arks advertising agencies more smiles and from Wilson Young a slight. But the editor of Kavanagh's Weekly had such a deep-seated sentiment for what he called 'the essential intelligence and warmth of the Irish mind, particularly the instinct of the women', that he refused to be discouraged.

'Let us put our cards on the table,' he said; 'people think we are being supported by the Communist Party (their headquarters were right across the street from us), others that we are being supported by the fascists, and still others by the opposition party. Let's explain in a Leader that only *you are supporting the paper and our wealthy readers will rally around.'*

The Leader was duly written but the only response was a begging letter to the publisher from some library or other. But the editor refused to accept the situation for what the facts showed it to be. 'Let's say we will continue only if we get a thousand pounds,' he told me, 'that will surely get a reaction'. While the edition carrying this information was going through the press something else happened which snapped my patience completely; our printer put on too much censorship pressure. Admittedly he was the most liberal printer in Ireland but he was frightened by the power of Big Business and the pressure of the distributor that he leaned too heavily on his censorship pen.

Even the editor as he tried to rub the pain out of his back after two hours at the stone, admitted that it was beginning to appear that I was right in the first instance — there was nothing in Ireland except flabby minds that stung like jellyfish when you came close to them. They had no real backbone. Their minds were corrupted by commerce and by listening for generations to political speeches and bad sermons. We both agreed that even if we did receive a thousand pounds we would not continue. It so happened that this promise was not put to the test because we did not receive a thousand or even a hundred. We got about ten pounds. So we prepared our final edition.

I was somewhat angry so we decided to limit the final edition to five hundred copies. When the edition was printed we decided to limit it by fire to one hundred copies. Of this edition only twenty copies were issued to the public — to intelligent friends and a few libraries. We returned whatever money we had received.

Had we continued we could have become a commercial success but what value would that be? That was not our purpose. We wanted a paper which would be subsidized by a wealthy patron and which would appeal to the *discriminating few. There are no patrons in Ireland for intelligence so we closed down the paper. Patrick Kavanagh closed his apartment and went to London and I returned to America for, whatever, its defects, America has energy. Ireland was never so defeated even under the so-called oppression of the British. It is at the moment one huge racket centred in Dublin. Everyone has fled the rural part of the country to some to the factories of industrial England and the rest to Dublin to join the racket. So it is that the greater Dublin area contains nearly half of the Irish population. The country areas are being taken over by retired English and Indian army officers. You could travel the length and breadth of Ireland without seeing a farmer even with the aid of a telescope. That is why Ireland has to import New Zealand butter. Under the rule of de Valera the whole basis of Irish society has broken down; in the course of the next ten years Ireland will probably be well on the way to its pre-historic barbaric state. Only a revolution can save the country. Had our paper continued we might have achieved just that.*

Chapter Nineteen

Pawing the wind

I hadn't been long back when I got interesting news. Patrick wrote me telling of an anonymous article published in a Dublin Weekly called *The Leader* in which both Patrick and myself were defamed. The article was entitled *Profile* and was written in a manner that made it clearly libellous in Irish law though by American standards the piece was not at all libellous. Here is the opening paragraph:

'A pard-like spirit beautiful and swift' is hardly the phrase that would occur to the mind of the casual observer watching Mr. Kavanagh hunkering on a bar stool, defining alcohol as the worst enemy of the Imagination. The great voice, reminiscent of a load of gravel sliding down the side of a quarry, booms out, the starry-eyed young poets and painters surrounding him — all of them twenty or more years his junior, convinced (rightly, too) that the Left Bank was never like this — fervently cross themselves, there is a slackening, noticeable enough in the setting-up of the balls of malt. With a malevolent insult which, naturally, is well received, the

Master orders a further measure, and cocking an eye at the pub-clock, downs the malt in a gulp which produces a fit of coughing that all but stops even the traffic outside. His acolytes — sylph-like red heads, dewy-eyed brunettes, two hard-faced intellectual blondes, three rangy university poets, and several semi-bearded painters — flap: 'Yous have no merit, no merit at all' — he insults them individually and collectively, they love it, he suddenly leaves to get lunch in the Bailey and have something to win on the second favourite. He'll be back.

Behind this seemingly innocuous essay we knew were those representing the most evil elements in Irish society. There was now a moral issue at stake and Patrick decided he had no choice but to sue for libel. I also had been libelled in the Profile but Patrick decided he had the stronger case. Besides, there was no point in risking us both in the same battle. Apart from the moral issue there was also the prospect of heavy punitive damages. This was cheering.

I agreed with Patrick that he alone should sue and so I promised to go over and give evidence if needed. Patrick assured me my presence would be necessary. This was encouragement enough for me. For some time I had been casting longing glances towards London, wondering if I could make a success there. Here now was my opportunity, so I packed my trunks once more and set out for London.

With Patrick's help and somewhat to my own surprise I got myself a job as a writer and editor for a large engineering company. I was now on the scene to watch developments. Patrick came to visit me once or twice. He seemed run-down but I was unaware at the time how sick he was.

Because of *Kavanagh's Weekly* Patrick seemed especially newsworthy and he was asked to read some of his poems on Radio Eireann. Although we had thoroughly abused the Irish radio in our weekly and Patrick had promised never to appear on it, yet he accepted. He saw an opportunity to interpolate in his reading a further exposition of his poetic point of view. Here is an extract:

For a man in Ireland to have the label 'poet' attached to him is little short of a calamity. Society when it has established a man as a poet has him cornered within narrow limits. If he looks like having too much scope in his little corner marked 'poet' he will be still further narrowed by having an adjective in front of poet — such as County poetry poet, Catholic poet and so on. He becomes a sort of exhibit, not a man in and of the world. If he happens to be a dilettante without a passionate faith he will enjoy this position but if he is a genuine poet it is an indignity and something much worse. Therefore I announce here and now that I am speaking as a journalist. I have resigned from being a poet and I hope that my resignation will be accepted.

In so far as the poet is thought of in Ireland the idea is that he is either an uproarious drunken clown, an inspired idiot, a silly schoolgirl type or just plain dull. He is in no way to be taken seriously.

The Irish ideal of a literary genius — weak, charming and a challenge to nobody. The poet does not seek misfortune; the poet does not pursue experience, experience pursues him. The poet does not go searching for beauty or intensity; these things happen to him. But that is a long story.

The logical collateral of these several and joint ideas regarding the poet is that poets are quite common in Ireland. They are never mentioned except in batches of a dozen or more. Fourteen hundred are reputed to have been present at the famous Assembly at Druim Ceat, and not long ago in one of the Irish papers I saw a list half a column long, of modern Gaelic geniuses which for a moment deceived me into thinking it was the list of chief mourners at the funeral of some noted patriot or industrialist.

It was a patriotic gesture, for patriotism does include belief in the importance of literature. Yet poetry has nothing

264

1960: England (Devon, *The Sunday Times*).

to do with patriotism, nor is it interested in any special language; it is universal. Even allowing for the unfavourable circumstances it is remarkable that in a thousand years Ireland has not produced a major poet or indeed a good minor poet. There was no audience for the poet's high dignity.

The poetic view of life is a view based on a true sense of values and those values must be of their nature what are called unworldly.

Furthermore a man may be a poet in prose as well as in verse or in merely talking to people. To narrow the poetic spirit down to its expression in verse is equivalent to narrowing religion down to something that happens on Sundays.

A good idea of the nature of the poet is to be found in E. V. Rieu's Introduction to his new translation of the Four Gospels. He remarks of St. Luke: 'St. Luke was a poet. I do not mean by this that he embroidered his narratives but rather that he knew how to distil truth from fact'. Rieu goes on to refer to Luke's 'poetic insight into reality' and to his realisation of the part played by Woman in the revelation of the Divine Idea.

That is the poetic mind.

If I happen to meet a poet — and I have met poets — I would expect him to reveal his powers of insight and imagination even if he talked of poultry farming, ground rents or any other common-place subject.

Above all, I would expect to be excited and my horizons of faith and hope widened by his ideas on the only subject that is of any real importance — Man-in-this-World-and-why.

He would reveal to me the gay imaginative God who made the grass and the trees and the flowers, a God not terribly to be feared.

This may seem awfully solemn. It is anything but.

Roughly two classes of people abhor the imaginative sense of values. There is the sound businessman whose solid worth *finds expression in the trivialities of the newspaper, and there is the literary mediocrity who must deny the existence of Parnassus if his little dust-heap of biographies and novels are to mean anything. The sound man of the world never reflects. Not to reflect is what is considered sanity. Yet without this reflective centre man is a savage and will not be long revealing his savagery if you touch the hollow beneath the conventional dress of respectability. And that touching or stripping of the hollow heart is what the poet willy-nilly does and is the thing which makes him hated by the world. In every poet there is something of Christ writing the sins of the people in the dust.*

As I have said one of the Irish ideas of the poet is of the uproarious clown. I am sorry to say that I have hardly ever heard an Irish admirer of Gaelic or of any other poetry speaking of the poet that he didn't give the impression that he thought it all a great joke.

The idea of the poet is of a man who at the drop of a hatpin would run off with another man's wife.

The note of the poetic mind is a moral one, and it is this moral quality which the world cannot stand for it is a constant reproach to inferior men — and inferior men let me explain who are committed to inferior things, who lack the courage to pronounce a judgement in defiance of their own petty vanity. The world loves the wild uproarious fellow who is made in its own image and will when it comes to the test take him to its bosom and confer upon him all the worldly privileges. Display a touch of this kind of irresponsibility and you're home and dried. The world knows it is not genuine.

After all these high claims for the poet you might be pardoned for expecting him to utter high and stupendous truths. But that is not the way of truth. Truth is very disappointing; we expect it to come transfigured and are inclined to ignore it when it comes simple and humble.

What therefore are the high and important things in this world? What are the immortal things?

Some foolish people in the writing business get worried in case their work lacks the stuff of permanency, and they write about things they think permanent and important and in doing so they only turn out ephemeral journalism or dead ponderous matter. They think immortality is in the future. But they are wrong; immortality is not in the future; it is in the timeless Now.

A blossom is immortal within its moment. A flash of summer sunlight is immortal. Moments of happiness, grief, or joy are immortal.

A man is immortal when his ideas are exciting to the young. Not to be exciting to the young, not to be loved by women is death. Not to be loved by all good men and women is death.

Poetry is experience, is reality. Beauty is the absence of ostentation, not to try to appear larger than you are. Beauty is humility, and poetry is the courage of humility.

* * *

My own autobiography, *Beyond Affection* (pp. 145-164), now takes up the story of the law case and Patrick's subsequent operation for cancer of the lung:

The law case opened on 4th February, 1954. Patrick was tense and fearful. He had not expected the case to go to trial, nor did his lawyers — the libel was too obvious and there could be no defense. But Patrick and his lawyers had underestimated the fury of the opposition, the intense hatred Kavanagh's Weekly had generated. I had added my share to the hopper but Patrick was the main target — he seemed to stand more than I for morality, for poetic position. In every word he wrote, they saw their own mean attitudes mirrored. Patrick had to be destroyed. They had planned for a year on how that might best be done and were not willing to accept a settlement however small the damages might be.

Our Statement of Claim followed the usual formula in

such law suits. The article in *The Leader* held Patrick up to odium, hatred, ridicule and contempt; it portrayed him as of limited literary ability, of intemperate habits, vicious and dissolute. And so it went on. Patrick had no choice except to follow the course set by his lawyers who had taken the case on a contingency basis.

Those who claimed to be Patrick's friends gathered around and helped him formulate a defense. They drank with him, blathered a lot, but gave no strength. They were, as was later to be discovered, secret enemies. He was to be a gentleman, they assured him, virtually a non-drinker who patronized coffee shops, not pubs. He was the kind of average, decent person most people would like to associate with. In retrospect it is clear Patrick would have done better had he taken his own advice, swing freely, be totally himself. The line of defense forced on him by his friends left him hamstrung and awkward. Just the same and in spite of that he put on a magnificent performance.

At Patrick's invitation I came over from London for the trial. I found him in a state of great agitation. He sensed the ordeal ahead and was fearful. He was vociferous as he detailed his strategy to me: he had to convince himself. He was tense and overwrought and began to blame all his troubles on me. He could defend his own point of view but not mine. I would be his ruination. Although I had some frustrations of my own I managed to absorb most of Patrick's.

Had there been a third party present with a good sense of the absurd, much laughter and amusement might have been extracted from the scene. There was I, dressed in my best Saville Row suit, bought for interview purposes, standing in this large, dirty and mostly unfurnished Dublin flat, being denounced as a disgrace and being warned by Patrick not to appear in public with him lest I damage his reputation. I was being ordered around like a serf and told to jump to it. Those who did not understand how intimate our relationship was might wonder why I stayed around, why I didn't leave. Patrick, of course, knew me better than that.

On the morning the trial opened Patrick borrowed my new Burberry showerproof and my briefcase, then set out alone for the courthouse, dressed as he imagined a high executive would dress on his way to the Stock Exchange. I followed fifteen minutes later wearing an extra inside shirt to make up for my loss of an outer coat.

By the time I arrived at the Four Courts Patrick was already inside after being photographed in his borrowed attire. There he was in the court, sitting with his good friends as they gave him final instructions on how he should set the angle of his jaw, and how his demeanour should be. By rights I should have been bursting with laughter at this grotesque comedy: instead I could see only the tragedy of the situation with myself powerless to help. Patrick had been brainwashed by those claiming to be his friends. Patrick was like that, always easily influenced by slick outsiders — though never for long. By indirection I myself was also brainwashed and saw myself as an awful person, undignified and vulgar. I hoped not to be called as a witness.

The jury was drawn from the upper-lower class of Dublin shopkeepers and one look at them was enough to convince even the most optimistic of us that only a miracle could save us. Patrick was doomed.

The trial took on the aspect of a social event and hundreds gathered outside the court each day to get a seat. The opposition counsel was John Costello who had recently been Prime Minister. His defense of the libel had been modelled on Carson's defense of the first Oscar Wilde trial. No one noticed the similarity until it was too late, not that we could have done much about it if we had known. His tactic was to attack Patrick as if he were the defendant. For ten days he kept Patrick in the witness box cross-examining him on the most minute aspects of his life, even on misprints in some of his essays.

He used every courtroom trick to admit to evidence items wholly inadmissable. Patrick's lawyers were not alert enough to forestall such tricks. Taken all in all, it was a disgraceful performance by Costello and his aides. He regretted it later, but that is another story. At the time he was representing the most evil elements in Irish life and was enjoying the experience.

As the days of cross-examination lengthened it was becoming apparent to Patrick that he had little chance of success and that the advice of his friends had been false. He began turning back towards me for help. He had done very well considering the premise he had set for himself.

It was the classic confrontation between the poet and the rabble. My suggestion was to end the ordeal as quickly as possible and that this could best be achieved if he were to allow himself to break down in court. He would have no difficulty: he was sick and exhausted, could swallow only with difficulty and was desperately holding back from a breakdown.

The trial came to an end quickly. Our fate was fore-ordained.

While the jury was deliberating Patrick and one or two of his friends went off to the Four Courts restaurant to rest, leaving me to await the result in the courtroom. The decision came within an hour. No, no, no, no to every question. I rushed out to tell Patrick. He could not believe it and was very shocked. And I the bearer of bad news! Later he complained that I should have broken the news to him gently, passing over the possibility that my sensibilities were equally devastated.

The newspaper reporters found us and asked for pictures. Now he was willing to be photographed with me. Pictures were taken and a statement prepared, though on the advice of counsel was not issued. There would be an appeal. As a matter of law the jury decision could not be allowed to stand. What the jury, correctly perhaps, might have done was to *find for Patrick but give him contemptuous damages, leaving him to bear all the costs. Appeal against such a decision would be virtually impossible. We went home together and fell asleep.*

Patrick had not been so engrossed in the law case as to desert his lover — poetry. The previous evening and early that morning he had been working on his poem Prelude. He gave it to me and I handed it in to The Irish Times so that while the announcement of his losing the law suit appeared on the front page a small box announcement advised readers to 'See poem on page 6'. The Prelude had been cut by the Editor but it was good even cut.

Saturday morning we both walked into town. A woman came running across the street to Job's comfort Patrick but he hurried away. He hadn't got a penny in his pocket. I went to the bank, changed some dollars, and gave him three pounds. He went to Mitchell's Café while I went to Bewley's. There in Bewley's I ran into a priest from Cavan who insisted on discussing the case. 'I hear he never goes to Mass,' he said. I didn't respond.

Back in our bleak and dirty apartment that evening we lit the fire, made tea and sat down to discuss the case. The comedy of the decision grew in wonderment as we talked. We began to smile, then to laugh, and finally we both fell into uncontrollable paroxysms of laughter. We roared until we were almost ill, and the more we tried to sober up the wilder the laughter became. Patrick shouted sternly at me asking that I desist. If we keep this up, he warned, we may lose our sympathy. This remark only made matters worse until finally I raced out the door and went downstairs.

Earlier when the mood was not so hilarious we received several crank calls, jeering at our defeat. No problem figuring out who the callers were although they were anonymous.

After the weekend I gave whatever money I could afford to Patrick and returned to London to battle it out there. We would keep in touch by telephone. There had to be an appeal against so outrageous a decision and I would be around to participate in it.

There was no difficulty in finding legal grounds for appeal. The decision went against commonsense: the defenders of the libel, for example, did not call a single witness and yet won their case. The main problem was to find the cash needed to take an appeal. At least seven copies of the transcript would be needed — one for each of the five judges, one for our side and perhaps one for some other purpose. The trial lasted ten days and the transcript would be lengthy.

Patrick hadn't a penny and I had only my newly acquired salary. But even if I had money Patrick would object to my spending it on his law suit. There would have to be a public subscription. A committee was formed, letters were sent out and a little money brought in. T. S. Eliot contributed twenty-five pounds, others much less. Some refused to contribute and denounced Patrick into the bargain. Eventually enough money was collected to buy the transcripts and the case went to appeal, opening 16th November, 1954. I was able to take time off from my job to be present.

There was not the same excitement on this occasion as there had been when the case first went to trial. The galleries were occupied but not packed and there was no queue outside hoping for a seat.

Here were some of the legal grounds on which this appeal was made: that no reasonable jury could have found as it did; that the finding of the jury was against the evidence and was perverse; that the judge had misdirected himself in law in allowing (over objection) cross-examination of Mr. Kavanagh directed to prove the alleged truth of libellous statements of fact, and in allowing the truth of such statements to be an issue when justification had not been pleaded. The judges trying the case were Martin Maguire, Conor Maguire, Cecil Lavery, Kingsmill Moore and

Cearbhall O'Dálaigh — the latter eventually be become President of Ireland. O'Dálaigh was in fact a friend of Patrick or at least an acquaintance. Kingsmill Moore was a Trinity College Protestant and it was assumed he would be on our side. Lavery was nothing much in particular..

These three Justices tried to keep the appeal along literary lines and they vied with each other in asking questions that demonstrated their knowledge of English literature. Would it be a libel on De Quincey to state that he was a drug addict? Would it be a libel on Ben Jonson to describe his drinking habits in the Mermaid Tavern? Good literary questions are hard to come by and once asked were certain to be asked again. On the second time around we had our counsel primed.

Kingsmill Moore — 'Would it not be legitimate to discuss the drinking habits of Ben Jonson in the Mermaid Tavern?'

T. J. Connolly — 'No. Such a party was entirely private. Jonson himself made that quite clear when he wrote On inviting a friend to supper.'

"And we will have no Polly or parrot by
Nor shall our cups make any guilty men
But at our party we shall be,
As when we innocently met."

Connolly spoke these lines from memory somewhat casually and his quotation brought the house down with applause and with laughter.

After seven days of hearing the court reserved decision. Three months later judgement was handed down and even though a higher drama was being enacted in our lives during this interval we will record the result of the appeal. The Irish Times, 5th March, 1955, reported as follows

'Reserved judgement was given in the Supreme Court, Dublin, yesterday afternoon allowing with costs the

1956: Advertisement, Feb., 21st.

1954: **Cartoon** in *The Irish Times.*

BY-LINE

He hasn't been mentioned . . .

275

appeal of Patrick Kavanagh. The Chief Justice and Judge Martin Maguire were in favour of dismissing the appeal, while Justices Lavery, Moore and O'Dálaigh were of the opinion that the trial was unsatisfactory and that a new trial should be ordered.

The court was filled for the judgement but Mr. Kavanagh was not present. He is a patient in a Dublin hospital . . . '

The majority opinion corresponded with that given by Kingsmill Moore who said that the impression conveyed to him by the article was that Mr. Kavanagh was somewhat of a poseur, unsubtle, opinionated and overbearing. He found it difficult to see how anyone could come to any other conclusion than that Mr. Kavanagh was held up to ridicule and contempt. He said that the jury could easily have been confused on a delicate distinction: they might have confused a justification of the facts to prove fair comment with a justification of libel as a whole and to regard cross-examination as to credit as if it were an attack on the plaintiff's character to justify a mitigation of damages. The defense did not plead justification.

There was to be no new trial, no victory. Momentarily the curtain dropped and then went up again on a more ghastly drama.

Chapter Twenty

Now is the hour we rake out the ashes
Of the spirit fires

I was about to recover from the trauma of the law case when disaster struck. Patrick became ill — not some casual disease but what appeared to be cancer of the lung. I was thunderstruck, heartbroken. The thought that Patrick might suddenly die had never entered my mind; now here I was faced with that awful possibility. Could I survive it, so closely had my life been woven with his? I was young and tough. Undoubtedly this was to the good but such a wrench as his death would cause to my whole being was not to be taken lightly. I might not survive it. To ease the shock I assumed the shadow reported on his lung to be no more than indication of T.B. I wrote a memo of the incident on the 6th March, 1955, which now picks up the story:

On Monday, 21st February, I phoned Patrick and he told me of another communication he had from (Prime Minister) Costello. He had just posted me a letter on the subject and he hesitated to mention its contents on the phone. When I had received the letter, he suggested, I might give him my views on it.

Wednesday morning I called from the office. He had been invited to see Tierney, President of University College, he said. I advised him to take a strong line.

At six in the evening I phoned again but there was no answer. Fifteen minutes later I received a call from him. Tierney had offered him a job giving lectures — one a week — for a fee of five pounds because, as he said, he felt that a man who could write a poem like the Prelude should be supported. The fee might be increased later. Patrick was in a tired mood. Then he told me the bad news.

He had asked Dr. Brendan O'Brien to examine his sinuses because of continuous catarrh. O'Brien declared there was nothing wrong with his sinuses and ordered an X-ray of his lungs. I was stunned. I said I would be over to see him on the week-end.

I arrived in Dublin on Saturday morning. Arrangements had been made he be given a bronchiscope inspection later in the morning. Pat O'Connor, then Curator of the Municipal Gallery, promised to drive Patrick to the appointment at the Rialto Hospital.

When I arrived at the apartment Patrick was still in bed. In addition to the rags, dirt and ashes usually associated with his apartment, this time there were many whiskey bottles lying around. Others heard of his illness and had barged their way in the night before. They held a party 'to cheer him up'. Patrick was very angry over it and told me he would call the police if they ever attempted the likes again. He was also worried that they might have searched his flat and read his private correspondence.

When he heard the sound of my arrival he called me into the inner room where he was lying on the bed (a mattress, really). He told me he knew the illness was serious. He was depressed though hardly as depressed as I was.

Six months before this he had felt a pain in his back near the shoulder and had gone to Baggot Street Hospital to have it looked at. The House Surgeon examined him and pronounced him all right. Now it seemed that the House Surgeon was wrong. He chatted about my job in London and was cheered when he heard how successful I had been in acting as Press Agent at the wedding of the Chairman's daughter. This was the kind of news that cheered him up and that he wished to hear.

It was by now almost nine in the morning. He got up and dressed. There was nothing at all to eat in the house. That did not matter, he explained, since he was not supposed to eat before taking the medical tests later. Pat O'Connor arrived in his car and we all set out for the Rialto Hospital along the canal bank. At the hospital we met Dr. Keith Shaw. He questioned Patrick on his symptoms as Patrick sat wearing his overcoat, his hat and scarf. 'For the past six Months', he began, 'I have been suffering from the delusion that I had catarrh'.

Patrick wanted us to wait for him — he'd be right with us immediately after the bronchiscope test. It wouldn't take a budge out of him. I persuaded him it would be best if we left now, and came back at noon to pick him up. Meanwhile he would rest at the hospital.

On his way back into town Pat told me that a priest friend of his had visited him a week before with the exact same story — he was suffering from a fatal disease. The priest was scared. Patrick, on the other hand, was very philosophic about it and told Marthe (Pat's wife): 'Very likely it is cancer and it will kill me, but to tell you the truth, Marthe, I don't give a shite'.

Back at the apartment I made an assault on the dirty conditions. I gathered up all the empty bottles, swept the floor and lit the fire. The weather was stormy but fortunately Patrick had coal. I fixed up a bed for him in front of the fire and aired the bed-clothes. They were very damp. Then I picked up Pat O'Connor and we went back to the hospital.

279

The House Surgeon informed me that the tests indicated cancer. Not much could be seen. The tube going into the upper left lung was blocked, causing periodic collapse of the lobe.

Patrick I found to be tired and dopey. He was not anxious to leave and had to be persuaded to come along. Back at the apartment Patrick objected to the arrangement of the bed in front of the fire. It was too low to sit on the edge. We both wrestled the couch into its place. There Patrick sat before the fire. I went to the shop and bought supplies. I made him an egg-nog. I myself hadn't eaten that day so I went into town for lunch. When I returned Patrick was still groggy though hardly less so than I.

Sunday morning — Patrick was awake ahead of me. I hurried out for the Sunday papers and on the way back borrowed a cup from the lady downstairs, Mrs. Burrows. I boiled water in a new saucepan I had bought the day before and used the saucepan also as a tea-pot. Our minds were on the results of the tests and not on the idle conversation we engaged in.

I went to Mass at 11.30. Patrick did not come along as usual because he feared the draughty church. After Mass Patrick and I talked till lunch time.

After Patrick had gone I phoned Dr. Shaw and discussed the diagnosis. Shaw was not hopeful. The operation itself was not dangerous. The question was how far the growth had travelled, and whether it already had become involved with vital parts. Could it be operated on at all? The chances of survival beyond six months was one in five. All depended on whether or not the cancer could be excised, including the cancer not visible.

I mentioned the possibility of getting Patrick a private room at the hospital but he told me this was not possible. He could only have a cubicle — to be shared with one other patient. I agreed to this arrangement. Then I called Dr. O'Brien, the referring physician. He gave the chances of

Patrick's survival as poor but better after the operation than before.

We sat before the fire in our apartment until midnight. With his consent I called my sister Mary in Carlow. She would be up on the first train in the morning, she said.

28th February. Monday. We both were up at nine. I hurried off to Kingsbridge Station to meet Mary. She was shocked at the news. By taxi to Bewley's of Grafton Street. We talked of cancer and the probabilities of secondaries. Our best judgment that an operation offered the best chances. Mary was well informed — she was the Matron of the Fever Hospital in Carlow. She explained that if the disease were allowed to follow its normal course death could be very painful.

Patrick lunched with us at noon and then went off on his own — to get sympathy, he remarked facetiously. Mary and I went shopping for those articles he might need in hospital. At three o'clock we met again and had further conversation. I then left Mary at the train and returned to 62 Pembroke Road.

There was a note at the flat. Brendan O'Brien wanted Patrick in the hospital immediately, that very same evening. When Patrick arrived home and heard the news he was distressed. He would not go this evening but would go tomorrow, he said, even though that was the day of the Leopardstown Races which he had hoped to attend and have a last fling. Exact plans had to be made at once. First, his Will. This he wrote out and brought up to Searson's pub, there to be signed by him in front of two witnesses, the barman and a policeman. He had a few drinks, bought a half pint of whiskey and came home. He asked if I would leave for a while: he had a girl who was to call on him. I arranged to go out to dinner. We discussed intimate things, what I should do if he died, who were his friends, and such like. I tried not to show my distress.

When I arrived home at 9.45 p.m. I found Patrick dazed

and sick-looking lying on the couch. The girl had not shown up nor had she called. My own nerves were on edge. I begged him to sit up and talk to me. He made an effort and sobered up. We growled a bit and Patrick said: 'You are the only person that means anything to me'.

I had planned to return to London but decided I would stay over so I could take Patrick to hospital.

1st March. Tuesday. Up before nine. After breakfast we began to sort out Kavanagh's Weekly so that no outsider could pick up a set. Patrick then asked for some time on his own. I began cleaning the bathroom and left fifty-eight milk bottles outside the door to be picked up.

While I was thus occupied Patrick had written a special verse dedicated to me which he wanted included in the Prelude. I was too distressed to read what he wrote but put everything away safely. We then had a conversation on a number of sensitive matters.

Patrick and I went into town to lunch at Bewley's. He left me for fifteen minutes to go to Confession and returned in good form. We walked home through the rain. Then gathering up all the manuscripts lying around we packed them into an old suitcase, checked on everything in the flat and set off for the hospital.

As we reached the hospital my stomach became nervous. Ward Four, that was our destination. A nurse directed us to an empty cubicle. Patrick sat down in the greatest gloom. He took a sip of wine. A nurse came in and handed Patrick a book of rules. She took his particulars: Occupation: author, penniless. He asked for special consideration. If you meet us half-way, she replied. Patrick felt that perhaps he should escape from the place. Judicious coaxing brought him to a settled mood. The matron came and the conversation was repeated. She seemed decent enough. The House Surgeon stuck his head in shyly: 'Come in, come in,' Patrick called. I urged Patrick to be a little considerate of the staff and this point of view cheered him. When I left he was in a settled condition. 'Pity I didn't bring my clock'. I gave him my watch. He gave me a list of people he would not object to visiting him. Then I left.

I hurried back to our flat, collected my baggage and off I went to catch the night boat at Dun Laoghaire. By morning I was back in London.

2nd March. Wednesday. I had a phone call in the office from Rory O'Connor, the solicitor, saying judgment would be given on Friday. Would I come over? I said I would consider it. In the evening I got a message by phone that Patrick would prefer I did not show up for the judgment. It would give the law case too great an importance.

4th March. Friday. At one in the afternoon I called the London office of The Irish Press who told me we had won the Appeal! Not especially elated. At 5.30 p.m. Rory O'Connor called and said Patrick was thrilled and he himself was dancing with joy. Patrick called later and was in excellent spirits. Tests so far for cancer by bronchiscope were negative, he told me. There was still hope.

5th March. Saturday. Read the judgment in the newspapers. Patrick phoned in the evening. He said that he was being pumped full of penicillin. If the shadow on the lung decreased then this disease is T.B. If not, then it is cancer. He warned me about being too hopeful.

The operation was performed on Thursday, 31 March. Patrick phoned me the night previous to it asking that I not come over while the operation was being performed. He would feel more at ease if he had not to consider my worried condition. Ideally, he said, he would like to think of me standing at some corner waiting for a girl-friend while he was being operated on. I followed his wish in not going over; the second could not be arranged. Keith Shaw, the surgeon, promised to call immediately after the operation and I had the switchboard alerted to connect at once with any cross-channel call.

The phone call from the surgeon came at one in the

afternoon. He had had to remove the whole lung, he said. There was cancer there. My heart began palpitating. That could mean death within days or at best months. The surgeon assured me that he had excised all the cancer, as far as he could tell. Patrick had survived the operation well and was resting comfortably.

As soon as possible I was on my way to Euston Station, then the long train journey to Hollyhead and the night boat to Dublin. I arrived around eight in the morning. By ten o'clock I was out at the Rialto Hospital.

Patrick was under an oxygen tent, the first such apparatus I ever saw. He was happy to see me but could barely speak because certain of the nerves that operate the vocal chords had been cut. He held my hand; I suppressed my tears. This noble body, the object of all my affection, energy and admiration — wrecked! He thanked me for honouring his wish that I not come over the day before. Alas others were less sensitive. The first object he saw as he came out of the anesthetic was the head of a friend peeping over the curtain! His privacy invaded! It was a violent insult to his ease of mind, but he refused to be bitter about it.

I stayed only a few minutes, then came back later and visited him again. And so, on through the weekend. By Sunday I could sense an improvement and felt there was no immediate danger. I went back to London taking with me — on his orders — the suitcase of manuscripts I had stored with the O'Connors. On reaching London I took the bag at once to Barclay's Bank and put it in a safe-deposit vault. When the assistant-manager saw what I was handing in — an old, torn and string-tied suitcase with papers sticking out — he looked at me in amazement and called the manager. After some discreet checking, and finding me a particularly good depositor, they sealed the bag in some way and took it into their custody. That much would be safe even if Patrick were to die.

284

1965: Patrick Kavanagh. Drawing by Pirozca Szàntò. [Courtesy, Desmond O'Grady].

The following weekend I was back again in Dublin — and the following week also. Patrick was making progress but he was still desperately crippled and weak. He gradually became cheerful and told me the book I had sent him to read had saved his sanity. It was called 'Minerals in Industry' and was issued by the Kensington Museum of Science, and was all about gems, how to recognize them, their properties, and much else. It was precisely the type of book to rest his mind in these circumstances.

As he improved and talked of getting up, he asked that I buy him a suit so he could walk around the wards and, later, out the hospital. When eventually he put on the suit I had bought him he was unable to carry its weight, except with difficulty — so weak had he become. But he wore it on a few occasions around the corridors and amused himself and the officials as he posed as a bed-pan salesman!

What he needed, he advised me (pathetically), was a cruise. Alas, he did not know what a cruise entailed, the sea-sickness, the dull companions, the boredom, the lack of privacy. I said a cruise could be arranged when he was ready for it. In the meantime, he could not go back to 62 Pembroke Road. For one thing, he could not climb the many steps. A friend provided the ideal answer to this problem — an offer to keep him in the Merrion Nursing Home for three weeks or so.

These arrangements were changed slightly; first he would put him up in a suite of rooms at the Hibernian Hotel. This was the kind of luxury living that would raise Patrick's spirits. He phoned me up and was all praise for this fellow's generosity. Two days later came an emergency call: the friend was nowhere to be found and the management of the hotel was about to evict Patrick for not paying his bills. Would I pay it? I sent the money by Express advising Patrick that he move at once to stay with his sisters in Longford. He balked at this suggestion and instead stayed a day or two with Mrs. Burrows in the flat underneath him at

62 Pembroke Road. Finally he had no choice but to go to Longford. He was so well treated that he was back in Dublin within a month, able to operate on his own.

There was still the law case to be taken care of. A new trial had been ordered. Patrick consulted with me and we agreed to an out-of-court settlement. A news item to this effect appeared in The Irish Times, 24th May, 1955.

The terms of the settlement were not announced — the embarrassment was too great. Everyone knew Patrick hadn't a cent to his name and that his lawyers were operating on speculation. What surprised Patrick and myself — and filled our lawyers with dismay — was the revelation that the opposition was almost as broke as we were. The Leader's assets consisted of its masthead while the printers, Argus Ltd., had only about £800 and even that was tied up in debentures. The shock, the swearing and eventually the weeping among the lawyers involved was a comedy that even Menander could not improve on.

Patrick's vocal chords had been injured in the operation. Now when he tried to speak it was in a hoarse whisper. He had constantly to keep clearing his throat and his breathing was so laboured that you wondered if the next breath might be his last. It was very painful being in his company especially for me who knew him as a cross-country runner and as a person of great strength. He seemed a very tragic figure and when on 1st May 1955 John Costello arranged with Dr. Tierney of U.C.D. to appoint him as extra-mural lecturer at 400 pounds a year no one seemed jealous — *he wasn't long for this world*, they thought. The funeral arrangements they had made while he was in hospital still might not be a wasted effort. They had planned to give him a sort of state funeral with the body lying in state in the Mansion House. Ten years later Patrick was still laughing at the antics of these people.

Costello was a generous fellow despite his tactics in the courtroom — he had a conscience, had a sense of shame, qualities unknown in many people. He loved the limelight of the court, longed for that one big case that would perpetuate his name as an advocate, another Pitt. Kavanagh versus *The Leader* was such a case. His sense of fairness had to be cast aside — he was an advocate and his obligation was to win. What matter that his client was a scoundrel and that he was an advocate for the lowest elements in Irish society.

He won but, having won, his victory did not seem as important as it should. Even his peers censured him for his handling of the case. Costello, however, was a man of courage and integrity and when he saw his error he did what he could to make amends. He helped Patrick at a critical moment. Patrick too had no grudge. He met Costello as he emerged from a polling booth. *I hope*, Costello said to Patrick, *you hold no grudge against me*. Patrick answered, *On the contrary, I just voted for you.*

For two or three weeks Patrick diverted himself by travelling over the south of Ireland with someone who was selling his services as a spray painter. He also came to London to pay me a visit. We were walking down Charing Cross Road when we were accosted by a fellow we had known from the Palace Bar of the forties — Ewart Milne. He wrote verse and frequently appeared in the correspondence columns of *The Irish Times*. There were many Job's comforters around and Patrick had asked that if possible I should protect him from them. So it was that when Milne made his approach I tried to shoo him off. Meanwhile Patrick had reversed his instructions without informing me and gave Milne an enthusiastic greeting. In *Irish Writing* 1956 Milne writes of this encounter:

I ran into P.K. in the Charing Cross Road. I saw him at a distance, just as he went into Collet's Bookshop, and there could be no mistaking that big figure. He was dressed in a pair of bogman's great boots, a pancake trilby hat, nondescript baggy trousers, (the little man Charlie) and either a bright blue blazer jacket or blue waistcoat. All in all,

288

a startlingly correct picture of a lumping stage Irishman. But there was nothing stage-Irish about that great craggy face, which, I noted with some concern in myself, was of a greyish pallor. I noted, too, how as he stood in Collet's glancing from book to book, he would put his hand up and touch his solar plexus regions, as if something inside there was hurting. Duodenal? I had heard he had been in hospital, with various rumoured ills, but this was the first time I had actually seen him since we last met in Dublin, on a Donnybrook tram, round about 1942. Then, he had been alone, and we had talked warily, both of us knowing, I imagine, how greatly we disagreed, but saying nothing of it. Now, however, he was with a companion, a thick-set, rather pleasant and good-looking man that somehow I knew I knew quite well, but couldn't for the life of me place. Wasn't it his brother? Or just a body-guard? I mean of course a bodyguard, an unofficial male nurse, a friend for his sick body, and because being ill he had to have somebody around? When they turned and came from the shop the companion recognised me first, and I said to him: 'Isn't your friend Patrick Kavanagh? At that moment Paddy himself said 'Ewert Milne' and the companion said, 'Strange that two such men as you should meet here. Maybe it was, outside the Old Bomb Shop, but after all, Charing Cross bookshops are likely, and indeed inevitable, meeting places for literary types. P. K. would not discuss his lawsuit, and was angry when I mentioned it, but in fact I was only being polite (not remembering for a moment that with my countrymen politeness doesn't count) and I was glad when he refused to talk about it. I asked him how he was, saying I had heard he had been ill, and he said he was better. Then suddenly the craggy face seemed to quiver, and he said with sudden bitter ferocity 'But I'm in no shape for standing much of the savage streets of London'.

The savage streets of London? Could any phrase sum them up more exactly? I suppose, though, that I myself looked like part of them; where both P.K. and his bodyguard friend could not be mistaken for anything other than complete foreigners, bogmen, mere Irish, and, to the undiscerning ninety-nine per cent of the British, stage Irish at that. But as for me I am the chameleon type in more ways than one, and no doubt, without actively attempting to do so, I have taken on something of the look of the Londoner prowling his savage haunts. Just then I realised Paddy was asking me, rather diffidently and doubtfully, if I would like to come for a drink somewhere. I said I couldn't very well as I was going to catch a train, and after a few more words we parted. I was annoyed, in a way, because I wanted badly to talk to him, but the large-sized and — I felt — disapproving presence of the bodyguard disconcerted me. Like a fool I had at first tried to be hearty, clapped the friend on the shoulder and tried to bring him into the conversation (short as that was), but your stolid man simply stood there and oozed disapproval of and at me. Or so I felt. Anyway, we parted soon and in silence, and I never said what I wanted to say, which was to ask P.K. — if he wanted to get away somewhere quiet off the savage streets — to honour myself and my wife by coming and spending a day or two or a weekend with us in our house in North East Essex. 'Is it nice there? he had asked when I told him where I was living and had lived since the late war. Yes, on close inspection he really did look really ill, but then that could be explained by the fact that he had, after all, just come out of hospital. Nothing organic. I'm not sure, though. Whatever sickness he had would have begun with the nervous system, I felt sure. And there is nothing small about Patrick Kavanagh. There is, however, something tragic, and something that is not exactly weakness but allied to it. He had kicked hard at the traces, but he had not kicked quite hard enough. The kick he needed to kick off his particular yoke, however, was double or treble the kick I had needed to give to throw off mine. So I needn't talk!

In a letter to me, November 1978, Milne makes these further comments:

I was very conscious of P.K. in those days (the 1940s), conscious, I mean, that he was a sort of outsider, and was called rather sillily, the 'peasant-poet'. But then I was a sort of outsider too, as I'd come up out of the great oceans, to be a poet. And I had another sort of bond with him, as in my youth I'd been on a farm in Wicklow . . . . Yet in our approach to politics we were poles apart. And in our poetry? Well, his marvellous way with words in English fascinated — and indeed humbled me. He seemed to me to write beautiful classical English with nothing at all of that spurious Gaelicism of the nineteenth century poets with the emphasis on Irish. He was always European in his thought and phrasing.

Chapter Twenty-one

Once more born again

Back in Ireland Patrick recuperated by lying on the banks of the Grand Canal near Baggot Street Bridge:

Most days last summer in the beautiful heat I lay there on the grass with only my shirt and trousers on. I lay on that grass in an ante-natal roll with a hand under my head. And because that grass and sun and canal were good to me they were a particular, personal grass, sun and canal. Nobody anywhere else in the world knew that place as I knew it. There was a branch in the water and it is still in the immortal water in my mind. And the dent in the bank can never be changed nor the wooden seat. When I raised myself on my elbow I saw Leeson Street Bridge. Only by a miracle could anyone ever see Leeson Street Bridge as I saw it. I report too on the corner of St. Stephen's Green (the Grafton Street entrance) where between the hours of two and four every day last summer I lay in the same ante-natal roll. It would never rain again. I got up, put on my Panama, then went into Robert's for a cup of coffee.

(*November Haggard*, p. 45)

292

In October 1955 I resigned my job in London and returned to the United States. I had consulted with Patrick's doctor and he gave me the startling bit of information that — while Patrick had a good life expectancy — he feared that the stress I was under, and would continue to be under if I stayed around, would finish me. I did not tell Patrick of this — it would only worry him and cause tension perhaps between him and his doctor. His friends on hearing of my departure rushed in with sympathy agreeing that it was an awful thing for me to have done. I was approached by concerned friends. I explained nothing. Where Patrick was concerned I didn't need to explain anything.

Clearly you were right to go back to America, he wrote me in a letter, *for the English mediocre mentality is terribly dull and a blank wall. No adventure.* His doctor had been right too, because within a few weeks I was in hospital for an operation and back again six weeks later for a second. Now Patrick was doing the worrying. *I wrote to you yesterday but write again today to say how relieved I am to know that you are over the operation, for an operation is an operation and there are no absolutely safe ones.*

He had made a collection of his poems and sent them to Macmillans. They not only turned them down but even went so far as to renounce all copyright in his work. Why they made their rejection so final I cannot say — apparently they saw no future in his work.

Patrick's letters now pick up the story once again:

62 Pembroke Road, Dublin, 8th February 1956
I spoke to a debate the other night and made a wonderful speech which I have sent to Nimbus and I am sending you the cutting which was the press reception. I am sending on the other copy today, now.
I have planned to give a series of lectures on:
The Poetic Situation in Ireland

What good is Poetry?

Thomas D'Arcy McGee, Carleton, Cervantes, Moby Dick, etc.

I wrote a damn good article for The Irish Times. I must send you a copy when I get a copy myself. It was supposed to be about Waiting for Godot but of course it was about myself arguing. Another wickedly amusing attack on what I called the Ireland writers and why no one gives them any heed.

The Archbishop came to see me at Christmas. I told him that if I got a cold I'd have to get to a hospital or Nursing Home. He arranged with Matron of the Mater that I will have a private room complete with everything any time I want. I hope I don't want but it is nice to know.

He had enclosed a Press cutting from *Nimbus*:

I note that in the promotion sheet of this meeting I am the only one who has a profession attributed to him — Patrick Kavanagh, Poet. This puts me at a disadvantage: how am I to know that one of the other debaters isn't an ex-heavyweight boxer with a nasty temper? This is a typical Irish kind of bad manners. A large number of people, particularly newspaper illiterates are always trying to imply that the term poet and silly idiot are synonymous. This is an attitude I will only accept from very beautiful women. . . .

As for the Censorship it does not concern the creative writer. The Censorship operates in a lower-middlebrow milieu. The one organisation that I would be terrified of getting into power is that which calls itself the Friends of Civil Liberty . . . . It is my duty to tell you that these people are the enemies of liberty. Liberty is largeness. Liberty is positive. You are not supporting literature by negatively attacking the Censorship; you support it by supporting with cash a writer of talent if you know one. I know that when a test came a couple of years ago when I was fighting a cause before a judge and jury in Dublin there wasn't one of these

1960: Peter Kavanagh with his own hand-built press. [*New York Times*].

Friends of Liberty, opponents of the Censorship, complainers about the power of the Catholic Church who didn't work night and day to dishonour, discredit, humiliate, and utterly destroy everything for which the word 'poet' stands.

* * *

Some Reflections on Waiting for Godot

(The Irish Times, 28th January 1956)

> The Existentialists declare
> That they are in complete despair
> Yet go on writing.

AUDEN

To those of us who cannot abide the theatre with its flatulent pieties, its contrivances and its lies, 'Waiting For Godot' is a wonderful play, a great comedy. I do not set out to interpret Godot, merely to say why I like it, which is probably the only valid criticism.

Take a play like 'The Bishop's Bonfire' which was well received in Dublin. There you have the old unhappy shibboleths paraded, the theme of 'Ireland' as a moral reality, and the last refuge of the weak, the theme that our failure to ramble out into those flowery lanes of liberty which O'Casey is always talking about, is due to forces outside ourselves. In O'Casey's case the restrictions of religion are the villain of the melodrama.

All of us who are sincere know that if we are unhappy, trying to forget our futility in pubs, it is due to no exterior cause but to what is now popularly called the human condition. Society everywhere today and its beliefs are pastiche; there is no over-all purpose, no large umbrella of serenity.

This world-wide emotion has seeped through national boundaries. It flowed into Ireland many years ago, but the

296

'Ireland' writers continued as if nothing had happened. Now and again one noticed their discomfiture; why, they seemed to be asking themselves, was no one giving them any heed?

These 'Ireland' writers, who are still writing of course, could not see that the writers of Ireland were no longer Corkery and O'Connor and the others but Auden and George Barker — anyone anywhere who at least appreciated — if he could not cure — their misfortune. Saying this is liable to make one the worst in the world, for a national literature, being based on a convention, not born of the unpredictable individual and his problem, is a vulnerable racket and is protected by fierce wild men. A national literature is the only thing that some men have got and men will not relinquish their hold on the only thing that gives them a reason for living.

It is because of its awareness of the peculiar sickness of society and a possible remedy suggested that I like Beckett's play. The remedy is that Beckett has put despair and futility on the stage for us to laugh at them. And we do laugh.

I am not going to say that Godot is a great illuminating hope-creating masterpiece like King Lear. But then, that is the present condition of humanity. Beckett is an honest writer. Academic writers and painters are always ready to offer the large illuminating symbol; they give us gods and heroes and they write and paint as if society were a solid unified Victorian lie.

I know that I am not being very direct in my statements about Waiting For Godot but that is part of this play's importance; it both holds a mirror up to life and keeps reminding you, if you are interested in sincerity, that the reason you couldn't endure the theatre hitherto was that it was tenth rate escapism, not your dish at all. Having seen Godot you begin to see that for one who can enjoy, say, a poem like —

My love lies in the gates of foam
The last dear wreck of shore

there is nowhere to go in the evening except to the pub.

You relax with the thought that there is refuge until you remember the television screen, and you go out into the street screaming hysterically in verbal disarray.

* * *

62 Pembroke Road, Dublin, 28th February 1956
I have started my lectures and last Tuesday, the first, was a great success. Got a terrific ovation and the university authorites were delighted. I speak again tonight on 'Poetry in the World'. Will send on cuttings in due course but at present have no other news.

As far as Extra Mural is concerned I am in for life, but I have hopes to be put on the staff next year. Once I have these lectures finished I'll have a repertoire that I can spout anywhere. The first was on 'Poetry in Ireland', never mentioned anyone but Yeats and Joyce. I am doing ten. The university spent a lot of money advertising them in all the papers, swanky ads on the Leader Page, under theatres. It is a helluva big job but worth it.

P.S.: My popularity with audience is terrific. Physics Theatre packed on stormy night with heavy snowing. The cutting will show you. Write soon.

P—.

* * *

And what else did I do? I need a constant supply of counter-irritant worries.

As I told you, lectures are going well. I must send on all the relative writings. I typed all out and interpolate as I go along.

* * *

62 Pembroke Road, Dublin, 19th March 1956
Got your latest letter today. P. Swift sent poems to David Wright, Editor Nimbus also co-Editor Faber Book of 20th Century Verse. He said: 'I am incoherent with enthusiasm,

he is not an Irish poet, he is the poet. This is the goods. All my life I've been wrong about P.K.'

Obviously, Macmillans have made a balls of themselves for the poems will get published.

PATRICK

* * *

P.S.: All well. Will send cuttings and lectures in due course. I'd be using the lectures many times again, please God — in the U.S. maybe. Hard going first time. When those silly, provincial-minded publishers see vast selection of poems in Nimbus they'll start getting interested.

* * *

62 Pembroke Road, Dublin, 15th May 1956
I got your cheque. I sent by other mail an hour ago to you some cuttings relating to lectures (10) now concluded; also a photo — recent — to show you how I fattened.

My ten lectures got a bad press but that was the press's error. Nothing like the reception I received was ever known, in Ireland — with, someone said, the exception of Parnell. It was like a Secret Society every Tuesday, an orgy. It was a great success with the authorities. Also it was fame, the rumour going around, in contradistinction to the notoriety of the press. I could not over-emphasize this. The final night they all came. I am in good form and would like to know how you are. Not much in your letter. Presume you are O.K. I am just on my way to London to renew contacts.

* * *

12 June 1956
I have really nought to say. I am in good form though as you can realize, one lung is not the equal of two and one gets depressed, somewhat frustrated; there is some discomfort always. But I am not by any means complaining.

* * *

299

Bornes, French Riviera, 14th July 1956
I have been here for a week — on the Riviera. The boredom is great and every day I am saying I will leave. I was brought here in the entourage of an American named Farrelly. Came by air — there are the man and wife, two small children, George Barker and wife, myself and three maids. We live in a converted castle up in the mountains overlooking Lavandon, a tourist sea resort. Nobody speaks English. I took my lectures and papers with me in the off chance. So far the place is too distracting. I didn't tell Mrs. Burroughs to send on mail as I didn't decide to stay. Still I hang on. I hope you are well. I wrote a few good poems lately, better of course than the dreary rubbish in A Soul For Sale. I suppose I'll stay another week or so.

* * *

62 Pembroke Road, Dublin, 12th September 1956
It is about time I wrote to keep in touch. Here's how I stand. Health good. I spent two periods comprising five weeks in France with U.S.A. friends. The woman in the case is at present visiting me. She returns to New York Saturday. She is planning my going out in Winter for a holiday. She is arranging to have my flat painted etc., a real patron.

* * *

62 Pembroke Road, Dublin, 27th October 1956
I finished the lecture book. I hope to go to New York soon. I am sending in the lecture book tomorrow. It is exceedingly interesting and readable. I'll send you a copy.
I am looking forward to seeing you in New York. I am in good form and weighing fourteen stone.

* * *

62 Pembroke Road, Dublin, 30th October 1956
P.S.: I am just like you, living like a millionaire, flat done

300

*up, costing 300 pounds by Mrs. F. Electric plugs and fires
and cookers throughout. Finished with spits.*

* * *

62 Pembroke Road, Dublin, 7th December 1956
Dear Peter,
   *I'll be seeing you P.G. before Christmas. Will phone you
on arrival about 19th.*

* * *

Patrick arrived in New York on 19th December. He came by
boat travelling first class. His patron put him up at the
Algonquin Hotel. He phoned me as planned and I went to visit
him. He had improved from when I last saw him but was still a
very sick man, and drinking whiskey at a rate somewhat above
moderate. He was excited and delighted with New York. He
didn't want too many people calling on him, he said, except his
intimate friends — none of the riff-raff of literature. After a few
days he phoned me up and accused me of isolating him from
people. He now asked me to let it be known that he was in
town.

That meant calling Patric* Farrell. If you want to meet
anybody in the world of art, music or literature he will be happy
to make the introductions. He is an artist in the field of
introducing people. So I called up Farrell and within twenty-
four hours he had upwards of fifty or even more press
representatives talking to Patrick and asking him questions. He
was brilliant in his repartee but it was unsuited to American
journalism. No one at that time wanted to be told that Churchill
couldn't write anything better than a passable cliché. Only the
Daily News carried a story, a poor one, under the caption, *The
World is Ruled by Idiots* (28 Dec. 1956).

After a week's stay at the hotel he moved in with his patron's
family, Mrs. Farrelly, who had a house at Third Avenue and
72nd Street — no relation to the Introducer.

---

* *Sic.*

After eating and drinking for three months and not performing in whatever manner was expected of him, he was shunted to a small flat on 86th Street, near Madison Avenue. From there he was shipped back to Ireland at the end of April, this time travelling steerage.

Every day he visited with me at my flat on 29th Street. I found him a satisfactory guest though like all sick people inclined to be cranky at times. My clearest memory of him is lying on the couch in the living room, his feet up in the air bicycling, repeating with amusement, *Baby Doll, Baby Doll,* referring to a movie he had seen which was black-listed by the Archdiocese of New York. Being a visitor, he explained, he didn't come under the prohibition.

I had a friend of mine, Ann Keeley, who worked for N.B.C., arrange that he do a reading of his verse on records as a memento of his visit. He agreed but was so sick that morning that the taping wasn't very good. Just the same I have made copies since, one of which is in T.C.D. library.

I asked Mr. Patric Farrell to write his impressions of meeting Patrick and though his account has some curious aspects I give it as he wrote it:

When Patrick eventually made his visit to the U.S. in 1956 we were informed of his arrival by Peter and told that he was staying at the Algonquin Hotel. When Peter gave the signal we arranged a Press Conference for him at the Algonquin at which a large crowd showed up — McCandlish Phillips of the New York Times pored over all his work for six hours including Kavanagh's Weekly etc., called in a photographer and wrote what many at The Times considered the finest interview ever to cross desks at The Times. But the interview was killed as too iconoclastic. Harvey Breit, Editor, critic and columnist for the Book Review thought it so exciting and colourful that he tried to have it published in The Times Book Review but only a short excerpt was allowed to get into this section. After his return to Ireland Patrick blasted The

Times and Breit thought it so ungrateful that he publicly commented on Patrick's bad manners.

Our first sight of Patrick was in the lobby of the Algonquin with Mrs. Farrelly. He in his incarnation was even greater than our high image of him — elemental, profound, spirited, wise, and this was reinforced during the interview. He was a massive man with strength and dignity, a noble head, big eyes locked into innocence and wonder. Later in an upstairs suite an interview was attended by The Times, all the Wire services — but only the Daily News printed anything the next day. They sub-titled the story 'Everything But the Kitchen Sink'. His interview was extra-terrestial and all there will remember it as one of the most exciting and colourful experiences — his grasp of poetry, life, politics.

My next memory is of Patrick at a party at the Albert Clayburghs. The latter was a son of the famous singer — friend of the Franklin Roosevelts — Alma Clayburgh. It was for Richard Eberhart, poet at Dartmouth and a staunch admirer of Patrick. Patrick had great presence at the party. He was a lion with his wit and wisdom. On New Year's Day bitter and raw we called at the Farrelly's home on East 72nd Street for Patrick to take him to a salon, open house celebration, at the home of the Aerosol heiress who had an art collection of note. The party was so filled with high personages of art, literature and the social world that Patrick inquired of me if I thought it was safe to leave his overcoat with the butler who had tried to take it from him. It was precious to Patrick. Because of the bitterness of the day and Patrick's post-operative condition as he was fitting on the garment I solicitiously asked if he thought such a coat would be warm enough for such a bad day. He indignantly scowled at me and asked 'What's wrong with this coat? It is thornproof!' And this in the fashionable silk-stocking district.

During the party he made his way with great aplomb until

303

he met James Johnson Sweeney to whom he had spoken probably because of Sweeney's family resemblance to his brother John, Librarian at Harvard University whom Patrick had met. But James did not respond with any enthusiasm to Patrick's attitude. This year I reminded Sweeney, formerly Director of the Museum of Modern Art and the Guggenheim Museum etc., that when Patrick spoke to him that long-ago day he didn't seem to know who Patrick Kavanagh was. Sweeney replied: 'Well, I certainly know who he is now!'

At a party of Tambimutti the Ceylonese poet in an East Eighties walk-up (Tambi the founder of Poetry London, publisher and poet) Patrick was in great form with his comments on English, American and classic poetry until he had a little too much to drink. Most of the guests had left and Patrick remained slumped in a chair. Tambi said to me: 'Get him out of here — I don't want him here all night!' This was from a man who was not always a graceful guest himself. So I upbraided Tambi. Then Willard Roosevelt, grandson of Teddy Roosevelt, cousin of Franklin, son-in-law of E. E. Cummings, who had relished the talk of Patrick all evening and relished him very much also chided Tambi. Together in Willard's car we got Patrick back to his room in East 86th Street near Park Avenue.

Whilst Elsa de Brun and I were living at the Chelsea Hotel Peter and Patrick called on us one afternoon and Patrick was in stimulating talking form until he imbibed too much holy water. Then he began to abuse Peter until Peter, despite his great control and patience, could take it no longer and left. His departure sobered Patrick a bit and out he came with one of the finest eulogies of another man and spirit that I have ever heard or read, fitting of Catullus. He went on and on with such a show of deep love of his brother the teacher, proud of him and dear to him, that Elsa and I were touched forever.

After Peter left we called up William Troy, a famous critic

Patric Farrell and Dame Elsa de Brun [Swedish Consulate].

1965: Chicago, O'Meara's house.

who lived at the Chelsea and his poet-wife Leonie Adams. He had wanted to meet Patrick and came right down. He was a severe critic, did not suffer fools gladly, but he seemed enraptured by Patrick's understanding of the meaning and forms of poetry and his response to the highest masters of literature. It was a good meeting.

One night at our shebeen at East 81st Street Patrick came and we had also Conrad and Mrs. Aiken. It was a meeting pregnant with fire. Aiken had reviewed the work of Patrick and because he did not call it the greatest ever he feared Patrick's wrath knowing how severe and cutting Patrick's irony and scorn could be. But it turned out they had so much in agreement that it ended by being an exciting encounter.

Also present that evening were two members of the Irish Consulate, Paul Keating and Eamonn Gallagher — Paul now Irish Ambassador to the United Nations and Eamonn Deputy Director of the Common Market. Peter and Patrick in their Weekly had derided some of the Irish diplomatic corps and we feared there might be another Donnybrook but Paul and Eamonn responded to Patrick the man and they had a high time. So much so that when Patrick suggested he might like to see the St. Patrick's Day Parade the next day Eamonn gave his official card for a seat on the reviewing stand. Again, Patrick had a little too much to drink on the Saint's Day and was refused his rightful seat.

On that same day Mr. and Mrs. Bernard Reis met Patrick. They had one of the great art collections of the country at their house on East 68th Street. They were old friends of Peggy Guggenheim and everyone who mattered in the art world. They did not know much about Patrick or his work but liked the quality of the man and at once invited him to a party they would hold in his honour. It turned out to be a gay and festive night and Patrick held court surrounded by the Picassos, Matisses, De Koonings, Rothkos, Stamos, Courbets, large and small Lipschitzs, with some thousands of small sculptures from primitive to the present. All the art

306

and literary world came, the Horace Gregories, museum directors, theatre directors, Edward Albee. Bernard Reis at that time was adviser to Mike Todd and their son-in-law had just won an Oscar for the film 'Round the World in Eighty Days'.

Patrick did not seem to be in sympathy with or appreciative of what we tried to do for for him so we were almost knocked off our seats when he phoned us the day before he returned to Ireland and profusely and gratefully thanked us for our kindness to him. Of course we sensed that Peter was behind the call but even so we were deeply touched.

We never saw Patrick again until one night in Rome in 1965. We met the poet Desmond O'Grady on the Spanish Steps; he told us he was expecting Patrick early that evening and that he would be staying with him during the Congress of European Writers to which Patrick was a delegate representing Ireland. Desmond called us that evening and told us Patrick had arrived and asked if Elsa and I would come over. I asked Desmond to determine if Patrick wanted to see us as we had had some disagreement with Peter over the Quinn Letters publications, or he had with us, and knowing the allegiance of the brothers to each other we were apprehensive about Patrick's attitude. But Desmond insisted that we come and put Patrick on the telephone; he promptly asked us to come and told us to bring some drink. When we arrived the Associated Pressman was trying to interview Patrick who was so blotto he made no sense. Then the A.P. man talked to us and as he was the same man who had interviewed Pound at Spoleto and annoyed Pound with some of his statements we got our licks in on Pound's behalf.

If anyone ever had the curse of the drink it was Patrick. It destroyed more of him than Dylan Thomas because he was so much a better poet than Thomas. For many years we did not speak to a number of our closest friends, America's foremost poets, because they had heard that Patrick was not house-broken and would not receive him — the absence of

307

cloacal etiquette offended them — as in our bathroom at the Chelsea where he urinated into everything but the bowl for that purpose. However, after his collapse in O'Grady's we thought he would not recover for weeks. The next morning as we sat at the Congress waiting for Sartre to call the meeting to order there appeared me bold Patrick larger than life, the most heroic and commanding presence there — so much so that three younger men during the intermission asked us who that extraordinary man was who spoke to us. And when we told him Patrick Kavanagh they begged to meet him. They knew his poetry and greatly admired it. The young men were the Scandinavian representatives from Sweden, Norway and Denmark. Although Patrick was aloof with us when he was sober that morning partly because of his devotion to Peter he consented to meet these three writers and we have wondered since what happened when Patrick and the boyos went out that night. We had to leave the next morning.

Chapter Twenty-two

The man they couldn't kill

Patrick liked to state that he was born as a poet on the banks of the Grand Canal Dublin in 1955. The banks of the East River in New York were perhaps an equal factor in this rebirth. There he lazed under the hot sun and dreamed his personal dream.

For six months he had free housing, free food, the best of company in an exciting city and more whiskey than he could drink. Until then he drank very little, one reason being that he could not afford to. He assured me he never liked the stuff and I believed him. I remember when I returned from England, a year or two before this, I wondered why I was able to drink half a bottle of whiskey even though the stuff did not appeal to me. I then discovered I had an internal problem that needed repair. So it was with Patrick. It was an anaesthetic against the pain.

Going back to Dublin, bleak, inhospitable, where he had no friends was also an awakening experience. The lectures he had delivered at U.C.D. the previous year were to have been published by the university. They never appeared. When Robert Frost visited the country and was entertained by the President of Ireland Patrick was not invited.

62 Pembroke Road, May 4, 1957

Boat trip awful. Bad storm and nobody in steerage but resentful beaten Irish labourers and girls. I was the odd man out and as out-of-place as in Shamrock Bar on your corner. Out of the question for any man of sensitivity to travel with those unhappy people. Had some luck in roommate. Dipso but intelligent and understood my fellow travellers. He pointed out that they saw in me the images of the men who pushed them around.

Young U.C.D. lecturer telling me yesterday Tierney called him aside last December said: 'I believe you are a friend of Mr. Kavanagh. Would he fix up that lecture Ms.?' No word of it coming out. Expect not.

I am in good form but inclined to feel uncomfortable when I try to write.

* * *

62 Pembroke Road, Dublin, 13th May 1957

I got a wonderful reception. Hundreds welcomed me back. All my friends knew I was away — the others did not. Good test. Poor Myles was at bottom of Senate poll and he thought he'd get in. I'm in good form today and not whiskeying too heavily. Just writing for the fun of it.

* * *

62 Pembroke Road, 11th June 1957

Incoming mail situation is worse than ever. Dede Farrelly has not written and has possibly ditched me.

Robert Frost is here. Reception for him by President O'Kelly. Was not invited.

* * *

62 Pembroke Road, 6th July 1957

Hope the weather is cooler. Hot enough here. Have no news except that I miss New York and wonder when again I will be walking down 3rd Avenue & 42nd Street. Hope soon.

* * *

The Farrellys dropped me completely. Didn't reply to my letters.

There is no such thing as modern poetry only among chancers in America. Enclosed photo of myself and Liam O'Flaherty at the races. O'F. in extreme right wearing peaked American cap. I don't suppose you ever catch sight of the Farrellys. How is P. Farrell? Who got Harvey Breit's job? In today's Observer I see pictures of various New York buildings including the Tishman. It is Sunday and rather cold. Compared with New York Dublin is rather shivery. That new PEN Anthology is out and is very entertaining. I wish I was back in New York for the winter but will get there again soon and this time I mean to go as Somebody, not all as one as the last time when in fact I was nobody and got nowhere.

Spender in Observer notes that if you paraphrase Dylan Thomas poems you would have no meaning, no nothing. Dante before writing verse wrote a prose statement, his argument, he points out. I find myself being regularly attacked by nasty-minded envious people on the street. Not often but occasionally. A defect of Dublin.

I keep very broke. Can you recall where we met last Christmas Day? I think I visited your apartment.

I do write a monthly article for a fashion magazine and next month I'm drawing once more on little old N.Y. —

Patrick's normal reaction to a difficult situation was to write. This time he responded with an additional burst of energy. He had been holding back until he had first achieved bourgeois success. That hope was now gone. Cancer had struck and the great literary push could be postponed no longer. When most people are faced with death they are inclined to hold on to the world. *This world will take some beating*, a rich woman on her death-bed told my sister Mary who had been speaking of the glories of the life to come. Patrick held on only because he had a destiny to fulfil, one that went beyond the material. He

311

grasped quickly at the time remaining to him. Hence a new series of poems beginning with *To Hell With Commonsense*. Other more exotic poems followed, poems better than any he had previously written.

> *62 Pembroke Road, Dublin, 14th October 1957*
> *I started writing a new kind of poems with new words. Sent some to Encounter and received this answer: Dear Mr. K., I have been to Tokyo and have only just received your To Hell With Commonsense and I would very much like to publish these in Encounter. Is it too late to do so? Please let me know. Many congratulations on these violently beautiful poems. Yours sincerely Stephen Spender.*
> *Here is the new kind of poem, one of the Encounter ones, 'Canal Bank':*
>> *Leafy-with-love banks and the green waters of the canal*
>> *Pouring redemption for me, that I do*
>> *The will of God, wallow in the habitual, the banal*
>> *Grow green with nature now as before I grew . . . .*
> *and*
>> *The important thing is not*
>> *To imagine one ought*
>> *Have something to say*
>> *A raison d'etre, a plot for the play.*
>> *The only true teaching*
>> *Consists in watching*
>> *Things moving or just colour*
>> *Without comment from the scholar.*
> *This is entitled IS.*
> *To write, particularly verse, one must be in great form. I am now better than while in the U.S.*

* * *

> *62 Pembroke Road, Dublin, 24th February 1958*
> *Got your latest. Bad about the colds. What about multivite tablets? Seems I hit on good time to see New York. Those*

poems of mine should be in Encounter in April. From the proofs they seem to be doing me proud — display title and author's name large at page top. They are awful good poems, and as you note visible in colour. . . .

The poems appeared in *Encounter* and while they were praised, no book publisher wrote offering to issue a collection. There was a vague suggestion that a private press in London was interested but nothing came of it. Patrick wrote to me (5th Dec. 1957):

. . . . I've had offer of de luxe publication of poems by David Archer (The Parton Press, London). He originally printed Dylan Thomas. George Barker wants to design production. I am not wildly enthusiastic since I started to write noo pomes. But it shows up those collections of American shites who are totally without opinion. Pound is as big a cod as e.e. cummings.

It was at this moment that I started my own publishing venture. Why should Patrick be depending on the judgment of some book publisher who essentially is no more that a merchandizer? It was a scandalous situation and I intended to bypass that system. I began with a selection of his new poems, naming the book *Recent Poems*. The printing was amateurish and the errata many but even so it was publication. At his request I sent him twenty-five of the printed sheets which he planned to have bound in Ireland and which he hoped to sell there. I saw the binding job later — really horrible, bound in a kind of linoleum. I don't know if he sold any. The remainder of the sheets I bound up in my own style and had them copyrighted. It is now a very rare edition.

62 Pembroke Road, Dublin, 17th June 1958
The printing is excellent and a great idea. I suggest that you omit Adventures in a Bohemian Jungle, and a number of

others. I suggest short ones like Shancoduff. I'll send on ten new poems. Then we'd have a neat sweet collection about fifty pages. Could be bound cheaper here, and twenty five copies offered in Miss O'Flaherty's (Parson's Bookshop) at ten guineas a time. Would get it here. Think up some non-committal name for the Press as the Johnson Press or the Anvil. Your name would stultify you. No news here worth much. I'm doing a weekly column for the Irish Farmer's Journal — six guineas a week. (Begun 14th June).

* * *

62 Pembroke Road, Dublin, 27th June 1958 Got pages to 9. As you'll have thought too, about now, the thing is to print and indeed the more mistakes — or nearly — the better. Spender wouldn't correct a word or grammar. Printing is good. Glad you like new poems which incidentally are written in spirit of it doesn't matter. So, by printing! If it is understood, O.K. Some bastards here, the Jesuits and that U.C.D. crowd, very petty. You have to be cute. I am. Weather wet for two months. Was in Cork yesterday for Farmer's Journal. I have merely written to say — don't re-set except when complete botch.

* * *

62 Pembroke Road, Dublin, 18th July 1958 Got book. A number of mistakes which ruin the sense. Pre-cooked in Requiem for a Mill not pre-cooked. Should be division between sonnets on page 9 but not essential. Page 11, 4th line: 'arsing' not arising. Page 12: 'Leers' not sleers; and 'fires of comedy' not vanity. Sonnet page 4 was mis-typed in Encounter. 'Now I am sure' is part of previous line but with full stop after 'youth passing'. Can you not correct a word without doing the whole page? The 4-line poem on page 11 should go on separate page in hand-printed book. About fifty copies would be enough and not for sale. I like those new poems as compared with the old, that I would like to

314

1958: Portrait by The Green Studio.

write more and include mainly only them. You needn't necessarily finish the book — sort of work in progress — keep adding. This one could be part of one. Get the idea? I think I may go to Inniskeen today but on the other hand, nothing in common.

Best wishes PATRICK
P.S.: Should you put New York on cover or not at all? Something should be on extra flyleaf; and don't autograph any of the final twenty five which is about all I want to have. Ten or so around.

* * *

Meanwhile in the spring of 1958 he delivered his second series of lectures at U.C.D. They were well received by a small coterie of curious people. This time he was more cautious than before: he wrote them out exactly and let me have them — ten in all — an extraordinary exposition of the poetic and his gospel. I published them after he died in *November Haggard* (1971). He wrote (14 Feb. 1958):

I am at present giving a series of public lectures, four before Easter and some later. Enthusiasm good, but nothing like the first time. Press are ignoring me but what are the Press? I am well. I wish I could get back to old New York. May do so in Fall. These lectures are good printable stuff.

I am trying in these lectures to be autobiographical since I came to Dublin. Something for a book.

I am in good form and remarkable I should have taken this new start.

Despite his occasional success, life continued to be very gloomy, even depressing:

62 Pembroke Road, Dublin, 1st September 1958
Dear Peter,
Strange thing about letters — they are unnecessary. I have

316

little to say. As you know, I work for the Farmer's Journal and now make around twenty pounds a week. I am in good form except that as my income increases I spend more and more.

Life here has never been duller and I'm beginning to have no one to speak to. I invented several friends and gave them words to say, but they just keep falling apart.

I had been thinking of travelling about the country but didn't get down to it. The curious thing is that I am more popular with the women now than before when I was younger. This is not sentimentality.

In October 1958 he made a big break with his past: he left 62 Pembroke Road where he had lived and suffered for fifteen years. Leaving the flat, he wrote, was like a death:

I will confess that I walked into each room in turn and prostrated myself on the floor, concentrating the while that this would be my last look out the window. I gazed out the window and concentrated and tried to fix in my imagination all those images. And, if the truth must be told, I wept.

(*November Haggard*, p. 10)

He moved to 19 Raglan Road nearby, a high-class lodging house he had lived in for a time in the spring of 1943.

19 Raglan Road, Dublin, 18 October 1958
As you'll see I have gone back to that place I stayed in many years ago. I owed a lot of rent — 100 pounds — and got out. I could have paid it but got to hate the place. They gave me a clean sheet to go. I intend to get a more civilized apartment on the ground floor.

Guinness here gives three small annual prizes for the best poems of the year — 300, 200 & 100 pounds. I got none though the four poems in Encounter were good. One Irish poet comprised the three judges so what chances were there.

They offered me five guineas fee for one poem 'October' for
their Guinness Book of Poetry. No dice.

He could afford the expense of high-class lodgings since apart
from the U.C.D. sinecure of four hundred a year he was getting
an additional six pounds a week from *The Irish Farmer's
Journal* for writing a weekly column about country life. It was
an interesting and amusing column concerned mainly with his
early youth and experience — but he hated writing it as
beneath his dignity and essentially a lie of *The Green Fool*
variety. He continued the column for four and a half years,
having little choice for he needed the money. New York had
taught him to live even farther above his income.

I went on with my printing and was now at work on my
Dictionary of Irish Mythology. I sent Patrick a copy of the first
fascicle. He was so enthusiastic that he wrote an Afterword for
the final fascicle and later on mentioned the dictionary
frequently in his column.

19 Raglan Road, Dublin, 29th October 1958
*Your book is the most beautiful I have ever seen. I don't
imagine such printing has been done anywhere this century.
In mine you were experimenting, learning. The stuff is good
and sometimes gay. 'Tis myself could write about twenty
articles out of it, but shan't.*

*I am well. Was down in Mucker for four lovely Indian
summer days last weekend. I got the start of a book out of it.
I'll send poems corrected. One or two are badly mixed up. L.
Robinson died. He hated my guts. G. Fay's Theatre book
loudly leaves you out. The man you steal from — you know.
It's only published in Dublin. Annie and Mary have made a
job of the place. It would have fallen if they hadn't come.
Eager to know about you. I pointed out that the purpose of
civilized folk was to have no job. Jobbery is false value. Pat
O'Connor leaves, I gather, on 3rd November. (Curator,
Municipal Gallery, Dublin). He is right to go. Rotten job in*

arse hole of the world. And come to think of it, what a rotten job. I wouldn't dream of taking it now. (He had once applied for the job — in January 1955).

* * *

19 Raglan Road, Dublin, 27th November 1958 I am just better of a bad cold. Working away for Farmer's Journal. That rascal Alan Ginsberg has made news with the Beat Generation. There is a great future for those Beat writers. You have only to roar and use bad language. I am genuinely thinking of having a go.

* * *

19 Raglan Road, Dublin, 8th January 1959 This is a terrible ignorant country in which no sensitive person can survive. Hence no poetry. But you knew that. Ran into Frank O'Connor. Affable and silly. The defect of Ireland is a weakness of character very common. If you are anybody, frustrated fellows roar at you. They cannot stand alone.

* * *

19 Raglan Road, Dublin, 21st January 1959 You make a mistake in putting your book forward as scholarship — it is mighty entertaining. I'm writing about it in the Farmer's Journal. What was that false entry? I seem to remember that you called the Lady Bird garrigan and garrivogue. A slight defect is that you do not sufficiently hint at the larger complications. The Jewish day also begins at sundown. The word scrape in ploughing is the English word scribe. The production is lovely Paddy Pigeon (Padraic Colum) is here and giving a Yeats Memorial Lecture. Right stupid bastard and loathes me, I hear. Last week New Statesman in review of Oxford Book of Irish Verse was very friendly to me.

* * *

In the course of writing for *The Farmer's Journal* he gave details of a racket he had some knowledge of. The underworld reacts the same in every country: an attempt was made to murder him, first by drugging his drink and then throwing him into the canal at Baggot Street Bridge one frosty November night in 1958. If he failed to drown it was assumed he would die of pneumonia since he had only one lung. But he didn't drown. As he hit the water he became semi-conscious, climbed onto the bank and scaled a seven foot wall, though he was without one shoe and without his glasses. He made his way to the flat of a doctor friend (Dr. Murphy) where he was treated for exposure and put to bed.

The following week he wrote an account of the attempted murder in his column:

The Man They Couldn't Kill

I am at present, 1959, planning to write the complete story of the past twenty years of my life. The thing that I find missing in my life is action. There are not enough plots.

Now, I sometimes wonder if actions and plots are not inventions of chaps in newspaper and publishers' offices. The goings on of film stars are all made up by the press agents. Nothing is real there. But I still have sound material.

If you find yourself hated, then you will also find yourself loved. In fact people are hated because they are loved The human male resents nothing so much as another of the sex making off with the honey of love. For that a man will be murdered, as an attempt recently was made to murder me (of that more in times to come). At any rate it was action that I hadn't bargained for.

If a man is known to take the odd drink it is the oldest and most popular of methods to throw him in a river or a canal: 'He fell in' will be the verdict.

In London recently several people said that I was the most powerful man they had ever met — because I had supernatural powers on my side.

Yes, it is true that my drink was drugged and I was thrown over the bridge wall into the canal. Yet such is the nature of the subconscious mind that even when our ordinary consciousness is out we are not helpless.

So it was that everything that happened was recorded automatically as on a screen, like photographing the other side of the moon. The whole scene, and what was said and who were there: all was recorded.

I climbed out and clambered over a seven-foot wall, got to a doctor's house and safety. Later that evening one of the scoundrels peeped into the pub where I was sipping a drink. I saw his horrified face in the mirror. He had seen Banquo's ghost and ran out in terror.

The ostensible reason for this dreadful affair was something I had written about the Dublin underworld, but I believe it was basically something to do with envy — envy of the poet.

One woman on hearing this tale said to her husband, a poet, 'Why don't you get thrown in the canal?'

Well, whatever the immediate outcome, I do have one chapter full of plot and action. Why, I could sell it to one of the Sunday papers. Make sure you order your copy when my wicked, wicked life is running.

Then there was my other miraculous escape when I had the world's most popular and most deadly disease. Yet here am I on this thrilling beautiful, frosty November morning in my native place in Monaghan feeling in terrific form. The frosty sunshine glitters on the little hills.

I do not say, the devil thank the begrudgers. I merely note that there are supernatural powers and woe to him who has made them his enemy. How does a man acquire these friends? Through suffering.

The one thing I find most a-wanting in Ireland (I suppose I mean Dublin) is enthusiasm. Enthusiasm is like a fire where we can warm our minds. There is too much criticism and resentment for my liking.

In London where I have been for a couple of weeks, there are always little enclaves of enthusiastic people. They are enthusiastic for what is good and that is what enthusiasm is. It is almost impossible to be enthusiastic for what is bad. Badness is mean and cold.

I forgot to mention that earlier in my life I had a very bad dose of Typhoid — which I overed. I believe you can only die when you have done whatever you came into the world to do. If you have something to do, you will not turn your back to the wall and die.

But we need enthusiasm. For the sake not merely of our mental but also our physical health. It doesn't much matter what we are enthusiastic about, whether it be pig-fattening or the philosophy of Plato. It is always a good sign.

It is difficult to write about the compensatory side of a life of suffering and hardship, that world of intense happiness and love. It has to be looked at sideways.

That chapter will be titled, 'The Women in My Life'.

How did he survive that fall into the Canal with a drop of fifteen feet? What was the supernatural force he spoke of? He told no one but myself and then only in pieces and with hints, fearful of stepping on the sacred Otherworld with clayey feet. But he let me know just the same and — in the face of the coarse laughter of an unbelieving world — I can say that his father came to him and bore him up safely from the waters of the Canal. Laugh away, friend. That is what he told me and that is what I believe.

Patrick made friends with his would-be murderer and even forced me to shake his hand. When some time later a child with some defect was born to this same fellow, he asked Patrick to come and lay his hands on the child, fearing the defect was the result of his sin. Patrick gladly consented. I have no knowlege of the aftermath.

322

Chapter Twenty-three

O Child of Laughter, I will go
The meadow ways with you

Patrick had not got a 'cause' in the vulgar sense of the word. What he had was a point of view — seeing the world from the upper slopes of Parnassus. Whenever he got a chance he would re-assert this point of view, or as he called it, his statement. It was always the same: that poetry is not entertainment but a profound and holy faith, the equivalent of prayer. This poetic statement did not go down very well with the public but Patrick never gave up stating it. He thumped for it, not earnestly but sincerely, even comically. The pursuit of anything too earnestly, he often said, even of God's truth, is an error, a sign of weakness, unsureness, the headlong hurried way to failure. To demand affection is to drive it away.

To an extent he had given up on his own generation. He was speaking in the belief that a future generation, free of the lies and shibboleths that surrounded himself, would hear and understand — in fact placing his faith in readers of this book who can view him stripped bare without the penumbra of lies.

Here he is speaking in 1957:

The Poetic Spirit

It is an embarrassing thing to be put in the role of a prophet. Prophecy does not consist in forecasting events, but in faith, and of being able to sit at the heart of that faith and explore its infinities. Prophecy is personality: it is a man giving the essence of himself. A prophet lying at the heart of the emotion burns himself up, and he comes out of the orgy in a state of shame and collapse.

That is why he needs the protecting love of devoted disciples, otherwise an audience. He needs around him a group which has hitherto prevented the development of a poetic passion in Ireland. But today such a group is beginning to appear. The people who rely on the ingredients of nationalistic local colour are fighting a rearguard action. But today in 1957 large numbers — which is to say about two percent of the population — know only too well that the spiritual adrenalin which the poet produces is not to be found within nationalistic formulae.

The audience is evidence of morality. The audience knows when its poet has arrived and is willing collectively and individually, to submit. The audience is Blake's cut worm.

The poet's arrogance and authority are hated by vain fools who will not submit to the will of God and be themselves. As a result you have counter-poetic movements. Class hatreds set up little vulgar gods. The mean and vain cannot reach the poet's unapproachable soul.

The poet's soul seems so intimate, so immediate, so easy to approach, but around is an invisible protecting area. And malicious envious man seeing this rare thing unprotected dashes towards it and, when repulsed is astonished and angry with hate in his heart. The soul is hurt but it remains intact, poised in all its Parnassian authority.

The ordinary non-poetic man has a high degree of insultability because he has no central security. The poetic man can be wounded but not easily insulted.

Peter Kavanagh, 1977 [Hans Nemuth].

The poet's secret which is not a secret but a form of high courage is that he in a strange way doesn't care. The poet is not concerned with the effect he is making; he forgets himself.

The immoral man will not accept. The poet teaches man worried about his position and his validity to cease to worry and then he will have a valid position.

Parnassus is a point of view. In the presence of the Parnassian authority we are provincials nowhere.

There is no hatred equal to that aroused by a man with the Parnassian faith. The malicious and envious rally around their god and when that false god of his nature disintegrates they create another. This is the counter poetic movement which has always been strong in Dublin. Those who set up false gods do not love them. No man ever loves a false god. The object in rallying around the false god is to wound the true God. The malicious are always looking for a 'poor man's poet'.

Malice is only another name for mediocrity. No man needs to be a mediocrity if he accepts himself as God made him. God only makes geniuses. But many men do not like God's work. This is another of the things the poet teaches: that every man has a purpose in life if he would submit and serve it, that he can sit with his feet to the fire of an eternal passion, a valid moral entity.

One of the principal reasons why the human male will not accept the small but unique genius that God has made, is vanity as regards woman. A woman who has not been corrupted by ideas of actors and fiddlers and painters has the ability of the poet to see only the cowardly little self hiding behind the mask of a giant, and the man is in a worse state than ever.

Insincerity is boring. Masks are boring. We all seek the simple reality of a man. The poet — and I mean the poet in the widest sense — is non-boring because he is himself; he is volatile, immediate and full of gaiety.

326

To be a poet in Ireland and not have several books of poetry published is, as Patrick remarked, to be a soldier without a gun. Not since 1947 when *A Soul For Sale* appeared had he a book published, if you except the hand-printed limited edition, *Recent Poems*, published by me. People he associated with were constantly remarking to him: *You haven't published anything lately*, while at the same time he was writing away prolifically. This could become very irritating; it reduced the public's confidence in him and lowered his credit rating — very serious for a man like Patrick who lived so close to the edge.

The problem was that no publisher would touch him and, as was seen in his letters, Macmillans turned him down permanently. They saw no future in him as a money-maker or as prestige. Publishers do not publish poetry for money: they publish it generally to conceal the fact that they are making a fortune selling popular vulgarity. The head of the firm is a businessman and sees literature only as a commodity. He has advisers and when he sees the need, say for a book of poetry, he calls one of these fellows up and places his order. Nor does the adviser on such matters himself know much about poetry —usually he makes it his business to know about poets and it is on this personal basis that a book of verse is ultimately published. In 1959 Patrick was unknown in England. His nineteen poems published in *Nimbus* in 1956 made a ripple only but it did make him known to David Wright, editor of the magazine.

In a letter to me (January 1979) David Wright recalls meeting Patrick for the first time:

. . . . I forget the year but not the place where I first set eyes on Kavanagh. Probably the year was 1952; certainly the place, the very small trianglar public bar of the Duke of Wellington at the corner of Old Compton and Wardour Street, at that time and for no particular reason the Soho rendezvous, George Barker's querencia, where you'd see MacBryde and Colquhoun, David Archer, Jimmy Burns

327

Singer, John Heath-Stubbs and the rest of them. It was there one winter evening, Kavanagh found his way. A dense mob in that small bar; but overborne, like an erratic boulder breaking the smooth of a moorland, by a looming figure, horn-spectacled under a farmer's fairweather hat, arms crossed, palm-clasped elbows — 'Here's Kavanagh', George Barker said.

This must have been one of his earliest post-war forays from Dublin to London.

It was some time after this meeting that I became involved, through Tristram Hull, whom I also met in the same public bar, with a magazine called Nimbus. It was Tristram's magazine, backed by a rich man called John Trafford who also owned the Trafford Gallery. Nimbus was run on a shoestring: so far as I recall, the backer would pay its printer's bill (which was considerable) while the moneys received from sales (which were not considerable) went to pay contributors. As time went the magazine prospered — or more likely, the backer decided it was worth a larger stipend — and Tristram was able to rent a sixth-floor garret off St. Martin's Lane for an office, and employ me as co-editor at a salary of £1 a week. We published poets like Hugh Mac Diarmid, Stevie Smith, W. S. Graham, Geoffrey Hill, Dannie Abse, and George Mackay Brown; not a fashionable crowd then, for it was the era of consolidation, conversational tone, and what was rudely known as The Movement.

One day in the spring of 1956 I was in bed with flu when the afternoon post brought a thick brown paper parcel. Inside was a bound book of carbon typescript poems, with no name on the cover and no letter from the sender. I began reading with what reviewers call mounting excitement. Although I'd never seen them before, whose poems they were became clear after the first two or three: Shancoduff, Kerr's Ass, Lines Written on a Canal Bank, Intimate Parnassus — all the poems in fact that were later to appear in Come

328

Dance With Kitty Stobling, the magnificent late harvest that
Kavanagh began to garner after 1954. Next day came a note
from Patrick Swift to say he had dispatched the collection of
Kavanagh's new verse to my address.

For the editor of a literary magazine it was treasure-trove.
Nimbus published nineteen of the poems in its next number.
Yet as I learned after his death, at the time Kavanagh was so
neglected and overlooked that he thought himself lucky to
find an English magazine to publish them. Au contraire,
Tristram and I thought ourselves lucky to have Kavanagh to
publish. . . .

Most of my recollections of Kavanagh have to do with
pubs. After all, they were our offices and drawing rooms.
When he came to London he sometimes stayed with the
Swifts in their basement flat at Westborne Terrace; and then
I would either see Kavanagh a prone silhouette stretched out
on a camp-bed in their kitchen, or else upright in the Archery
Bar, a quarter bottle of whiskey in his raincoat pocket, for
the time had come when beer or Guinness no longer worked
for him.

Three years later (1959) he sent David Wright his newest
collection including all the later poems that had been published
by me in *Recent Poems*. Wright who by now was announcing
to everyone who would listen that Patrick was not just an Irish
poet but was *the* poet, passed this newest collection on to
Thomas Blackburn, reader for Longmans. Blackburn, himself a
writer of verse, wrote immediately to Patrick saying he liked a
number of the pieces and was recommending thirty or forty of
them for publication by Longmans.

Thirty or forty! Less than a third of what he had submitted.
To make matters worse, those selected were nearly all thirty-
year old poems from his farming days — as Patrick explained it,
a real Englishman's selection. Even *The Prelude* and most of
the Canal poems were excluded. To cap it all, they wanted to

name the book *Shancoduff!* This would make it worse than no publication. Patrick wrote as politely as he could to Longmans:

> *Publication of a book of verse can give little pleasure if the poems published are not the author's choice generally. The essence of poetry is honesty and to publish thirty-year old poems as if they represented my present mood would be the opposite of honest.*

The correspondence dragged from March 1959 without any formal contract being submitted. Patrick had no leverage. Then on 22nd June the situation changed:

> *NEWS FLASH: I am to become one of the three judges in Guinness Poetry Award July 1959-July 1960. Honorarium 150 guineas and full expenses for about five trips to London. Keep this quiet for a while as it is partly to be a secret who the judges are. I am in Inniskeen for a holiday and have left Raglan Road, for the present anyway.* *

This appointment gave him some slight influence in the poetry field. At least he had a vote. Furthermore, when he next visited London it would be at Guinness's expense, with the right to stop at Brown's fashionable hotel.

The contract now was not long in coming and Longmans dropped their demand that the country poems predominate. Patrick, they said, could make his own selection, but not forty-five — only thirty-five poems to be included. Patrick took this half loaf. He handed them my publication *Recent Poems* and added a few more to make up the thirty-five. I still have the copy used in the typesetting. He also had his way with the title, an outrageous one: *Come Dance With Kitty Stobling*.

The book was the choice of the Poetry Society and was widely reviewed. Here is a review by Michael MacLiammóir from *The Sunday Times*, 24th July, 1960:

* According to the rules, one of the judges had to be a resident Irishman. The other judges were Stephen Spender and John Press.

When some Dubliner, with more malice than wit, nicknamed Patrick The Ploughboy About Town, it was generally accepted that the rustic aspect of the poet — those pendulous shaggy clothes, those lean arms interlocked athwart the chest, that battered hat crammed over the back of the skull, those porter-black locks of hair, that husky despairing voice, those lingering vowels — was all as deliberate an adoption as Baudelaire's green hair or Gérard de Nerval's chain-led lobster or Sarah Bernhardt's coffin, and that the town about which he so ominously loomed and boomed represented the brass tacks, so to speak, down to which he was getting.

The reverse of this, of course, is the case: the Ploughboy in Kavanagh is the reality, and the Town, and all it stands for, is the trap into which he would willingly let himself be caught if only he could find his way in. This, to me, is manifest in his new book, Come Dance With Kitty Stobling, and even when he (quite correctly) rhymes Canal with Banal one feels he is toying with images and ideas that have but little part in his true life and that if he could only live up to the instinctive wisdom of his

> *The only true teaching*
> *Subsists in watching*
> *Things moving or just colour*
> *Without comment from the scholar . . . .*

we would have a more consistent and complete picture of his nature.

To me he is a poet, not a philosopher, or a sage, and that is why I am left cold by his indignation or his constructive suggestions about how life should be understood, for example by his:

> *We want no secular*
> *Wisdom plotted together*
> *By concerned fools . . . .*

331

or by his:

> *. . . . Problem that confronts me here*
> *Is to be eloquent and yet sincere,*
> *Let myself rip and not go phoney*
> *In an inflated testimony . . . .*

Here, indeed, he seems to have almost succeeded in finding the snapping trap-door that fascinates the foolish moth. Yet I am conquered completely by the mood in which he cries:

> *I had been looking at*
> *Fields, gates, lakes, all that*
> *Was part and parcel of*
> *The wild breast of love.*
> *In other fellows wives*
> *I lived as many lives . . . .*

and by the splendour of his whispered talk with his mother:

> *O you are not lying in the wet clay*
> *For it is harvest evening now and we*
> *Are piling up the ricks against the moonlight*
> *And you smile up at us — eternally.*

There are many moments of an equal simplicity and passion, and I am at once intrigued and baffled by the man who, having given us such things, can waste his time by peering with such astounded bewilderment, into the Dublin pubs with their Paddiads and their Chestertonian Paddy Frogs, and the whole pretentious bag of their half-mastered tricks; he who ought to be out on the hillside with Ariel instead of snarling in a snug with a bunch of suburban Calibans.

It is, of course, an interesting problem, this of the countryman brought face-to-face with a world of literary-minded townies, towards whom, one suspects, he experiences an emotion half-envious, half-scornful — does he not recognise 'the devil Mediocrity' sitting among them? But somehow one regrets the risk of contagion and prefers, I think, to remember him in those moods, not of indignation against what he hates, but of delight in what he loves. One exception to this rule, it may be, is the important 'Auditors In' where the poet combines most subtly the wheels of passion and thought, and of praise and scorn.

At his worst, as in the Paddiad, he is a cautionary rhymester of the Belloc school — though without Belloc's accomplished humour — with a strong leaning to the wooden rhythms of the English translation of Struwwelpeter (but with Struwwelpeter the subject matter is superbly matched with the treatment).

At his best, as in the poem that gives the book its title and where all is deeply felt, there is a dreamlike quality, wild and gentle, alternately groping and flying, that is so close in spirit to the essence of Chagall that it would have been a miracle, or mayber a disaster, if Mr. Kavanagh had ever met that extraordinary painter.

The worst of him and the best: and the worst, as I think, is when he appears as a combatant in the sphere of thought — see how his Miss Universe, in the poem to which she lends her regrettable name, ensnares his feet and his tongue — at his best as a rhymer whose true life has its being not in his brain but in his sharp and delicate perception.

* * *

9 Westbourne Tce., London, 12 December 1959 Happy Christmas. I have more or less left Dublin for good as a permanent domicile. This is Saturday and I left Monday. Am well. Meeting of Guinness Poetry cod Wednesday next. Spent last week in Inniskeen. Put years on you. Decent but awful. Poems, some dated, from Longmans in the spring and maybe a prose book. Will let you know. Did you see new magazine X and Non Plus?

* * *

Inniskeen, Ireland, 27th January 1960
I read it all in London. Exciting, but costly to lose the books.
I suppose you saw the Daily Telegraph etc.*

I have been in poor shape lately — very tired but not losing weight. Gaining it in fact. I am here in Mucker for a few days. I had business. You said you might be coming.

I have all sorts of literary jobs, Encounter, the B.B.C. and the new magazine X. I am taking vitamin pills. I hope you are well. I have just written to the Editor of Independent and Irish Times objecting to giving your age as 53.

* * *

Inniskeen, Ireland, 30th January 1960
When I last wrote I was still in poor shape. Good as ever. Too much whiskey. Inniskeen is O.K. for health of body but awful otherwise. Socially plain hell. I just cannot communicate this to Annie. I talk to all but no communication.

I am at home in London. I have a contract to do 15,000 word job for Encounter and also B.B.C. Ireland is barbaric and very malicious, no place moreso than hereabouts. The X Magazine didn't arrive in New York yet it seems. Gotham Book Mart sold copies of Non Plus.

* * *

Parson's Bookshop,** Dublin, 28th April 1960
Great Hunger being done on 3rd Programme on 13 May. I do a short introduction — fifty minutes the lot. Poems are May choice of Poetry Book Society — 1,000 copies fifty pounds. Am in good form now but had a bad winter.

---

* The publication by me in New York of The John Quinn Letters. The New York Public Library sued claiming copyright infringement. The case continued for years with indecisive results.

**Parson's Bookshop at Baggot Street Bridge and on the right bank of the Grand Canal is close to 62 Pembroke Road where Patrick lived. He had to pass there on his way into town. He made it his rendezvous, his convenience address, his library of current books and, occasionally, a place to shave. It is run by Mae O'Flaherty who still speaks with pleasure of Patrick's visits.

1962: Self-Portrait. [Photo courtesy RTE Guide].

*I have just finished marking 450 poems for Guinness —
the third batch. Mary is in England I think. Was down for
one day to collect books. Terrible place Dublin. No one to
talk to.*

* * *

9 Westbourne Tce., London, 5th July 1960
I am again a Judge of the Guinness Award for a further
year. Good job. Have been in London for three weeks. My
book has been out a couple of weeks but my author's copies
went to Dublin as I came to London. Otherwise I'd have sent
you a copy. Don't want to buy one. Am likely to get good
reviews. Observer is doing it about next Sunday. They are
also doing long interview with four poets. I am the first. A
bowsie American to be sure reviewed me in this week's New
Statesman, makes silly remarks but he did say nice things
that seven or eight of the poems would be remembered. I am
going to do reviewing for the Observer. Will send books soon.*

* * *

Inniskeen 24th August 1969
*Have been in London promoting my book which is in second
printing soon. Got good press. I hope your book did well. I
heard you had an ad in TLS. (One of my Hand Press
books).*
   *The big problem in autobiography is to evoke or create a
mood which gives the theme cohesion and character.
Very difficult. I don't think this one is your story. You have a
personality, sharp, observant, comic — like for instance
remembering Jimmy Hamill getting ball and with head down
running into clump of players etc. You should have another
go. This is written on the surface of the shibboleth — 'Irish'
etc. Lies. Green Fool at its worst. Have been in Inniskeen for
a few days. Am well. Hope you are.*

---

* The other judges were William Plomer and Cecil Day Lewis.

1 Wilton Place, Dublin, 6 October 1960
I have really nothing to say. If one stops writing letters for a while they seem unnecessary. Must go down to Mucker soon. Have been in London all summer promoting my book. Sold out 1st edition; reprinting. I have to be in London again soon as I am judging for the Guinness Poetry Award — a second term.

*   *   *

47 Gibson Square, London 29th November 1960
A line at Christmas. I am fairly well in body though not so hot in brain sector. Still, I did manage to write a poem for the Observer which I enclose. Gay wee thing, I think. I have stayed over in London for next Guinness Poetry Award meeting which is this day week, 6 December. Nice place this.
My poems are in the third impression but that needn't deceive you — impression is 500 or 750. They sent a few to America and they may be out there now. I got a wonderful press for them. Up to the present about 2,000 have sold. Good for poetry. America has no standard except bad ones. In literature I mean. They all go for the artificial verbalism of Richard Wilbur and such clan. Based on the old new criticism of F. R. Leavis. A fellow called Tomlinson failed to get a publisher in England. In America he was hailed, I hear. There are a few of those American critics getting published here and it is tiresome.
Interesting you say I go false in Mucker poems. They are lies. I never belonged there. Terrible, ignorant, vulgar place Inniskeen. You were largely protected by your learning, the schoolmaster. I shall hardly ever go there again except for a day or so.

*   *   *

1 Wilton Place, Dublin, 3rd April 1961
I should have written long ago but I am allergic to letters. I have your letter before me a bit torn. You are wrong about Phyllis McGinley. She is much better than e.e.cummings and

in fact you don't seem to be in touch with the vastness of American literary criticism. Miss McGinley does not get all the publicity, Robert Lowell, W. D. Snodgrass, etc., etc.

I have made a ballet* which will be done in the Olympia Theatre, Dublin, the first week in June. Scene is a casino and the players are part of the roulette wheel. Today is Easter Sunday. 1 Wilton Place will always get me though I live not there.

Had a mind to visit Inniskeen but doubtful. Nothing in London either, only contacts.

Poems in third printing.

Gave eight lectures at U.C.D. this spring. Mostly Americans came. New Statesman wanted me to review P. Colum's poems about Ireland but was too tired at the time to care. It wasn't reviewed, I think, at all. Colum is here I think. Studies for last Autumn had two articles on me; did you see them?

Will write if I think of anything; if I don't post this at once I never will.

* * *

47 Gibson Square, London, 18 August 1961
So long since I wrote that I hardly know your address. I am here in London and it is unlikely that I shall return permanently to Ireland. I have been in poor shape for some time in Dublin, probably psychosomatic. I am in great form today for the first time, hence my writing. I have nothing to say as you know.

Tarry Flynn is coming out in paperback from an outfit called Four Square Books. Gave me 150 pounds down and more to come I hope. I also did a recording of my stuff for which I got a century down. All within the last two weeks. I also found that there was twenty-five nicker waiting for me

---

* Produced at The Abbey Theatre, June 1st. Based on a poem, The Gambler! (See *Complete Poems,*' p. 302 ff.).

for an article I wrote several years ago on Liberal Education. Not too good. It appears in the next issue of X. Ostensibly I am here for the Guinness Poetry Award but I'll stay on I'm sure. I got another century for my ballet which was enthusiastically received. We don't know who is making the record of me — the man who paid me is an agent who'll try to flog it where he can. Ireland is bad news for a sensitive man or one prone to loneliness.

I would like you if you can get that person to give the name of the storeroom man in Dublin where her stuff is packed along with the Ms. of mine, I could sell this easily. Of course she's a real —————. I asked her when I was over and she was trying to use her knowledge as power.

Is is a beautiful day today as I look out on Gibson Square. This is the Islington of Dickens and Co. Lovely small squares. I hope you and all your friends are well. I was in Inniskeen for a few days but it is a terrible place. And a single copy of my poems never sold within a twenty mile radius of Inniskeen.

Tarry Flynn is terribly funny and true in most places. No one but me could have done it, and only when I did. Was at the Oval yesterday seeing a cricket match between the Australians and England and it did me a lot of good. Supreme health is the essence of genius. I could make money.

Sorry now I gave the Ms. to the National Library; could get large sums. The Guinness Award, the final on Monday and Tuesday next. Give my regards to Broadway. What new project have you on the press? The finalizing of your case* was reported in many papers this side. Well that's the way with some and more with others. The sun is shining. All the best as per usual. Bought a 'new' jacket for a pound.

* * *

---

* *The John Quinn Letters*

c/o Parson's Bookshop, Dublin, 29th December 1961
Received Ms.* but haven't studied it yet. Funny in spots. Parts missing were published in The Bell. You have them in those prose pieces. Nothing strange since I arrived from London.

I wasn't feeling too well as you noted, not fit for comic writing, so I entered Baggot St. Hospital yesterday. Nothing serious. I am being given an appetite and in general feeling secure after a lot of insecurity. I have written this in case you hear and think I was on my last. At present I am sitting up in bed, drinking bottles of stout. If I happen to be here more than a week don't change from Parson's who will forward all mail. Best love.

PATRICK

* * *

c/o Parson's Bookshop, Dublin, 1 January 1962
Dear Peter,

Happy New Year. I learn there is nothing organically wrong with me — just run-down through years of undereating. I have now got a terrific appetite. Am off Whiskey of course. Keith Shaw is here, you may know. I was in pretty bad shape when I came in and of course couldn't write.

We've had a white and frosty New Year. New Irish Telly started last night. Frank O'Connor has settled in Dublin 'for good', and it seems he is trying to revive the 'Ireland' myth. I haven't been in good enough form to take a roaring laugh at him in The Irish Times. But a lecture of mine printed in last X magazine is pretty near to it. I'll be here at least another week. All the best.

PATRICK

P.S.: You can tell by this letter I'm getting into pretty good form.

* * *

* Old novel Ms.

340

c/o Parson's Bookshop, Dublin, 5th January 1962
Dear Peter,

Still attending hospital. Just writing to say complaint is minor — gastritis which was caused by my drinking too much whiskey and eating too little. It is inflammation of the stomach. I am better now and better than I have been for ten years. I have to continue for a couple of more weeks with injections to keep the appetite going. News that there was nothing really wrong with me must have caused a shock. After this I expect to write as many books as Hugh Kenner (The American critic).

Chapter Twenty-four

*He dabbles in something and does
Not realise that it is his life*

The Irish Television authorities, impressed by the reviews coming out of England, decided it would be best if they included Patrick in some programme. There was a series running on Irish Television in 1962 called *Self Portrait*; Patrick was invited to take part in this series, the official letter carefully adding the proviso — if his script were *acceptable*, and *with amendments*. They would pay him twenty-five pounds on receipt of the *acceptable* script and fifty additional pounds on completion of the performance.

I happened to be back in Inniskeen at the time and he discussed the offer with me. He very much wanted to do the programme — to use it as a sort of literary Last Will and Testament. He felt he had not long to live. Some months earlier he had been in Baggot Street Hospital with pneumonia and at the time I was present he had severe gastritis along with his other ailments. The ill-mannered invitation insulted him and he wondered what he should do in these circumstances. This was part of the same dreary attitude he experienced in dealing with Longmans. And what did he get from being nice to them? Not very much. My advice to him was that he should assert his integrity and if that were not good enough it would be pointless to proceed. He took my advice and wrote as follows to R.T.E.:

Dear Mr. White,

I have now perused your letter about the Self Portrait. Your letter suggests that my script would have to be submitted to you for your approval. If this means matters technical, legal, etc., it is O.K., but concerning the matter and manner of my stuff, absolutely intolerable. There can be no censorship. I must have absolute freedom. I submit my stuff to no man. There can be no such thing as acceptable Ms. or amendments.

The usual attitude of people who ask me to write for them is one of correct humility: Give us something. I wouldn't be able to do a script unless I was completely free. I am responsible to myself for such a performance. Let me know if you accept my conditions.

R.T.E. gave him assurances and he went ahead with the script and sent it along. A week later he was invited to go to Dublin for a taping. He went full of misgivings. What should he do if they had altered his script? Just come home, I told him. He was back next day delighted with himself. Not only had they allowed it to go unedited they even permitted it to run five minutes overtime. Furthermore they had put the whole talk on a Teleprompter — a new machine at this time. He had made a good showing, he told me. No problem — he had only to read it off the machine!

The programme was to be aired on October 30th. Patrick went to Dublin to be on the spot to receive congratulations from those who saw him as a celebrity and in general to catch the moment of emotion in Dublin where he had endured such infamy. I stayed in Inniskeen to report on the reaction from the home front. I watched on a neighbour's television. He put on one of his greatest performances. Everyone was impressed, knocked over, that someone they regarded as such a clown had transformed himself into a great speaker, an orator. He made no slips and no one knew that he was reading it off the teleprompter.

He came back to Inniskeen the next day. I met him in Dundalk and was home on the bus with him to Inniskeen. As we got off the bus at the Mucker Lane and were standing on the roadway the bus driver leaned out and remarked: *Good man, Paddy! You didn't let us down!* We did not reply but looked at each other fascinated by the remark. Patrick was more startled than amazed, being aware of the attitude of the people towards him. In *The National Observer*, January 1960, he had written:

> *In my native district around Dundalk where I spent a lot of this summer the whole pleasure of the scenery and weather was spoiled for me by the positive malice towards me as a poet — that is to say, as a man who is not one of them and who can drink large whiskeys . . . . Even when you ignore them they publicly shout malicious remarks. I mean they did that to me. There is no protection in Ireland anywhere for anybody with a poetic talent. . . .*

Self Portrait was the high point of Patrick's career. First, he had asserted himself as a poet with the authorities and won; second, he had issued his statement to the public both in what he said and in his manner of saying it. Only the most obtuse could now say that he was a vulgar eccentric fellow. From now on nothing mattered very much, debts, publication or even his health. He would enjoy what days remained to him.

Here follow extracts from *Self Portrait*. The image at the end, being able to play a true note on a slack string, for which I have seen him occasionally criticised, was in fact part of my contribution to the talk.

> *I dislike talking about myself in a direct way. The self is only interesting as an illustration. For some reason, whenever we*

344

1965: Patrick Kavanagh in New York, holding his niece.

talk about our personal lives they turn out to be both irrelevant and untrue — even when the facts are right, the mood is wrong. . . .

The quality that most simple people fear — and by simple people I mean terrified, ignorant people — is the comic spirit, for the comic spirit is the ultimate sophistication which they do not understand and therefore fear.

When, under the evil aegis of the so-called Irish Literary Movement, I wrote a dreadful stage-Irish, so-called autobiography called The Green Fool, the common people of this country gobbled up this stage-Irish lie. When, years later, I wrote Tarry Flynn which I am humble enough to claim is not only the best but the only authentic account of life as it was lived in Ireland this century (a man shouldn't be afraid to tell the truth even when it is in favour of himself), the principal people who enjoyed this novel were literary sophisticates; its uproarious comedy was too much for the uneducated reader.

I am not trying to boost my wares. I am merely trying to illustrate a position. . . .

My childhood experience was the usual barbaric life of the Irish country poor. I have never seen poverty properly analysed. Poverty is a mental condition. You hear of men and women who have chosen poverty, but you cannot choose poverty. Poverty has nothing to do with eating your fill today; it is anxiety about what's going to happen next week. The cliché poverty that you get in the working-class novel or play is a formula.

My father, being a shoemaker, was probably less poor than the small farmer classes. What was called the 'dropping shilling' kept coming in. But as for the scradíns* of farmers with their watery little hills that would physic a snipe, I don't know where they got any money. But the real poverty was the lack of enlightenment to get out and get under the moon.

I am afraid this fog of unknowing affected me dreadfully.

* Sic.

346

But, as I have suggested earlier, all this is of little importance.

Round about the late nineteen-thirties, a certain prosperity came through and foolishly enough that was the time I chose to leave my native lands. I had no messianic impulse to leave. I was happy. I went against my will. A lot of our actions are like that. We miss the big emotional gesture and drift away. Is it possible to achieve our potential grand passion? I believe so. Perhaps that has been my weakness.

I came to Dublin in nineteen-thirtynine. It was the worst mistake of my life. The Hitler war had started. I had my comfortable little holding of watery hills beside the Border. What was to bate it for a life? And yet I wasted what could have been my four glorious years, begging and scrambling around the streets of malignant Dublin. I could have done my smuggling stint. I could never see my own interest. I could never see love on bended knees begging me to come. I was always in the fog.

When I came to Dublin the Irish Literary affair was still booming. It was the notion that Dublin was a literary metropolis and Ireland, as invented and patented by Yeats, Lady Gregory and Synge, a spiritual entity. It was full of writers and poets and I am afraid I thought their work had the Irish quality. . . .

No, part of my poverty-stricken upbringing was my belief in respectability — a steady job, decency. The bohemian rascals living it up in basements and in mountain hideouts horrified me. . . .

When I think of the indignities I endured in the cause of respectability I can kick myself. And me with health and strength to dig ditches, or to leap them anyway with a sack of white flour on me back. The Monaghan-Armagh-Louth border was not a severe test for a true stayer carrying top weight. I can kick myself for all the people I didn't kick then. Sometimes, when walking along a Dublin street, I might well *be noticed making wild, vicious kicks at emptiness and scringing my teeth at the same time. . . .*

A poet is never one of the people. He is detached, remote, and the life of small-time dances and talk about football would not be for him. He might take part but could not belong.

A poet has to have an audience — half a dozen or so. Landor, who said he esteemed ten a sufficient audience, was very optimistic. I know about half a dozen and these are mainly London-based. It may be possible to live in total isolation but I don't understand how. The audience is as important as the poet. There is no audience in Ireland, though I have managed to build up out of my need a little audience for myself.

The real problem is the scarcity of a right audience which draws out of a poet what is best in him. . . .

. . . I am wandering around Dublin when I run into a poetry lover.

'How are you getting on at all?' says he with much pity.

The instinct to do a day's good deed has always been a weakness with me, so I reply:

'Terrible'.

'Poor fella'.

'Sure what can I do?'

'And you're not writing any poetry these times. I never see anything by you in The Irish Times. The flash is gone. I say, the flash is gone.'

'I suppose so'.

'A terrible scandal that the Government doesn't do something for our Irish poets. There's forty or fifty major poets in this country today and if I had me way they'd all have a civil list pension. Is the health all right again?'

I cough hard and send him away happy.

I fear that the mood I have been evoking may give the impression that what happened to me is important and that I am important. Nobody is important. Nobody is major. We get to our destiny in the end. I am not in the least bitter over all this. In fact I am always in danger of bursting out laughing.

I merely state the facts. Of course I do not blame some of these people. I had been assailing the myth of Ireland by which they were managing to beat the artistic rap. I had seen and shewn that this Ireland thing was an undignified business — the trade of enemies and failures. . . . .

Among the other things I missed, one I regret was refusing the offer of Reuters to go in as a reporter with the Second Front.

Once again and as always, I was showing my cautious, respectable mentality. Instead of letting it rip. This has been a great defect in my nature.

Another great experience I had was my law case, hereinafter to be known as The Trial or Trial and Error, mostly error. Curious thing is that an event so seemingly large at the time disappears in the perspective of a few years. What seems of public importance is never of any importance. Stupid poets and artists think that by taking subjects of public importance it will help their work to survive. There is nothing as dead and damned as an important thing. The things that really matter are casual, insignificant little things, things you would be ashamed to talk of publicly. You are ashamed and then after years someone blabs and you find that you are in the secret majority. Such is fame.

Of my early Dublin experiences I have little of value to offer.

In those days in Dublin the big thing besides being Irish was peasant quality. They were all trying to be peasants. They had been at it for years but I hadn't heard. And I was installed as the authentic peasant, and what an idea that was among rascals pretending to have an interest in poetry. Although the literal idea of the peasant is of a farm labouring person, in fact a peasant is all that mass of mankind which lives below a certain level of consciousness.

They live in the dark cave of the unconscious and they scream when they see the light. They take offence easily, their degree of insultability is very great. . . .

In the beginning of my versing career I had hit on the no-caring jag but there was nobody to tell me that I was on the right track:

> *My black hills have never seen the sun rising*
> *Eternally they look north to Armagh.*

There are two kinds of simplicity, the simplicity of going away and the simplicity of return. The last is the ultimate in sophistication. In the final simplicity we don't care whether we appear foolish or not. We talk of things that earlier would embarrass. We are satisfied with being ourselves, however small. So it was that on the banks of the Grand Canal between Baggot and Leeson Street Bridges in the warm summer of 1955, I lay and watched the green waters of the canal. I had just come out of hospital. I wrote:

> *Leafy-with-love banks and the green waters of the canal*
> *Pouring redemption for me, that I do*
> *The will of God, wallow in the habitual, the banal*
> *Grow with nature again as before I grew.*

And so in this moment of great daring I became a poet. Except for brief moments in my very early years I had not been a poet.

The trouble is that there are so few who would know a poem from a hole in the ground.

It is possible on the other hand to recognize a poet, for the animal is recognizable. The main feature about a poet, if you ever happen to meet one — and that's a remote chance, for I can't be everywhere at the one time — the main feature is his humorosity. Any touch of boringness and you are in the wrong shop.

350

Recently a man was presented to me as being a great poet. He wrote in Irish. I expressed my doubts and the introducer said: 'How can you tell when you don't know the language?' That was a sore one, but I was able for it. I said, 'I can't bawl like a cow but I'd know a cow if I saw one'.

Shancoduff's watery hills could have done the trick, but I was too thick to take the hint. Curious this, how I had started off with the right simplicity, indifferent to crude reason and then ploughed my way through complexities and anger, hatred and ill-will towards the faults of man, and came back to where I started. For one of the very earliest things I wrote, even pre-dating Shancoduff, started this way:

> *Child do not go*
> *Into the dark places of soul*
> *For there the grey wolves whine,*
> *The lean grey wolves*

In that little thing I had become airborne and more; I had achieved weightlessness. And then I heard about having one's roots in the soil, of being a peasant. And I raged at Monaghan and the clay and all that. But Poetry has to do with the reality of the spirit, of faith and hope and sometimes even charity. It is a point of view. A poet is a theologian.

A poet is an original who inspires millions of copies. That's all education consists of — the copying of a good model.

Reverting at that to my public career, I must mention that adventure when I edited and wrote Kavanagh's Weekly in 1952.

Why do people engage in such madness?

But recently looking up the files I read something that has relevance here. On School Book Poetry I wrote — quoting Longfellow:

> *There are things of which I may not speak,*
> *How strange things happen to a man.*

351

> *He dabbles in something and does*
> *Not realize that it is his life.*

That was what I wrote then. And yet I had not yet been born, as I believe I afterwards was, though perhaps some folks may not agree. It doesn't matter. Anyhow, I did arrive at complete casualness, at being able to play a true note on a dead slack string.

Chapter Twenty-five

Handling all sorts of littleness

Patrick's newly formed philosophy of not caring was an excellent guide in aesthetic matters but those holding cheques marked *Return to Drawer* did not see it in this light. He was constantly living beyond his means and in a financial spin, borrowing money, writing post-dated cheques, signing agreements. He persuaded Hutchinsons to advance him one hundred pounds on an autobiography which he must have suspected he would not live to write. Occasionally his behaviour in these matters led to amusing situations.

In a London pub, just eight months before he died, he assigned to Barbara Rowland, for fifty pounds down payment, the film rights to *Tarry Flynn* which he already had assigned to McGibbons & Kee. That wasn't bad enough! Sitting beside him was an editor of McGibbon & Kee and he had him witness the agreement. Next morning when the editor realised what he had done he went into what might be imagined as a strong faint. Could it be that Patrick whom he thought close to his dotage had outsmarted him? The publisher denounced the agreement as invalid and called Patrick a smart-alec. The transaction was inadvertent on Patrick's part and when he heard himself being so abused he wrote to say how hurt he was. Had he been in his health he would have roared laughing.

Two or three years earlier when Patrick fell ill he had entered a Dublin hospital where he engaged the best room with a telephone service. The hospital authorities were so pleased with his patronage that they offered him the service of a psychiatrist to help him with his problems. This Patrick regarded as a most amusing suggestion but he politely declined. Some months later when he was approached on behalf of the hospital by a bill collector he remarked, *Now the hospital authorities could use the services of a psychiatrist.*

Here is a sampling of the numerous letters he received in the years 1960-1961

19 January: From Dan McNello: Your cheque for five pounds has been returned marked: 'No Account'.

15 August: From Hutchinsons Publishers: I am delighted that you are going off into the country to write your autobiography.

September: From Hutchinsons: Frankly, we'd rather pay the sum in instalments.

10 October: From the George Hotel, London: Three cheques of yours each of three pounds have been returned marked R.D. . . . If . . .

25 November: Patrick to Brian Farrell U.C.D.: I think my trouble with the Income Tax people is settled and I now can return to Ireland in the black. Perhaps you would send the cheque to me here in London.

25 November: To Dublin Bank Manager: The British Tax men have cleared me, and with a cheque from Hutchinsons I might be clear at the Bank to write more cheques.

20 February: From R. Mulderry: Get out of my flat by March 1st and pay damages for what you have done to it.

23 February: From John Morgan, Eimer Beer, Dundalk: Your cheque for three pounds has bounced and unless . . .

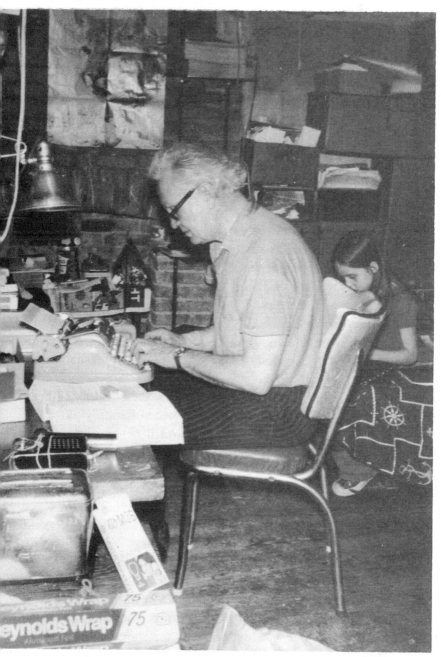

Peter Kavanagh, with Caomh, New York, 1976. [Photo, Keeling Kavanagh].

23 March: From Assoc. Rediffusion: What do you mean you are not interested in television plays? You would if I sent you some money in advance. From Peter Willis, Head of Drama.

25 March: To Rediffusion from Patrick: It is essential to get a refresher.

23 June: From M. Sweeney, George Hotel: I hold three cheques of yours for nine pounds . . . . I am a married man . .

7 July: From Hutchinsons: Dear Paddy, Any News?

21 November: From Hutchinsons: How goes the book?

29 March: From Hutchinsons: How about your autobiography?

Patrick's behaviour in certain of these circumstances could hardly be classed as strictly honourable. On the other hand he himself was being exploited by publishers, by the Income Tax people who garnished his U.C.D. sinecure, and even by his own intimate acquaintences.

He cared only about important matters and money was not one of those. He knew that death lay in ambush. Once cancer gets its grip, it is doubtful if it ever leaves. In addition to the residue of cancer, he was suffering from a series of other complaints — of the liver, the kidneys, the bladder, the heart and thrombosis of the leg. Yet as Brendan Kennelly stated in a letter, *If ever I saw a sick man with a healthy soul, it was Patrick in those last years when I had the privilege of meeting him a few times.*

A peculiarity of his character that didn't improve with age was his snobbishness. For as long as I remember him he was a snob and used to annoy his mother with this attitude. Were she to buy wallpaper he always knew the best — at ten times the price. And when once I drew his attention to the fact that his glasses were fake tortoiseshell he replaced them with the genuine article. Very fragile, they didn't last a week. In Inniskeen in the early sixties he tried to act the squire, occasionally giving someone a large handout while at the same time borrowing from me or his sisters.

When he visited New York in 1965 and we served him *Five Star* Haig & Haig he was satisfied until he had learned that there was a more expensive brand called *Pinch*. He was drinking heavily then, as much as he himself and his friends could afford. Often this amounted to a quart a day. This drinking had no apparent effect on him. I never saw him the slightest bit drunk. And in addition to the whiskey, he was taking all sorts of pills including the dangerous *Seconal*.

During the last three or four years of his life he began to display less of the outward signs of affection for me than he had shown in the past. No angry words were spoken but there was between us a sense of irritation. My sister Annie noticed it and told me she felt that Patrick had become jealous of me. I don't believe that. It is perhaps unfair to analyse the momentary resentments of a man as sick as he was. Just the same I give this explanation: I turned out to be a disappointment to him. Apart from natural affection he saw me as his life insurance. He wanted me to achieve all the things life had denied him; to be well-dressed and conservative. I myself drink very little but in 1957 when he was visiting me in New York I got somewhat tipsy on wine and he was outraged. He dreamed of my being rich, filthy rich, someone of whom he could boast and from whom perhaps borrow ten thousand dollars without an ugly murmur. My being a professor merely drawing a salary depressed him. Worse, I was making signs that I might enter the literary scene. Life could be simple if I supplied the finances while he supplied the genius.

At heart he was contemptuous of money and when I informed him that we were about to have a baby he scoffed at the notion of money. Here was real wealth, he said, the extension of my life — and his — by fifty or more years.

He liked the compliment of being given the best seat in the house — for him, the one nearest the door. He feared boredom and wanted to be able to make a quick exit. For the same reason he kept his hat and coat always beside him — an excellent strategy for him but not one designed to put his company at ease. Except in matters relating to literature he had a very weak will and was easily manipulated. On numerous occasions he publicly regretted this instability.

I mention these facts and surmises, not because I think they are important in establishing Patrick's character as a poet but rather as a gesture and an offering to the speculations of some future psychologist.

One effect of *Self Portrait* was that he was able to switch from writing for *The Irish Farmer's Journal* to doing a column for *RTV Guide*, the magazine of the Irish television and radio industry. He began this assignment in April 1963 and continued it until his death. Each week he looked forward to reading *his little piece*. He had become very tired of *The Journal* and the kind of writing its readership demanded.

After seeing his performance on television several literary scholars saw Patrick as a good subject for a colourful biography. Patrick was approached. At first he was pleased with the idea: it would add to to the general atmosphere of diversion that was becoming essential to his will to live. But he had second thoughts. What if the biographer were to write the book from the point of view of the pub-crawling, horse-betting character, the man living by his sensations, that Patrick was acting out in London? That could easily happen: there was enough evidence to justify it. Everything Patrick stood for, his personal and poetic morality were in jeopardy. He became so agitated that he even cabled me a warning to give out no information. After the dust had settled and he was in a calm mood he asked that I take on the job of writing his biography since *You are the Sacred Keeper of my Sacred Conscience* (*Lapped Furrows*, p. 250).

Immediately I set about the immense task, collecting letters, documents, photographs, that eventually was to lead to a series of books covering sixteen years and culminating in this biography. With his rearguard well protected by me Patrick threw himself once more, and with greater abandon, into the synthetic world he had invented for himself in London.

358

As has been observed, now that he was a judge of the Guinness Poetry Award he visited London more often. He began frequenting the literary pubs where publishers and the hangers-on of literature congregated. Despite his excellent credentials he was not accepted for a long while, was in fact regarded as a freak with his one lung and his hoarse voice. He was up against a public-school, *limey* mentality, a kind of hard scab difficult to get underneath. Ahead of him, stretching towards some undefined centre, each with a manuscript on his person, was a line of sycophants:

Who chant the praise of love that isn't
And bring their bastards to be christened
At phoney fonts by bogus priests
With rites mugged up by jounalists.

(*Complete Poems*, p. 275)

Eventually and without effort Patrick found himself at the head of the line and was confronted by the editors of McGibbon & Kee who by now had got the message that he was not the freak they had supposed but a poet of the first order. It was further noted that *Come Dance With Kitty Stobling* had been a success both with the critics and at the bookstalls.

What have you to say, my son? Patrick had nothing to say. How about publishing your *Collected Poems*, he was asked. Patrick replied that he was so ill and so tired that he would not be able to make such a collection. The publisher, pleasant and good-natured, guaranteed that he would have a senior editor of the firm do the editing. Patrick, well aware that good nature is the key to real villainy, was cautious — but when the publisher offered him fifty pounds in advance on royalties immediately on signing a contract, he brightened-up and agreed. The contract was signed on 11th November 1961. Patrick collected the cash and put the matter out of his mind. He was oblivious to the fact that he had not only signed away his publishing rights but also the digest rights, serial rights, translation rights, Book Club rights, broadcasting rights, film and dramatic rights — even strip-cartoon rights. No loop-hole was left.

The book, eventually published in 1964, was well received. However, not until some time after Patrick's death did the word leak out that behind his back the collecting and editing had been assigned to someone from Ireland who was utterly distasteful to Patrick. The secret was so well kept that he never suspected what was going on.

There are other matters not so easy to conceal, including a series of deals made by the publisher. The most offensive of these was the selling of fifteen-hundred sheets of *Collected Poems* to an American publisher whom Patrick also detested. I was keeping an eye on his interests in America; saw the announcement by the American publisher, and informed Patrick at once. He could scarcely believe the news, so confident had he been in the integrity of his newly-found publishing friends. He did not wish to face up to the embarrassment of admitting that he had been dealing not with friends but with businessmen — hard nosed merchants. Was this underhand dealing necessary? he asked somewhat pathetically.

It must not be supposed that because publishers are associated with literature they treat their clients with more kindness than the usual dealers in other types of commerce. But even taking this into account the discourtesy shown Patrick was exceptional. The uncovering of the motives behind this apparent abnormality I leave to some future scholar.

Shortly after I had made my revelation to Patrick of the unauthorised American edition I arrived back in Ireland (August 1964) for a holiday. I found him in a state of great agitation and frustration. His protests to the publisher had at first been met with excuses and when he protested further he was told by a staff executive to keep his views to himself, he had no say in the matter.

I may state here as a matter of information that once an author signs a contract with a publisher his copyright from then on is only theoretical: the publisher has what are called Publishing Rights.

Patrick felt that he had been taken advantage of in the contract but did not know what to do about it. Could I do anything, he asked, to defeat these people? When I told him that I held U.S. Copyright in those poems published in *Recent Poems* he began dancing with delight. *Great! Great!* he declared, *once more you have saved me.*

He made an immediate decision. He would give me Power of Attorney. If these people were able to do as much as they had done under his nose, there was no telling what else they might do. He felt he needed protection and giving me Power of Attorney would accomplish that. With that in my possession I could enjoin the American edition.

We went at once to Dublin and had an attorney draw up the necessary document; thence to the American Embassy to have it sworn-to, stamped and decorated with red tape. Here is the document:

Power of Attorney

To all to which these presents may come, Greetings.
Know all men by these presents that I PATRICK KAVANAGH of Inniskeen Dundalk, Co. Louth, in the Republic of Ireland, Poet and Author do hereby appoint DOCTOR PETER KAVANAGH of 250 East 30th St., New York 10016, in the United States of America, Publisher and Proprietor of The Peter Kavanagh Hand Press to be my Attorney and in my name and for my use and account should do the following Acts and things:

1. To commence, prosecute, carry on, maintain or otherwise engage in, in any manner whatsoever and in any court having jursidiction therefor in the United States of America, any Action whether Plenary or by way of Injunction open to process of Law, for the purpose of protecting my copy right in the United States of America in all or any of my literary works, either in prose, poetry, blank verse or of any other nature or description whatsoever and for the purpose aforesaid to claim, collect or receive damages in connection with any infringement of the copy right aforesaid or to compromise or settle any such proceeding or proceedings at any time during the course of such proceeding or proceedings.

2. To sign my name, set my seal and as my act and deed to execute seal and deliver any instrument, contract, discharge, release, or otherwise for effectuating any or all of the purposes aforesaid.

3. To receive, and sign and give receipts or discharges for any or all monies received in connection with the Prosecution of the power hereinbefore referred to and out of such monies to make such expenditure in exercise of this power as he may consider proper.

4. To stand possessed of all monies, property, securities or investments acquired by him under this power for my use.

5. To join with any other person or persons corporation or corporations in executing or completing any instrument or thing requisite to the purpose hereinbefore mentioned.

6. To pay on my behalf any claims or expenses which may arise out of the carrying out of the power herein conferred.

7. Generally to do, execute and perform all and every other act matter and thing whatsoever in any ways necessary or expedient to be done in any concerns and business in relation to the said copy right in the United States of America as fully and effectually as if I were personally present to do the same.

And I the said Patrick Kavanagh hereby agree and undertake to confirm all and whatsoever my said Attorney shall lawfully do or cause to be done by the virtue of these presents.

And I declare that this Power of Attorney is irrevocable for five years from the date hereof.

In witness whereof I have hereunto set my hand and affixed my seal this 28th day of August 1964.

Patrick, having signed this document, now felt a great sense of relief. He would leave the action to me and take the publisher at his word to keep his mouth shut.

(For those unacquainted with the procedure of filing an injunction I give here a short outline. After being presented with a wad of money, a lawyer fills in the injunction form, presents it to a judge, and immediately a temporary injunction is in effect. A week later, after a trial, if the injunction is made permanent, the opponent may decide to appeal, in which case he may demand that the petitioner post a sum of money equivalent to what he may have lost in the interval between the temporary injunction and the winning of the appeal. This can be a considerable sum and if the petitioner hasn't got it he loses out. Usually the person with the most money wins.)

When I returned to America armed with the Power of Attorney, Patrick wrote encouraging me to enjoin the pirate edition:

Inniskeen, Ireland, 3rd August 1964
McGibbon & Kee sold 1,500 sheets to Devin Adair. But it has always been my belief that a signed contract with the author is also necessary before you can publish. As I don't know the address of Devin Adair I am sending this letter on for you to address and post.

I wasn't too well or I would have prevented McGibbon & Kee from giving Garrity the sheets. But there is some underhand work going on as I have been unable to find out what was done.

There are lots of rights such as Television and Anthology ones.

What seems to have been done was that Devin Adair gave

McG. & K. 2,000 sheets of Tarry Flynn which they are publishing here and on which they gave me an advance. But no word about Adair or the Collected Poems in that contract.

After surveying the situation I came to the conclusion that a court battle was not to my taste or advantage. Furthermore, I was a bit frightened and intimidated by the extent of the power Patrick had invested in me. He had virtually handed over his soul to me. So sacred a trust had to be treated with the utmost delicacy and care. Therefore I decided not to go to court but to savage the edition privately by sending our warning notices of copyright infringement to newspapers, distributors and to bookshops. I first asked Patrick's permission and here is his reply:

> *Inniskeen, Ireland, 24th September 1964*
> *Dear Peter,*
> *You have my permission to do as you suggest but I think it a weakish idea.*
> *I am writing now to McGibbon & Kee reminding them that they are my agents for America only and as such bounded by the contract to get me an American contract, they merely get 10%. As they have acted, it is a swindle. I will be getting in touch with the Society of Authors. What about that lawyer Ernst?*

Eventually he came round to my way of thinking and agreed to the circular denouncing the pirate edition.

> *Inniskeen, Ireland, 9th October 1964*
> *You have my best wishes in any action you take though it would be best not to get too broke in the process.*
> *Of course I'm like you not interested in the 10%.*
> *I was in fact getting together a batch of unpublished poems for you. I think you might well print a selection as well as some from the collected.*

1966: Patrick Kavanagh. [Photo: *The Irish Times*].

I am in fair good shape and planning to spend the winter
in Halcyon Hotel, South Anne Street — three guineas a week.
It's awful lonely and depressing here. And the weather has
turned to winter. That's all for the present and good luck.

Patrick never mentioned a word of what was going on to the
London publisher: he kept on drinking and kept on blathering
about inconsequential things. A year later the same publisher
issued under the title *Collected Pruse* a selection from Patrick's
prose works. The word *pruse* was an old joke of his, based on
the affected pronunciation of the word *prose*. Once more the
collecting and editing was not done by himself and it turned out
to be scattered and without direction. This time, at least, he
knew who actually was doing the editing.

London had not turned out to be the haven he had hoped-for
and dreamed-of in his early years. From this time forward he
always referred to it as *Sharkland*. But *Sharkland* or not, a
large number of his poems and a chunk of his prose were in
print as a result of his sufferings there. Death could now do its
worst. It did.

Chapter Twenty-six

No flight in the light

Here follow a few letters illustrating his later years:

Inniskeen, 23rd Februray 1962
I thought you might be wondering how Patrick was. Well, I
went up to Dublin to see him yesterday and he is great. It
was his first day up and he was dressed. He was pleased to
see me though he pretended I might give him my bronchitis
which I've had for over two weeks — and which I might have
got from him originally. He had a good many visitors at first
but when you are in three weeks they thin down slightly. He
had a visitor while I was there so he is not doing badly. He
says one lobe of his lung is affected and it has still got a spot
on it. When he gets discharged he is coming straight down to
Inniskeen. He thinks he got this dose from sleeping in a
damp bed in Dublin the weekend he went up . . . .
ANNIE KAVANAGH

* * *

367

Inniskeen, 14th August 1962

Dear Peter,
You have written an interesting and maybe important work (John Scotus Eriugena*). I'm sure the B.B.C. Third programme would jump to get it. But how about showing it to Mr. Blythe? You have managed to get yourself into it. I am not enamoured of colloquialisms unmeddling or Inniskeen for verisimilitude purposes. It is too sophisticated for that climbing down. But this doesn't matter much. The production is beautiful. Stephen Spender would I'm thinking be interested for Encounter. Whatever you suggest, all should be done through me I think. Am in fair form. A wanderer. Did not see Telstar but that Ann reference was really big time on big occasion.

* * *

Inniskeen, 3rd December 1962

Dear Peter,
Patrick had a bad do the weekend you were travelling to America. He came back with a bad cold from Dublin and it got worse. He waked me up at 4 a.m. on Saturday morning. He was shivering. I put more clothes on him, got him a hot water bottle and made tea. He didn't want the fire on. Later on in the morning he felt worse and I decided to go for the doctor in Carrick. I took his temperature and it was 101.6 so we sent for the doctor. She came daily for four days and he recovered very quickly. He is keeping fairly well since. I see by the bottles, he has started drinking whiskey again. He is busy working this morning complaining of the heat of his room and throwing water on the fire. I expect he will be going out on the 2 p.m. bus . . .

ANNIE KAVANAGH

* * *

* John Scotus Eriugena, Number 3 in a catena. (New York, 1962). [Pub. note]

368

Inniskeen, 17th September 1963

Dear Peter,

Long time no write. About twelve months since you were here. I am well. Hope you the same. Am living in Dublin mostly and Parson's Bookshop, Baggot Street Bridge will get me. Was in Inniskeen yesterday with crowd. Was collecting papers for recording I'm to do.

* * *

37 Upper Mount St., Dublin, 24th October 1963
I'm staying at the above place on and off for last few years. In fair form. Gave up alcohol some time ago but have to take a little again. Have made an LP record which will be released next year sometime. One side prose devoted to Kavanagh's Weekly. Very funny first time, sad second time. I think the poems on the other side are well done. You'll have a copy when it comes out. Could let you have script of prose. Actually the recording company I did it for is a Guinness (Porter). Gareth Brown is the name. Costs nearly 1,000 pounds to float a long-playing record. Was on live television last Saturday and a great success by all accounts. Delivered my statement. All the best.

* * *

37 Upper Mount St., Dublin, 11th November 1963
Got somewhat depressing letter but on second thoughts, no. Only health matters. I was fair at last letter, not so good now. I am afraid I have prostate trouble, and that would mean an operation. But don't mention this. I may go to England. My above address is O.K. but doubtful. Write c/o Parson's Bookshop. Am well otherwise. Have seen doctors in Baggot St. Hospital but am afraid of results of tests to look in. It is the depression of it all.

PATRICK

* * *

c/o Parson's Bookshop, 20th November 1963
Dear Peter,
*Received your letter. Haven't been feeling too well since
and I'm afraid it is prostate trouble. Called to Hospital and
talked to Keith Shaw, but didn't return yet as I feel I know
alright. Haven't energy to send on script of record but will
try.*

*I'm not too well since I last wrote — something wrong in
kidney section. Pain in back. I have been tentatively seeing a
doctor in Dublin but didn't go for X-ray. Too much talk in
Dublin.*

* * *

47 Gibson Square, London, 8 January 1964
*At length I have taken the pen up. I have just got a report
from the Royal Free Hospital about the back pain — some
osteo-arthritis is the verdict and nothing else amiss. . . . But
it is good news, you'll agree. Heat treatment is the thing for
this pain. I never had thought it cancer come again but
rather what Macmillan had. Thank God.*

*I have been having that novel you rescued typed, or rather,
McGibbon & Kee my publishers are having it typed. I'll be
seeing it Monday. One bit I saw was very good, and the
Literary Editor of the New Statesman to whom someone
showed it was very excited and wants me to write for them.
As I was so depressed I wasn't interested.*

*But shall now I hope, for among other things the New
Statesman has great influence among the suckers of the
U.S. publishing world. There is a strong resistence to me
there, McGibbon & Kee said; they haven't been told I'm an
O.K. name.*

Thank God Christmas is over and the shortest days.

*I agree with the theory that Oswald was paid or organized
to do the murder. That's why he was done in before he
blabbed. Morality is hated.*

Another phone call, this time from my personal doctor

who got the report. Osteo-arthritis is very common after forty-five and isn't all that harmless but it isn't too terrible. There are tablets and exercises. I shan't stay much longer in London as I'm inclined to be broke. This isn't as bad a winter as last and now with the arrival of spring. Poor old McNeice died, you saw. Considerable person, I feel. Give my best to all your friends and I may write more often. PATRICK KAVANAGH

> PATRICK *(I thought I was signing a cheque)*
> *P.S.: This address will get me even if I'm in Ireland.*

* * *

47 Gibson Square, London, 21st January 1964
You are inclined to intrude on one's private world and use information acquired as a brother. Think of me as an acquaintence. It is hard to explain this but I know you are smart and get the idea.

I'd like to hear what you have on me useful re. biography.

Also some of those prose things you have would be useful to me here if you get copies.

A friend of mine, Tommy Marks of Guinness firm — he is Managing Director of Harp's lager — will be in New York next week. I gave him your tel. no. and he'll call you. He's the chap gave me the job judging the Guinness Poetry Awards and he is very friendly in other ways. I hope you like him.

I am in fair shape. If you and Dougherty discuss my ills I don't want to hear the answer. I'm in the hands of the leading European consultants. Bla bla.

I have had that old novel typed or rather McGibbon & Kee had. My poems will be out in two months or three. It will be a vast size — 300 pages.

I enjoyed the novel. I'll return to Mucker when and if I get a substantial advance from my publisher. Mild winter.

Write and let me know what you have pertaining to me, my biography.

371

The best. Spring is coming.

P.S.: A biography in which the subject isn't let down wouldn't be of much interest.

* * *

47 Gibson Square, London, 27th January 1964
It is a bit distressing to get a highly charged emotional letter from you. What I was trying to say was that I wanted a judicial rather than a brotherly report. The question of what is revelation and what is exposure is the problem and is one of the big snags in writing an autobiography — or biography. Only in verse can it be done.

Therefore I suggest that you send me typed copies of the letters till I have a look at them for they are worth some — a lot — of money.

You understand that in these matters what one wants is not love but usefulness.

If I could have typed copies of those prose pieces and stories I might make some money out of them.

I'm frightened of writing almost anything to you on account of your emotionality. That is why I have written so seldom in the past. You should understand that I don't want to worry or wound you. On several occasions I have signed my full name and surname — of second nature. Intent is everything.

* * *

47 Gibson Square, London, 31st January 1964
Am fixing up that novel* for McGibbon & Kee. Poems about 300 pages. They are trying to flog novel to U.S. I am in good form.

The point we must condole over is who is going to write my Life and what about myself, or keeping it in the family anyhow.

---

* The novel here mentioned was autobiographical. The Ms. had found its way into a private collection in America. I recovered it for him. He did not fix it up as he had hoped but after his death I edited it and published it under the title, *By Night Unstarred. (Co-published in Ireland by The Goldsmith Press, 1977: Pub. note).*

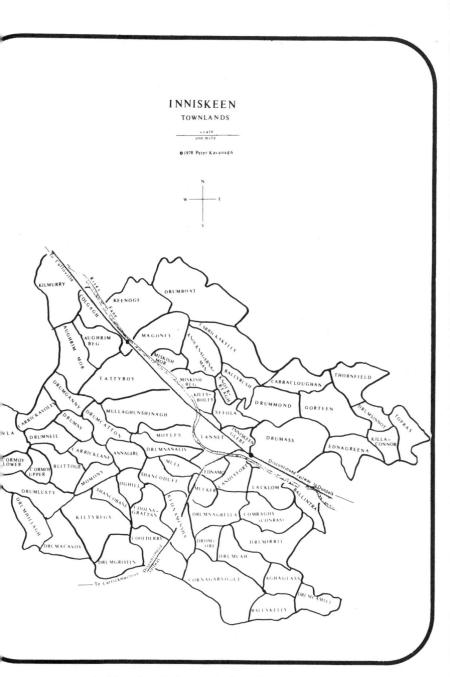

INNISKEEN
TOWNLANDS

scale
one mile

© 1978 Peter Kavanagh

KILMURRY

To Culloville

River Fane

COLGAGH

KEENOGE

DRUMBOAT

AUGHRIM MOR

AUGHRIM BEG

MAGONEY

CARRICKAKELLY

DRUMGANNY

TATTYBOY

MISKISH MOR

CARRA-KYGARRA-MAL

BALLYRUSH

CARRACLOUGHAN

THORNFIELD

MISKISH BEG

KILLY-BOLEY

KNOCK-EAGH

DRUMMOND

GORTEEN

DRUMSINNOT

TOPRAS

CARRICKAVOLEY

DRUMNY

DRUMCATTOS

MULLAGHUNSHINAGH

SEEOLA

KILLA-CONNOR

NLA

DRUMNEIL

MOYLES

LANNET

INNISKEEN GLEBE

DRUMASS

EDNAGREENA

CARRICKLANE

ANNAGIRL

DRUMNANALIV

CORMOY LOWER

CORMOY UPPER

BLITTOGE

MOMONY

MUFF

EDNAMO

Discontinued railway to Dundalk

DRUMLUSTY

OGHILL

SHANCODUFF

MEEKER

CANDLEFORT

LACKLOM

BALLINTRA

DRUMHILLAGH

SHANCOBANE

CODLNA-GRATTAN

KILNAMINSHA

DRUMNAGRELLA

COMRAGHS
(CONRAS)

KILTYBEGS

COOLDERRY

DROM-ORI

DRUMIRRIL

DRUMACAVOY

DRUMGRISTIN

Discontinued railway

DRUMCAH

To Carrickmacross

CORNAGARVOGUE

AGHAGLASS

DRUMCAMILL

BALLYKELLY

Inniskeen townlands: map by Peter Kavanagh.

I write merely to confirm your letter that we must thing the matter out.

I think now that the letters would have to remain absolutely Private as also the stuff in National Library of Ireland.

But Nothing From You

Who Are The Sacred Keeper Of My Sacred Conscience.

I wrote a Preface to Collected Poems yesterday. Though in bad form from whiskey (though very little I take now) it turns out a lively acrid piece in which I mention the English critics. There is a roadblock against me in America. Association with Devin Adair did no good but it runs deeper. deeper.

That's about it. McGibbon & Kee are trying to flog that novel in the U.S. and I think they'll find it hard. I don't mind for I'm going to make a real pleasant job of it. McGibbon & Kee of course want it. The makings of a wonderful novel in it.

Is there a precedent for a biography of a living writer who is still writing? A writer doesn't hand over his material. About a poet's work only — okay.

* * *

47 Gibson Square, London, 3 February 1964
After the fright our letters are crossing. Hope to hear you got my cable. None of the Ms. you have is of any use to me. That's all I have to say. Sorry for all but somehow you must for momentary insanities in me and stall hard.

I haven't been well this weekend but I imagine whiskey is the cause. I've had an ulcer for years but now it has been getting less tolerant of whiskey and from yesterday whiskey is out for good. Might even be able to take a New York trip.

* * *

47 Gibson Square, London, 8th February 1964
There is a new film in London called Dr. Strangelove, the

final nuclear war, the Russians have the Doomsday Machine with which they will wipe out the human race. The pandect is your doomsday machine that I didn't know existed and which I wanted you to trigger off. I have looked through it and it is too terrible for me to contemplate. But my lost life is all there and the hidden years. Any biography without that would be nothing. I had forgotten so much. It ends rather abruptly at 1958 but that will come no doubt. An American who wrote a play about Dublin (Brian Donleavy) after the war comments in an introduction to the play about meeting a man (me) in Dublin who talks about an attempted murder. The date was 27th October 1959. He doesn't mention me by name. I wrote a contemporary account of same which is in Inniskeen. I plan to go to Inniskeen next week. Of course I don't claim copyright in your letters. I also realize . . . that you were Kavanagh's Weekly.

Winter is nearly over. Mild compared. Will comment on pandect soon. Those letters are valuable. You own them of course, I have a few dozen of your letters in Inniskeen. Will send them on sometime.

* * *

47 Gibson Square, London, 10th February 1964
I can hardly face the pandect. But there are some awfully revealing things in it.

The pandect is the most terribly indicting document. Have it photostated, the letters I mean, and only send them in small quantities to the photo man. If you do nothing else but type out those letters it would be a life's work. But the pandect is good as it stands and readable by me and you. I did let myself down on many occasions. Little do people know that such a thing is in existence. Some break my heart. Deirdre!

* * *

c/o Parson's Bookshop, Dublin, 28th May 1964
Hope you are well. I myself have unfortunately got a bad
turn. I'm afraid your doctor was right. Very disturbed
physically and of course otherwise, but not that bad.

I still write a column for the Irish Television Magazine.
Did a small piece around some Irish pictures which are
going in Sunday Times colour supplement, next Sunday.

I'm in Dublin at the moment but was in Inniskeen for last
weekend. Collected Poems out 27th June I think. Must send
you a copy of my Self Portrait (Television address).

Will write soon if I pick up.

* * *

c/o Parson's Bookshop, Dublin, 5th June 1964
Dear Peter,
I am much better thanks to your letter. Great news*.
Forget about me. In fact I am physically better. But your
news is wonderful. I don't think one should talk too much.
Best wishes to you both and all, PATRICK

* * *

c/o Parson's Bookshop, Dublin, 23rd June 1964
Not much to tell about my physical condition which is as you
know a permanent affair I am afraid. I am beginning to
learn to put up with it, if it gets no worse. Reports of this
condition leak out and it didn't make me too happy with my
alleged friends.

I am in Inniskeen today and writing from there. As the 2
p.m. bus will be going soon to Carrick I'll stop. Collected
Poems coming out July 22nd. Guinness in London giving a
party to celebrate the coming out.

* * *

The Halcyon Hotel, Dublin, 6 December 1964
Dear Peter & Ann,
This is to wish you a happy Christmas and New Year. I

* The information that we were expecting a baby.

am in fair shape but not in writing form which demands energy. I have no news. Wasn't in Inniskeen to live for some months. Went to Belfast to lecture to Queen's (University) and I read them my record piece about K's Weekly. It doesn't wear well, I thought. Record will be out shortly. I must send you copy and also copy of De Luxe edition of Collected Poems, leather bound and signed.

* * *

The Halcyon Hotel, Dublin, 11th February 1965 Dear Peter, Ann, etc.: I have just come out of the Meath Hospital after near three weeks. Trouble was not prostate but contraction of bladder. It only held less than two ounces. They stretched by filling it with water or some fluid. Pumped it up. I am feeling much better these days. And I'll be ready for the U.S. in April. I hope you are all well. The weeks I spent in hospital were the worst of winter. I had a private room to myself, twenty guineas a week. I hope they get it. I am fit for work now and hope to have something to say. I just had a letter from Torchiana the professor at Northwestern University asking for title of my lecture. I am suggesting 'Yeats' luxurious background' the world of the rich Anglo-Irish. Even though he might have got little money from them they were still there. George Moore gives the background. I am still here at the Halcyon though it is likely to be closed shortly. However, letter will always get me here.

In April 1965 Northwestern University, Illinois, held a symposium to celebrate the centenary of the birth of W. B. Yeats. Patrick was invited to participate, all expenses paid. This was the first such invitation he ever received. He accepted eagerly and arrived in Chicago 20th April 1965 for a week-long session. He phoned me immediately on arrival and I tried to give him some useful advice on the university scene. As with most advice, it only helped the giver. His stay there was not too happy. America is a very conservative country. Keeping one's pants pressed is part of the economy. If you are a bohemian it is better to be a studied bohemian. Even the district in which Northwestern University is situated is *dry* — the sale of liquor being prohibited. So Patrick was an outsider from the start:

> *It takes two to make a row and it also takes two to make an agreement; there was none of that in that audience. They were antagonistic to my viewpoint. More antagonistic than an Irish audience. There is no comparison. There they are positively wrong. It is complete negation in America. You are never to mention Longfellow, Bret Harte or Vachel Lindsay, no one that's alive . . . . I made my own world. I lived with friends in Wisconsin and New York and I drank in the local bar . . . .*
>
> (*November Haggard*, p.97)

On April 30th he arrived in New York via the Kentucky Derby in Louisville. At that time our apartment was even smaller than it is now — one moderate-sized room and a tiny bedroom. When he saw our accommodation he informed us at once he would move out to a room in the morning. Six weeks later he was still with us. When we saw him putting things away tidy — including the eggs in their separate slots in the refrigerator — we knew he was satisfied with our arrangement. Three of us and a six months baby in so small a place! He loved being with us and he especially loved taking care of the baby, even bringing her down along the East River to play in the sun.

Every day he set out on his tour of New York and every evening around five returned home with a pint of *Old Crow* bourbon in his pocket. He was an engaging conversationalist on every subject and in general was a pleasant guest.

Towards the end of his stay he, the baby and I flew out to Wisconsin at the invitation of Dr. Lois Byrne. Patrick loved Wisconsin as much as I do and it was from there that he left for London on June 25th. He was short of cash but refused what I offered, telling me he would prefer I spent it on the baby. When

378

he reached Chicago he discovered that his ticket had changed in status from winter to summer rates with a consequent change in price. He was equal to the problem, having the airline phone Northwestern University. The University was glad to pay the extra amount and so he returned to *Sharkland.*

As soon as he arrived back he wrote to us saying how much he missed America and missed the baby. *I do wish you would send me a snap of her laughing and kicking up her heels. Let me know if she has got a tooth yet.*

Stories of Patrick's performance at Northwestern preceded him and at once the Government agencies moved to slap him hard for giving Ireland a bad name. The Income Tax people once more roughed him up and the authorities at U.C.D. reduced his sinecure — already reduced by a garnish — by a further one hundred pounds. *I presume*, he wrote the University, *it was those idiotic Americans with their stuff that done the job.* Patrick's reputation with respectable people was so low that Harvard University (The Poetry Room), recording writers in conjunction with the British Council offered him no more than $50.00 if he would do them a recording. If later he appeared on a commercial disc with a number of verse writers he would receive *a royalty of one halfpenny for each disc sold in respect of each minute of playing time of your work recorded* (Letter of 22nd March 1966). When Patrick asked for fifty guineas ($150.00) and a list of the *poets* that would appear on the disc with him, they dropped the matter and the recording was never made.

Not everyone took such a low measure of him. On 6th June 1966 he received a cheering letter from Christopher Fitzsimon, Executive Producer of R.T.E. television, proposing to do a half-hour documentary on Patrick and his work.

You may well wonder at our approaching you so comparatively soon after your television Self Portrait, but the form of the proposed programme is very different. We plan to record the script with voice only (as for radio), and later shoot appropriate film at the location referred-to in the text. It is also hoped that we may illustrate selected poems in the same way. Proposed recording date is mid-July and filming would take place in early August.

I do hope you decide to undertake the script. It would be a great pleasure to me to be connected with it, partly because of my admiration (since schooldays when I first was introduced to Tarry Flynn and A Soul For Sale) for your work, and partly because I know your corner of Monaghan well, though I lived mainly on the other side of the county.

The fee offered was fifty pounds and expenses. Patrick accepted eagerly and not just because of the money. He was cheered by the enthusiasm displayed in the letter, *the civilized approach* he would call it. Furthermore, he loved the idea of being a star in his native parish.

Chapter Twenty-seven

The tape goes up

The recording part of the programme took place on the 29th July and the video part was shot during the first week of August. I was in Inniskeen at the time of the filming. Patrick was bursting with suppressed pride and a bit on edge lest I or someone else steal the show. I understood his feeling and made certain not to intrude. He had come a long way before receiving such a compliment and I was happy to see him enjoy it.

But the truth must be told: he did not belong, even in a film about himself. He looked incongruous in the setting. He was not now the Tarry Flynn of the novel, nor the person who drove a horse and cart — he was an outsider who might just have newly arrived from Italy or Kazakhstan. The film had come too late except as a compliment.

Adrian Cronin, who directed the documentary, sent the following memoir:

From about 1962 I met Patrick on and off. I knew he had a curiosity about the whole television process though he never admitted it. When I progressed into the area of making documentaries, one of the first people I wanted to make a profile of was Patrick and at our first meeting when I put the proposition to him he was very flattered by the proposal even though he didn't show it but I could detect a quiet pride in the weeks that were to follow, particularly when he spoke to his friends and said such things as 'You know they are making a bloody film about me'. Patrick knew I was no literary egghead and therefore he was reasonably sure that I wouldn't make some arty-crafty programme with my own interpretation of his work and I let him know several times that I was only a technician in his hands and that I would be guided by him completely in the choice of material in the programme.

One way of making sure that Patrick would be on time at all the locations was to have him live with my wife and me and our baby daughter for the three or four weeks that were involved in the shooting. During that time I realised more than ever that Patrick's exterior was a complete disguise for the gentle sensitive man that he was. I think there was a programme called Meet The Clans on radio and he made some contribution to it. . . .

On not one single occasion was he late for any of the shooting or in any way unfit for the work.

Just before the documentary was aired on the 10th October Patrick mentioned it in his column in *R.T.V. Guide*. Here is part of what he said:

The film of my life and hard times to be shown on 10th is based on my belief that things of public importance are never of any importance.

Man is a small animal and it is just because of his smallness that he is important.

This film of my own smallness is founded primarily on a series of pieces which I wrote for the magazine Envoy in 1950. They were entitled Evocations of No Importance.

ERA

Drawings by Brian Bourke, Era Review (Kavanagh issue, 1978).

It is a summer's day and I am aged about twenty-two and I am drawing coal from the station . . . . There I was, my face black and the fields looking at me.

Almost no communication with the general public. Just evoking for myself.

I have seen and even liked this film in a run-through. I wrote the script and read the prose and T. P. McKenna read the poems with the exception of a couple of verses of Belloc's which I read myself. It is directed by Adrian Cronin . . . .

We did three days shooting in South Monaghan along the Fane River where Simon Weaver spotted an injured kingfisher, that most beautiful bird which I had never seen before . . . .

Then we did two days shooting along Pembroke Road, the Grand Canal and Haddington Road.

> *On Pembroke Road look out for my ghost*
> *Dishevelled with shoes untied*
> *Playing through the railings with little children*
> *Whose children have long since died.*

We got this with two pretty children in the picture . . . .

At all events I do hope you will turn on your sets on the tenth of the tenth and forgive me my trespasses.

On 24th February 1967 Patrick wrote what turned out to be his last letter to me. It stated: *I haven't been in good shape lately: moving from place to place. I'm going to London 13th March for the publication of my Collected Pruse.* * *It isn't a good collection as I didn't do it myself.*

Exactly two months later I received a letter from one of his Dublin acquaintences informing me that Patrick had just gone through a marriage ceremony in Dublin. Nothing came directly from Patrick. Seven months later, on 30th November, the Irish police phoned my apartment in New York to say Patrick was dead.

* Sic.

Of those intervening nine months I have no direct knowledge. What information I have comes from relatives. No one who was at his bed when he died would write me a memoir. The information I received from relatives and friends is now published separately in a book *Love's Tortured Headland* issued in New York, December 1978.

He had come down to Dundalk on his own to be present at the local production of the dramatised version of *Tarry Flynn*. There he took ill and was brought back to the family house in Inniskeen where my two sisters lived. They called the local doctor and, both being professional nurses, gave him the best treatment possible. He wished to die in his own home, he told them. They were anxious to have him but were overruled and he was brought up to Dublin to die in a Nursing Home. It was not considered necessary to put him in a hospital with intensive care facilities.

Before leaving Inniskeen he managed to find sufficient privacy to make an intimate statement to my sister Annie. Life had cheated him one last time. The pattern of his life had not varied — always failure in the end:

One day I asked God to give
Me perfection so I'd live
Smooth and courteous, calmly wise
All the world's virtuous prize,

So I should not always be
Getting into jeopardy,
Being savage, wild and proud
Fighting, arguing with the crowd;

Being poor, sick, depressed
Everywhere an awful pest;
Being too right, being too wrong,
Being too weak, being too strong;

Being every hour fated
To say things that make me hated;
Being a failure in the end —
God, perfection on me spend.

And God spoke out of Heaven:
The only gift in My giving
Is yours — Life. Seek in Hell
Death, perfect, wise comfortable.

(*Complete Poems*, p. 162)

I managed to get back to Ireland for the funeral and was able to salvage what was left of the wreck of his life. When I got back to the United States I resigned my university post and from then until the present have devoted all my time and energies to making sure that even if life betrayed him I would not. Hence the series of books I have produced since then.

He was buried in his native Inniskeen by his own wish and insisted-on by my sister Mary. I designed the grave as it now is.

He was sixty-three when he died.

Epilogue

by Patrick Kavanagh

I have had my fill of what is called tragedy. But tragedy is really the dung that fertilises the soil of life. There are probably many exceptions to this. We cannot all be Socrates.

I have lived in poverty for twenty years in the illiterate and malignant wilderness that is called Dublin. There I have lived among people who care nothing for the things of the spirit. They blathered about poetry and, as the fella said, they knew as much about poetry as my arse knows about snipe shooting.

Then in a law case in the Dublin High Court where before a jury of the same malicious specimens I was humiliated. This was really a black injury which nearly laid laid me low in tragedy's muck.

If that wasn't enough it was followed by an awful sickness of mind, body and spirit which gripped me for a year. I couldn't eat. It was awful. It was cancer of the lung.

387

But we survived. I say! Do you hear me? We survived to laugh another day.

But the self is not important except as an illustration. It would be an impertinence for me to recount what happened to me as if I were a General writing his memoirs. Only in so far as they can be squeezed for the comedy that is truth, are they worth mentioning.

But now that I look back on my own life and experience for the last twenty or more years in search of the tragedy, all my tragedies and misfortunes look up at me and laugh. While I try to concentrate on the many times I have been starving, the more I concentrate the more those glamorous compensatory gifts draw attention to themselves.

No sir, the tragic act is not my kettle of fish.

Appendix

Letters from Inniskeen to Peter concerning Patrick

1963
3 April: Patrick is away for at least four weeks if not five; he went to Dublin for one week and was then going on to London for good. I haven't had a line from him so I don't know how he is.
3 June: Patrick is back here since last Friday (31 May). He accidentally met Mary in Amiens Street Station. He was getting out of a taxi and Mary was looking for one on her way to the North Wall. She got the same taxi Patrick came in . . . . The starlings have made several nests under the eaves where the plaster is off and the first thing Patrick did was to get up on a ladder and seal the nests in.

1964
25 January: We heard from Patrick since the New Year and expect him momently.

9 March: . . . . *Patrick is back safe and sound since 24 February; he came straight from London to here. He is doing well, eating like a ploughman; a 2 lb. loaf barely does him a day. Also eggs, at least five, and the first three days he had a gallon of new milk delivered from John Lennon. He is complaining of gas on his stomach but with all his eating there isn't much room for gas. His lung is O.K. He was X-rayed and examined in London. He was in Dublin on Saturday and brought back a point* steak for his Sunday dinner. It cost him five shillings. I had already bought two point steaks — 7/6 the two — so we were well fed with steak. . . . He is off the alcohol.*

13 March: Patrick is as usual, keeping reasonably well, some stomach trouble and diarrhoea. Eats very well. He is in Carrick this morning I presume. He caught the 11 a.m. bus in that direction.

21 March: Patrick is still here. Went to Dublin yesterday but didn't come back last night.

7 April: Patrick is here on and off. He went to Dublin a week ago today and we haven't heard of him since. He is pestered with the Income Tax people.

29 June: I have heard the glad news (coming of Keelin). *Patrick was down here a week today and went back on the Wednesday evening. As he was going for the bus, I was in the garden at the back of the house. He came back a few yards to tell me the good news that he had heard from you. He couldn't keep it to himself. I said to him, are you thinking of taking a trip to New York? He is not drinking now but he backs horses and enjoys himself generally.*

3 July: Peter to Inniskeen: So Patrick blabbed! I really thought he could have kept quiet longer. Of course I had not put him under oath not to tell. I must say that I am astonished that he would take all this so excitedly. I had thought he would have been just mildly interested and was very ill and I felt he should know before he left this world. But apparently he has no sign of leaving.

* Sic.

Patrick Kavanagh's grave, Inniskeen.

15 July: Patrick flew to London yesterday. He says he won't be back for two weeks.

8 October: Patrick is with us most of the time. He goes up to Dublin some weekends.

10 December: Patrick is still in Dublin — Halcyon Hotel, South Anne St., directly off Grafton Street. We expect him down with your good news (birth of Keelin) anytime now. He will be thrilled with your news.

1965

15 January: Patrick hasn't been down since Christmas.

29 January: We haven't heard from Patrick since Christmas. He stayed with us from Christmas eve till the Monday after Christmas. He writes in the R.T.V. Guide each week but this week there is no article. It says he is on holidays. More likely he is in hospital for that operation.

9 February: We haven't heard from Patrick and are in the dark as much as you are.

12 February: Just had a note from Patrick. He is well. Was in the Meath Hospital for three weeks suffering from contracted bladder. They stretched it and he is now fine, so he says.

29 March: Patrick was brought down from Dublin by Dr. Murphy on Friday evening. He only stayed the night and was off at 2 p.m. on Saturday. He is flying to London today for a few weeks stay and will fly from London to America. He looks very well. Mary also knitted Patrick an Aran knit but he thought it too heavy for this time of year. We have no intention of giving Patrick any knitted articles to take over, especially when he isn't going direct to you. He would lose them or sell them . . . .

1 April: You will have Patrick to see you in a few weeks, however long he will stay. He is like a wandering Jew, up and down, in and out, God help him. He doesn't know what he wants.

13 April: It will be very nice to see Patrick. He was very interested in the baby's photos.

2 July: I see by this week's R.T.V. Guide that Patrick is in Wisconsin enjoying himself.

1 August: Patrick came home last Monday evening about 10 p.m. He looks well and is his usual self. He had a look at all the photos of Keelin but he says they do not do her justice. She is a lovely happy baby and does something to him but not the photos. Patrick has been in Dublin yesterday and Thursday for the day. He can't settle himself to do anything. He brought home a great pile of washing — now he is able to change shirts frequently and hankies ad lib. He is arriving now on the 2.45 p.m. bus from the village and I must get his dinner ready for him.

19 August: Patrick is still here, goes out every day, either to Carrick or Dundalk. He seems quite well.

24 August: We may expect you soon. Patrick was away the weekend and wants to know if there was any post. When we told him of the parcel of baby food he could name the brand. He is getting very excited and anxious to see you all, particularly Keelin.

13 October: Had a postcard from Patrick this morning. Still in Rome.

27 October: Patrick is in Dublin but we expect him down for Christmas.

17 December: From Peter to Inniskeen: I heard today from Patrick from an address at 136 Upper Leeson Street, Dublin. He asked me to send him some Ms. of his that I have been holding. I will send them to you at Inniskeen. You can tell him I am sending everything I have got.

29 December: The Mss arrived yesterday for Patrick. He wasn't down for Christmas nor for weeks before that. He is sharing a flat with a House Surgeon who works in Baggot Street Hospital. The doctor sublet to Patrick and even so he finds it very expensive. We are expecting Patrick any of these days after all the Christmas festivities are finished.

1966

7 February: Patrick called down two weeks ago. Arrived on the 11 a.m. bus and left on the 2 p.m. He is quite comfortable in Dublin. Three of them share a flat at 136 Upper Lesson Street.

20 April: Patrick is with us again since before Easter. He is quite well now but had a bad turn when he came to us. He said it was alcoholic poisoning. He isn't taking so much whiskey now and is getting fat and eating well. One night as he was sitting on his bed eating supper he got a fright. He was sure he saw someone whispering in his ears. He came up to us in the sitting room in a fright and shaking all over. We had to calm him down and Mary had to sit up that night with him he was so frightened. Well, no need to worry about him.

He is well again and has gone up to Dublin to open an exhibition of paintings in Dawson Gallery by Michael Farrell. We had a great time getting him ready, washing his white shirts and cleaning his sports jacket and having some clean handkerchiefs. Mary polished his shoes. Mary says not to worry about him. He can still bawl and when he is not able to do that we will telephone you post haste.

27 April: Just a few lines to put your mind at ease. Patrick is in great form now eating like a horse and drinking alcohol like a fish. He swore to me when he was in the 'jigs' that he would never take alcohol again — of course he is a dipsomaniac. When I told him that he bawled my head off. He went off to Dublin yesterday to back horses and of course to bend his elbow. He suffers periodically from laceration of the stomach. He was treated last summer in London for it. That is what he had here this time before he got 'the rats'. The alcohol is burning his insides and sooner or later it will finish him, but my guess is that he will see both of us down as he is as strong as a bull. His average is five eggs a day plus meat, milk etc. You can rest assured if anything unforeseen should happen we will phone you straight away but that is most unlikely. I gave Patrick the cutting and your kind regards and he was very pleased.

2 May: Peter to Inniskeen: According to the best medical information over here it takes two years off the booze to undo the damage caused by alcoholic poisoning — so damaging is it to the brain. So that if Patrick is now drinking again it means he has not long to live. This is the way it happened to Dylan Thomas, a Welsh poet who died over here. Same thing, alcoholic poisoning. He knows all this I assume, so it is useless to tell him. It is quite sad.

20 May: Patrick went to Dublin yesterday. He may be back tonight or he may stay until Monday. No change in his carry-on. He is up and down all night drinking milk, water and breadsoda. I told him the other morning to ease off the whiskey as he was putting a nail in his own coffin. He told me to go to hell and mind my own business. No use worrying — we do all we can.

25 May: Both of us as well as Patrick are thrilled at the idea of you and Ann coming over in July. Patrick is advising us already of the danger of the fire. Patrick is down here since April but he says he won't be here long.

24 July: Patrick is here with us since he returned from London. He keeps asking when you and Keelin are coming.

14 September: I was reading a poem on Patrick's table dedicated to his niece Keelin, all about minding her in New York and 2nd Avenue & 30th Street. Patrick went up to Dublin on Monday morning and came back last night. He is off again this morning with his bag and typewriter. We don't know if it's for good. He never said anything to us, just walked out as usual.

17 October: Patrick's film was shown on Telefís Eireann a week today. It lasted 20 minutes. It was quite good and its only fault was that it was too short and quick. We couldn't take in all the scenery. Only the back of the house was shown, Kednaminsha School, Inniskeen, the Station, Lockingtons, the Round Tower and church, the Catholic Church, Dan McNellos with Patrick supping whiskey; also that cross in Dan's wall given in 1798 to a Captain McMahon, Carrick convent was shown and all Patrick's haunts in Dublin, Pembroke Road, Baggot St., the Canal.

5 November: Patrick is still in Dublin. We haven't seen him only the once for an hour between 4.30 and 5.30 p.m. buses. He hasn't written in the R.T.V. Guide so he must have plenty of money left.

10 December: Patrick's play Tarry Flynn is running at the Abbey Theatre these last three weeks. It finishes next week and that is only because the theatre is putting on a pantomime for Christmas. We hired a car and went up to the Abbey last Tuesday week 29 November. We took John and Mrs. Lennon with us and Breda McLoughlin was staying with us and she came. We would have brought Josie with us but she was in England at the time. The play was great and true to life and there are packed houses every night. In fact people had to be turned away. A carload of Inniskeen farmers went to it as well as Dan MacNello.

For a continuation of these letters see *Love's Tortured Headland* (New York 1978).

Bibliography

Lapped Furrows: Correspondence 1933-1967 between Patrick and Peter Kavanagh: With other documents.Edited by Peter Kavanagh. 307 pp. New York 1969.

November Haggard: Uncollected Prose and Verse of Patrick Kavanagh. Selected and arranged by Peter Kavanagh. Illustrated. 229 pp. New York 1971.

The Complete Poems of Patrick Kavanagh: Collected, arranged and edited by Peter Kavanagh. 391 pp. New York 1972.

Beyond Affection: An Autobiography by Peter Kavanagh. 201 pp. Edition of 500. New York 1977.

By Night Unstarred: An Autobiographical novel by Patrick Kavanagh. Edited by Peter Kavanagh. 175 pp. New York and Ireland 1977.

Love's Tortured Headland: A continuation of *Lapped Furrows.* 45 pp. Edition of 600. New York 1978.

All the above books published by The Peter Kavanagh Hand Press, 250 East Street, New York 10016.

(Publisher's Note: The Goldsmith Press, in conjunction with Dr. Kavanagh, has published: *By Night Unstarred* (1977) and *Lough Derg* (1978). Also in 1978 they published *A Guide to Patrick Kavanagh Country* by Dr. Peter Kavanagh.)

Index

Abbey Theatre, 119, 204, 211, 226, 254, 338, 396
Abse, D., 328
Adair, Devin, 204, 363, 364
Adams, L., 306
AE (George Russell), 46, 47, 48, 49, 232
AE Memorial Award, 71-72
Aer Lingus, 259
Aiken, Conrad, 306
Aiken, Frank, 203-204, 210, 211
Albee, E., 307
The American Mercury, 254, 257
Ante-Natal Dream, 218-219
Aquinas, T., 252
Archer, D., 313, 327
Argus Ltd., 287
Arks, 259
Around the World in Eighty Days, (film), 307
At Swim-Two-Birds, (O'Brien) 119
Auden, W. H., 124, 220, 296

Baggot St. Hospital, 340, 370
Bard of Callenberg, 28-29
Barker, G., 297, 300, 313, 327, 328

B.B.C., 48, 62, 105, 146, 208, 217, 334, 368
Beauchamp, Mrs., 187
Beckett, Samuel, 297
The Bell, 89, 151, 155, 158, 159, 165-168, 168-170, 171, 174, 204, 228-236, 244, 340
Belloc, H., 333, 384
Bernhardt, S., 331
Best Poems of 1930, 54
Beyond Affection, 268-276
B. & I. Steamship Co., 85-86
The Bishop's Bonfire, 296
Blackburn, T., 329
Blake, W., 10, 324
Blois, Miss, 64
Bouch, Joe, 114-115
Briet, H., 311
British Council 210, 372
Brogan, H., 147
Brooke, R., 224
Brown, Harold C., 92-93
Brown, G. 369
Burns & Oats, 209
Burns, R. 246
Burns, Singer, J., 328
Burrows, Mrs. 280, 286

398

By Night Unstarred, 42, 75-81, 178-184, 372
Byrne, L. 378

Callan, M., 15
Callan, N., 13-15
Campbell of Drumcatton, 14
Campbell, T., 224
The Capuchin Annual, 107-108
Carleton, W., 244, 294
Carroll, Paul V., 73, 231, 242
Carson, 270
Cassidy, Miss, 21-22
Cassidy, Whit, 92, 94
Celtic Twilight Tradition, 46-47, 59
Cervantes, M., 220, 294
Chagall, M., 333
Charles, D., 204
Chaucer, G., 104
Chekhov, 229
Chesterton, C. K., 169
Chinese Lyrics, (Waddell), 56
Chuck, T. 26-28
Churchill, W., 301
Clarke, Austin, 158, 173, 188, 251
Clayburghs, 303
Collet's Bookshop, 288, 289
Collected Poems, 359-360, 374, 376, 377
Collected Pruse, 366
Collins, M., 125
Coloured Balloons, 165
Colum, Padraic, 146, 147, 319
Come Dance With Kitty Stobling, 329, 330-333, 359
Complete Poems, quoted 22, 24, 30-31, 62-63, 67-68, 88-89, 89-90, 97-98, 99-100, 121-122, 171-172, 196-197, 198, 199, 359, 385-386
Connolly, T. J., 274
Constables, 58, 59
Corkery, D., 297
Cooney, W., 11-12
Costello, John, 270-271, 277, 287-288
Courbet, G., 306
Cuala Press, 104
Cultural Committee, 209, 210, 211, 251-252, 256
cummings, e. e., 304, 313, 337
Curry, Peter, 115, 132, 134, 171, 189
Cronin, Adrian, 381-382, 384

The Daily Telegraph, 334
Dante, 311
Dark Haired Miriam Ran Away, 126

de Brun, E., 304
de Kooning, 306
Delargy, S., 232
de Nerval, G., 331
De Valera, E., 111, 148, 168, 261
Dickens, C. 220, 339
Dictionary of Irish Mythology, 318
Diplomatic Whiskey, 250
Doak, H., L., 84
Dolan, M., 147
Dostoievski, 48
Dougan, P., 237, 241
Dougherty, Renée, 237, 238-241, 242, 244, 245
Dublin Grand Opera Society, The, 251
Dublin Magazine, The, 48, 52, 53, 71, 89
Dunlop Rubber Co., 259
Dunleavy, B., 375
Dunsany, Lord, 244

Easons, 249
Eberhardt, R., 303
Eliot, T. S., 273
Emerson, 48
Encounter, 312, 313, 314, 317, 334, 368
Envoy, 203, 206, 207, 244, 247, 382; Article 213-226
Eriugena, John Scotus, 368
The Evening Herald, 48

The Faber Book of Twentieth Century Verse, 298
Farrel, P., 300, 301, 302-308, 311
Farrell, B., 353
Farrelly, Mrs., 301, 303, 311
Farren, R., 173, 188, 211
Farmers' Journal, 314, 317, 318, 320, 358
Fay, G., 318
Feehan, M., 257
Fitzsimons, C., 379-380
Fitzsimons, P. 187
Fleming, P. 62
Fleming, Ian, 62
Four Square Books, 338
La France Libre, 147
Freedom, 44
Freemasons, 83

Gallagher, E., 306
The Gallivanting Poet, 162-165
Ganley, Brigid, 102
Garvin, Miss, 66
Geary, 85

Gil Blas, 16, 48, 242
Ginsberg, A., 319
Goddard, Paulette, 137
Gogarty, Oliver, 59, 164
Goldsmith, O., 236
Graham, W. S., 328
Grand Canal, 292, 309, 320, 349
Greacen, Robert, 124-125
Great Hunger, The, 19, 103-107, 171,
    191, 204, 244
Green Fool, The, 15, 16, 42, 58, 59, 63
    64, 71, 231, 233, 237, 318,
    336, 346
Gregory, H., 307
Gregory, Lady, 347
Guggenheim, P., 306
Guinness Poetry Awards, 330, 333,
    336, 337, 339, 359

Hamill, J., 336
Hamill, P., 40
Hanratty, O., 31
Harte, B., 378
Harvard University, (The Poetry
    Room), 379
Harvey, N. S., 92-93
Heath-Stubbs, J., 328
Herbert, G., 221
Higgins, F. R., 147, 154, 155, 156,
    158, 162-165, 172, 173
Hill, G. 328
Hill is Mine, The, (Walsh), 92
Hiring Fair, 41
Hoagland, Kathleen, 152
Hollis & Carter, 191
Holloway, Joe, 118
Homer, 252
Hopkins, G. M., 234
Horizon, 103, 104, 160, 189, 190, 206
Hull, T. 328
Human Comedy, The, (Saroyan), 242
Hunger, (K. Hamsun), 240, 242
Hutchinsons 353, 354, 356
Huxley, J., 123

Inscription on the tomb of an Unknown
    Warrior, 97-98
The Intangible, 47
Irish Academy Exhibition, The, 102
Irish Academy of Letters, The, 226
Irish Hospital Sweepstakes, The, 252,
    256, 257
Irish Independent, The, 85, 92, 99, 334
Irish Press, The, 42-43, 64, 74, 118-
    122, 125, 128, 138, 283
Irish Statesman, The, 46, 47, 232

Irish Times, The, 73-74, 85, 92-97, 100,
    103, 107, 108, 111, 128-130,
    173, 187, 240, 244, 272, 274-
    275, 287, 288, 334
Irish Writing in 1946, 89
Irish Writing in 1956, 288
Is, 312

Jack Doyle, 121
John O'London's 'The Cobbler & The
    Football Team', 146
The John Quinn Letters, 334, 339
Joseph, Michael, 59, 67
Joyce, James, 164, 168, 172, 219, 220,
    254, 298
Justifiable Homicide, 121

Kavanagh, Annie, (sister), 357, 367-
    368
Kavanagh, Brigid, (Mother), 18, 19, 25
    49, 134, 135
Kavanagh, Cecilia, (sister), 18, 48, 50,
    152
Kavanagh, James, (father), 13, 16, 22,
    26, 47, 49
Kavanagh, Lucy, (sister), 41, 46, 49,
    126
Kavanagh, Mary, (sister), 281, 311,
    336, 386, 389, 392
Kavanagh, Patrick
    America in, 302-309
    Attempt on his life, 320-322
    Birth, 13
    Brother, and his, 9, 24, 202, 227-
        228, 254, 277, 357, 360-366
    Childhood, 15, 21-22
    Court Cases, (B. & I.), 85-86
        (Gogarty), 59
        (v. The Leader), 262-263, 276,
        283, 287, 288, 350, 387
    Death his, 385-386
    Dublin Society and, 71-72, 81-83,
        190-191
    Early works by, 54-57
    Epilogue by, 387-388
    Father, and his, 16, 322
    First poems, 25-31, 43-49
    Gambling, and, 201-202
    Illness, 41, 206, 271, 277-288, 311,
        342, 356, 371, 390, 394-396
    Journalism, his, 85, 92-97, 100-103,
        107-110, 135-144, 171-173,
        203-204, 213-226, 247-251,
        252-254, 296-298
    Journalists, and, 73'74, 161-162,
        250

Letters to his brother, 146-160, 186-189, 204-212, 293-301, 310-311, 312-319, 333-341, 367-377
Letters to his sister, 50-53
London in, 57-59, 62-67, 288-291, 358, 374, 375
Mother, and his, 25, 50, 134-135
Other writers, and, 124, 162-170
Physical appearance, his, 10, 71, 239, 288-289
Seeking work, 73, 81-83
Self Protrait, his, 344-352
Sisters, and his, 18, 50-53
Women, and, 124, 125-126, 196-200, 217
Word Pictures of, 228-236, 238-241, 242-246, 302-308, 327-329
Youth, his, 22, 25, 40-41, 42-43
See also names of individual works
Kavanagh, Peter, (brother)
America, in, 145-146, 293
Audience and Critic, as, 43, 178
Birth, 13
Childhood, 24
Diary, 110-116
Education, his, 49-50, 122, 131
Illness of Patrick (memo), 277-287
Letters to (Concerning Patrick) 389-396
Newspaper started with Patrick, 247-261
Power of Attorney given, 360-366
Printing Books, 313
Teaching, 57, 60
Kavanagh's Weekly, 244, 247-254, 263, 268, 282, 306, 369, 375, 377
Keating, P., 306
Kednaminsha, 90
Kednaminsha Primary School, 21
Keelan, Dick, 40
Keenan, G. 237, 244
Kelleher, D. L., 114
Kenner, H. 341
Kennelly, B., 356
Kensington Museum of Science, 286
Kenny Estate, 19
Keyes, Margaret, 12
Kiernan, T. J., 62, 72
Kilfeather, John, 237, 241-246
King Lear, (Shakespeare), 297
Kipling, R., 224
Kneafsey, Miss, 134
Knights of Columbanus, 83

Landor, 348
Lapped Furrows, 29, 58, 146-160
Lavery, C., 273
Lay of the Crooked Knight, The, 138-144
Leader, The, 262-263, 269, 287, 288
Leavis, F. R., 337
Leitch, George, 131
Leslie, Howard, 136
Lewis, Cecil Day, 336
Lindsay, V., 378
Lipschitz, 306
The Listener, 89
Little, Patrick, 127
Little, Philip F., 127, 128
Longfellow, 351, 378
Longmans, 329-330, 335, 342
Lough Derg, 85-88, 109, 112, 114, 191
Lough Derg, 109-110
Love, Oscar, 92-93
Love's Tortured Headland, 385, 396
Lowell, R., 338

Mac Bride, 327
Machado, Antonio, 9
Mackay Brown, G., 328
Mackey Brown, G., 328
Mac Liammóir, M., 251, 330-335
Macmillans, 54-56, 104, 148, 156, 171, 176, 178, 187, 204, 243, 299, 327
Macmillan, Harold, 64-67, 124
Maguire, Bernard, 57, 88, 128
Maguire, M., 273, 276
Manchester Guardian, The, 256
Mangan, 210
Marks, T., 371
Martin, Eamonn, 89
Marx Brothers, The, 229
Mc Caffrey, A., 102
Mc Connell, 259
Mc Entee, Mrs., 83
Mc Gibbon & Kee, 353, 359, 363, 364, 370, 372
Mc Guinness, Norah, 102
Mc Hugh, Roger, 209
Mc Kenna, T. P., 384
Mc Manus, M. J., 188
Mc Neice, L., 371
Mc Nello, D., 353, 396
Mc Quaid, John Charles, 83, 115, 117, 118, 178
Meegan, P., 40
Meet the Clans, (Radio), 382
Méryon, C., 232

Messenger, The, 231
Methuen, 111, 176
Milne, Ewart, 173, 288-291
Milton, J., 166
Minerals in Industry, 286
Moby Dick, (Melville), 16, 48, 242, 294
Mooney, Ria, 209
Moore, G. 377
Moore, Kingsmill, 273, 276
Moore, T., 210
Morgan, J. 354
Morrow, Larry, 154, 159, 188, 228
Moult, Thomas, 54, 58
Mulderry, 354
Murphy, Delia, 72
Murphy, Dr., 320, 392
Myles Na gCopaleen, (Flann O'Brien), 92-93, 94, 102-103, 118-119, 242, 310
My Wild Irish Weekly, 254-261

Nation, 161
National Observer, The, 344
New Art Patronage, The, 128-130
New Statesman, The, 161, 319, 338
New York Times, The, 302, 303
Nimbus, 294-296, 298, 299, 327, 328
Non-Plus, 244, 333, 334
November Haggard, 31-39, 292, 316-317, 378

O'Brien, Dr. Brendan, 278, 280, 281
O'Brien, Flann, *see* Myles Na gCappoleen
Observer, The, 64, 311, 336
O'Casey, Sean, 164, 177, 208, 219, 296
O'Connell, Daniel, 170
O'Connor, Frank, 48, 89, 104, 105, 111, 148, 150, 152, 153, 156, 165-168, 172, 206, 233, 297, 319, 340
O'Connor, Lir, 94
O'Connor, Pat, 278, 279, 318
O'Connor, Rory, 283
O'Dálaigh, Cearbhall, 274, 276
O'Donnell, Peadar, 89, 148, 152, 155, 158, 168, 204
O'Faoláin, Seán, 89, 233
O'Flaherty, Liam, 168, 170, 311
O'Flaherty, Mrs. Mae, 313, 334
O'Grady, D., 307, 308
O'Kelly, S. T., 310
Old Moore's Almanac, 231
Olympia Theatre, 338
On Raglan Road, 126

O'Sullivan, Seamus, 48, 58, 71
O'Sullivan, Seán, 232
Oswald, Lee H., 370
Oxford Book of Irish Verse, 319

The Paddiad, 188, 190-191, 206, 333
Palace Bar, 73, 74
Parnell, C., S., 299
Parson's Bookshop, 314, 334, 340, 369
The Parton Press, 313
P.E.N., 226
P.E.N. Anthology, 311
Petrified Forest, The (film), 136
Picasso, P., 229, 306
Pilot Press, The, 158, 176, 178, 187, 204
Pitt, 288
Plomer. W., 336
Ploughman, (1), 54
Ploughman, (2), 62
Poetry Book Society, The, 334
Poetry Chicago, 48, 189, 190
Pound, E. 307, 313
Prelude, 272, 329
Press, J., 330
Pye Radio, 259
Pygmalion, (film), 136

Queen's University Festival, 239
Quinn, Brigid, 13
Quinn, Jimmy, 46

Radio Athlorie, 57
Radio Eireann, 62, 151, 154, 263
Recent Poems, 313, 327
Reeve, Alan, 81
Reis, B., 306, 307
Restaurant Reverie, 122
Rialto Hospital, 279, 284-286
Rieu, E. V., 266
Rilke, 71
Rimbaud, 236
Robinson, L. 318
Rodgers, W. R., 48
Rodin, A., 230
Roosevelt, 132, 303, 304
Roosevelt, 132
Rothko, 306
Rowland, B., 353
R.T.É., 340, 342-352, 379, 382, 395
R.T.É. Guide, 358, 376, 382-384, 396
Ryan, Desmond, 148
Ryan, Dr., 146
Ryan, J., 206, 209, 211

Saturday Evening Post, The, 92

402

Searson's Pub, 281
Self-Portrait, 246, 342-352, 376, 379
Senan, Father, 107-108
Shakespeare, W., 220, 252
Shaw, Keith, 279, 280, 283, 340, 370
Shelley, P. B., 166
Shevlin, M., 53
Sinatra, F., 229
Smith, S., 328
Smithson, A. P., 229
Smyllie, 73-74, 148
Snodgrass, W. D., 338
Some Reflections on Waiting for Godot, 296-298
Soul for Sale, A, 104, 148, 171, 327, 380
Spectator, The, 62
Spender, Stephen, 312, 330, 368
Stamos, 306
Standard, The, 43-44, 97, 105, 108 109, 115, 116, 118, 122, 132, 150-151, 156, 171, 178, 189, 239
Stendhal, 81
Stephens, J., 48
Stony Grey Soil, 90
Dr. Strangelove, (film) 374-375
Struwelpeter, 333
Sunday Press, The, 250, 257
Sweeney, James Johnson, 304
Sweeney, M., 356
Swift, J., 164, 220
Swift, P., 298, 329
Synge, J. M., 163, 347

Taaffe, B., 53
Talbot, Matt, 253
The Talbot Press, 84
Tambimutti, 304
Tarry Flynn, 10, 25, 66, 111, 121, 127-128, 153, 158, 159, 160, 161, 174-178, 187, 202, 231, 240, 241-242, 338, 339, 353, 364, 380, 385, 396
Thomas, Dylan, 229, 307, 311, 313, 395

Thomson, Francis, 52
Thoreau, 216
Tierney, 278, 287, 310
Times Literary Supplement, The, 336
Tit-Bits, 232
Todd, M., 307
To Hell with Commonsense, 312
Tomlinson, 337
Tomorrow The World, (film), 137
Torchiana, 377
Trafford, J., 328
Troy, W., 306

Ulysses, (Joyce), 214, 219

Victory of Mediocrity, 248-249

Waddell, Helen, 52, 56, 58, 59, 20
Waiting for Godot, (Beckett), 294, 296-298
Wake of the Books, The, 171-172
Walsh, Maurice, 89, 92
Walsh, Roisin, 84, 89, 160
Weaver, S., 384
Weekly Independent, The, 44, 231
Whitman, W., 48
Why sorrow?, 88-89
Wilbur, R., 337
Wilde, Oscar, 250, 253, 270
Williamson, Bruce, 148
Willis, P., 356
Wilson, Young, 259
Wood, W. 19
World is Ruled by Idiots, The, 301
Wordsworth, W., 166

X magazine, 244, 333, 334, 339, 340

Yeats, J. B., 103
Yeats, W. B., 48, 147, 166, 172, 210, 214, 254, 298, 347, 377

Zozimus, 236